C000075827

The History of the Gwydir Family and Memoirs

Welsh Classic Vol. 4
Series Editor   Lynn Hughes

Sir John Wynn of Gwydir, with coat of arms

(William Sharp)

THE HISTORY
OF THE GWYDIR FAMILY
AND MEMOIRS

Sir John Wynn

Edited with Introduction and Notes by
J. GWYNFOR JONES

GOMER PRESS
1990

First Impression — May 1990

© J. Gwynfor Jones

British Library Cataloguing in Publication Data
Jones, J. Gwynfor
    The history of the Gwydir family, and memoirs.—
(The Welsh Classics; 4).
    I. Title   II. Series
929.209429

ISBN 0-86383-596-1
ISBN 0-86383-697-6 W

This volume has been published with the support of the Welsh Arts Council.

Printed in Wales
at the Gomer Press, Llandysul, Dyfed

I Enid
a fagwyd ym Mertheos,
ffermdy ar hen ystad Gwedir
ym mhlwyf Dolwyddelan

CONTENTS

ILLUSTRATIONS

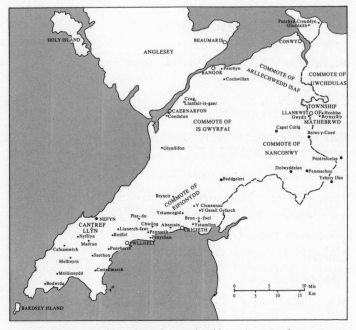

North-west Wales, identifying chief locations in the texts
(Richard Jenkins)

PREFACE

THE *History of the Gwydir Family* and *Memoirs*, written by Sir John Wynn of Gwydir in the Conwy valley, rank, in Welsh historiography, as the most imaginative historical sources to have been composed in the sixteenth century. They were written during the years after 1580 when Wynn inherited the vast Gwydir estate, and both works, judging by their style and content, took some time to compile. It appears, however, that the *History* was never finally completed and, as it stands, it reveals graphically the manner in which Tudor gentry in Wales viewed and interpreted the background to their family history in the later Middle Ages.

The *History of the Gwydir Family* is the only chronicle of its kind to be written in sixteenth-century Wales and, on that count alone, is considered noteworthy. Also, the emphasis on kindred loyalties and animosities and on the practical impact of war, social dislocation and revolt gives the work an instant appeal. At the same time it obscures many of the developments—as modern historical research has shown—which accelerated change and recovery in the post-Glyndŵr era. Wynn's vivid portrayal of his chief characters, most of whom were repressed by a restricted and disintegrating social environment, gives his narrative a buoyancy and appeal which, regardless of the emphasis placed on lineage and kindred integrity, discloses elements of a society—confined by the mountain fastness of Gwynedd and adjacent regions—which was perpetually torn between the forces of the old and the new world with which conservative clan groups found themselves in difficulty.

The strains and tensions of war and revolt as well as the rise of a new generation of landed gentry determined to aggrandise themselves through the acquisition of landed power and regional authority, exposed fresh and exciting dimensions which offered aspiring propertied individuals wealth and control based essentially on their new-found loyalty to the Tudor dynasty. The career of Maredudd ab Ieuan ap Robert, Wynn's ancestor and founder of the Gwydir family, symbolized such a shift in emphasis, and the *Memoirs*—which were written in the early seventeenth century—serve to show how members of the ecclesiastical and landed order in Gwynedd had, in late Tudor and early Stuart times, become representatives of a new and dynamic age involved in establishing reformed religious practices, developing educational skills and exercising military talents.

The *History* dwells on the past and considers divine providence and status to be the principal modes of social advancement. The *Memoirs* record the achievements of individuals whose forbears, for the most part, had contributed significantly to establish the basis of the landed structure in Tudor society. Both works are, in that sense, inter-related and highlight the broad cultural and dynastic interests of a squire whose family had achieved prominence in the public affairs of sixteenth-century Gwynedd.

EDITORIAL NOTE

The text of the *History of the Gwydir Family* in this edition follows the original autograph manuscript deposited in the South Glamorgan County Library at Cardiff (MS.83 [now MS.4.101]). Every attempt has been made to reproduce Sir John Wynn's text as closely as possible, editorial changes being limited to the up-dating of personal and place-names and to some technicalities considered essential for grammatical accuracy. The text of the *Memoirs* follows that included in NLW Add.MS.27 (c.1720), the earliest known copy of an original which has not survived. Since both manuscripts often lack adequate punctuation the editor took it upon himself to reduce some over-long and frustratingly confusing dependent clauses into sentences which entailed some minor technical emendations. This was done only in places where it was considered to be absolutely necessary. Elsewhere, the constant use of the semi-colon for clarification has enabled the editor to retain the original intact and to preserve both works as they had been compiled. Changes, where they occur, are indicated in italics, square and sometimes round brackets.

I incurred many debts during the period when this study was written and wish to express my appreciation of the courtesy shown to me by many individuals. I am indebted to library assistants at the National Library of Wales, Aberystwyth, the South Glamorgan County Library, Cardiff, Gwynedd Archives Service and the libraries of the University College of North Wales, Bangor, and University College, Cardiff respectively, for their unfailing courtesy at all times. Mr. Bryn Jones and Mr. Alun Giles Jones, in particular, need to be mentioned for their conscientious attention to my requests. Dr. D. Huw Owen, my former colleague, now Keeper of Pictures and Maps at the National Library of Wales, read the work in typescript, and Mr. Brian James, formerly Keeper of the Salisbury Library, University College, Cardiff, read the complete work at

proof stage. I wish to thank them both for their generosity in undertaking such onerous tasks and for dis-
cussing many aspects of the project with me. Mr.
Philip Wyn Davies of the National Library of Wales
also gave me much needed assistance on manuscript
material, and Professor John Percival, Head of the
School of History and Archaeology at the University of
Wales College of Cardiff gave liberally his help with
Latin translations. I appreciate their polite and enthusi-
astic attention at all times. I also wish to thank Mr.
Richard Jenkins for drawing the map, Mr. Lynn
Hughes, the general editor of the Welsh Classics series,
for his support and guidance and especially Mr. Dyfed
Elis-Gruffydd and Gomer Press for their courtesy and
expertise in producing this volume. Last, but not least,
I am deeply indebted to my wife, born and bred in the
heartland of the Gwydir domain, for her support and for
allowing Sir John Wynn to 'reside' in our home for such
a long period of time.

J. Gwynfor Jones
University of Wales College of Cardiff

ABBREVIATIONS

AC	Archaeologia Cambrensis
Ann.C.	Annales Cambriae
BBCS	Bulletin of the Board of Celtic Studies
BL	The British Library
BMW	Boroughs of Medieval Wales
BT	Brut y Tywysogion (Pen. MS. 20)
Cal.Anc.Pet.	Calendar of Ancient Petitions relating to Wales
Ca.MS	Cardiff MS
CCQSR	Calendar of Caernarfonshire Quarter Sessions Records
Chron.M.	Chronica Majora
CPR	Calendar of Patent Rolls
CSPD	Calendar of State Papers Domestic
CSPF	Calendar of State Papers Foreign
CSPI	Calendar of State Papers Ireland
CWP	Calendar of Wynn (of Gwydir) Papers
DNB	Dictionary of National Biography
DWB	Dictionary of Welsh Biography
Dwnn	Heraldic Visitations of Wales
Eifionydd	Eifionydd: a Study in Landownership
EHR	English Historical Review
ELl	Enwau Lleoedd
ELlSG	Enwau Lleoedd Sir Gaernarfon
GC	Giraldus Cambrensis (Itinerarium Kambriae)
GCH	Glamorgan County History
GLM	Gwaith Lewys Môn
GST	Gwaith Siôn Tudur
GTA	Gwaith Tudur Aled
GWC	Gwaith Wiliam Cynwal
HC	Historie of Cambria
HGF	History of the Gwydir Family
HGK	Historia Gruffud vab Kenan
HMC	Historical Manuscript Commission
HPF	History of Powys Fadog
HSt.A	History of St. Asaph
HW	History of Wales
IGE	Iolo Goch ac Eraill
JMHRS	Journal of the Merioneth Historical and Record Society
LS	List of Sheriffs

MWS	Medieval Welsh Society
NLW	National Library of Wales
NLWJ	National Library of Wales Journal
PACF	Pedigrees of Anglesey and Caernarvonshire Families
PH	Parliamentary History
PRO	Public Record Office
RC	Record of Caernarvon
RCAM	Royal Commission on Ancient Monuments
Rot.Chart.	Rotuli Chartarum
Rot.Claus.	Rotuli Clausarum
Rot.Parl.	Rotuli Parliamentorum
RWM	Report on Welsh Manuscripts
SHD	Survey of the Honour of Denbigh
SW	Statutes of Wales
TAAS	Transactions of the Anglesey Antiquarian Society
TCHS	Transactions of the Caernarfonshire Historical Society
TCS	Transactions of the Honourable Society of Cymmrodorion
TDHS	Transactions of the Denbighshire Historical Society
TYP	Trioedd Ynys Prydain
UCNW	University College of North Wales
WATU	Welsh Administrative and Territorial Units
WG	Welsh Genealogies
WHR	Welsh History Review
WRE	Welsh Reformation Essays
WWR	Wales and the Wars of the Roses

INTRODUCTION

The Wynn family of Gwydir in the Conwy valley, north Wales, was one of the best known landowning families of early modern Wales—the sixteenth and early seventeenth centuries—the period sometimes referred to as the 'golden age' of the Welsh gentry. The survival of a large corpus of source material, chiefly in the form of private correspondence relating to several heads of the Gwydir household, reveals them as astutely opportunistic in the acquisition of property and offices. Land lust was a preoccupation of the age among the privileged families.

Outstanding among the generally distinguished Wynn family was Sir John Wynn (1553-1627). A country squire, he wrote the charming and informative chronicle history of his antecedents that was subsequently entitled the *History of the Gwydir Family*. In spite of its shortcomings it is a work that has appealed to generations of historians for its vivid portrayal of fifteenth-century social life, with its graphic accounts of bloodshed and intense family rivalries in the remote commote of Eifionydd in south-east Caernarfonshire where, within the medieval Principality of North Wales, Wynn's ancestors had set down their roots.

The *History* needs to be used with caution. It records events in a manner and style whose specific design is to elaborate the author's primary motive, namely promotion of his family's interests, which presents the historian with a chronicle that is as stimulating as it is perplexing. Nevertheless, the later generations of historians have regarded it as a broadly accurate social commentary. W Llewelyn Williams, writing in 1919, believed from his reading of Wynn that, by the end of the fifteenth century, 'the Edwardian Settlement had hopelessly broken down'. Howell T Evans comments in 1934, that 'such misdeeds as we read of in the lively pages of Sir John Wynn of Gwydir are only such as might be found in the records of a modern police court'. Idris Jones, likewise, in the opening paragraphs of his

Modern Welsh History (1934) relies heavily on Wynn's *History:* 'Compared with England, conditions in Wales were in a more chaotic state'. Wynn had evidently conceived for him a most persuasive picture of the strife, bloodshed and anarchy that prevailed in Wales in the period immediately following the outbreak of the dynastic wars in England.

In addition to the *History*, Sir John Wynn wrote his *Memoirs.* They mainly consist in a number of biographical sketches of local and contemporary celebrities, including members of his own family. Among them were William Thomas, the Caernarfonshire soldier who fought and died in the Netherlands; Richard Davies, a native of Y Gyffin near Conwy and Bishop of St David's; William Morgan, the translator of the scriptures into Welsh and Bishop of St Asaph; and Sir William Jones, Chief Justice of the King's Bench in Ireland and a native of Llŷn. The *Memoirs* are not as well known as the *History*; even so, both works do contain much the same kind of material, most of which is biographical and genealogical and derived from Wynn's own reading and interpretation of sources. The antiquarian aspects, while not wholly dependable, typify the somewhat self-indulgent methods of a well-educated Welsh country squire of these times.

As Tudor-period family histories are rare in Wales, the *History* has understandably been subject to closer scrutiny than would otherwise have been the case. Its entailed importance, therefore, has increased its status as the prototype of historical writing in sixteenth-century Wales, and despite the local and precise nature of its reference—Eifionydd, Nanconwy and the western fringes of the Lordship of Denbigh—its application can be more widely and generally assumed. It adds an extra dimension to the study of Lancastrian and Yorkist Wales as seen by a man whose ancestors were closely involved.

Sir John Wynn's kinsmen could really only have traced their ancestry and ascendancy to a group of freeholders from Pennant and Penyfed townships in four-

teenth-century Eifionydd, though he himself would
have his readers believe that his stock had descended
from Gruffudd ap Cynan (c. 1055-1137), King of
Gwynedd. According to Wynn, Maredudd ab Ieuan ap
Robert of Y Gesail Gyfarch in Penyfed, who was
fostered by an unknown freeholder in the vicinity of
Caernarfon, settled at Dolwyddelan castle in the upper
reaches of the commote of Nanconwy round about
1485. He then built for himself and his growing family
a new house at Penamnen in a secluded valley to the
south-east of the present village. His small band of
spirited followers—some of whom had dubious back-
grounds—were settled in vacant bond holdings which
their master had succeeded in acquiring from the
Crown. In addition, he purchased lands from the long-
established Coetmor family of Betws-y-coed and
Llanrwst in the upper Conwy valley, built the original
mansion-house of Gwydir and laid the basis of an estate
which became one of the most splendid in north Wales.
Maredudd ab Ieuan became a country gentleman who
set himself the task of ridding the countryside of
thieves and brigands and creating order out of anarchy.

Maredudd was followed at Gwydir by his eldest
legitimate son, John Wyn ap Maredudd (d. 1559). He
was the first head of the family to achieve prominence
in local government as member of parliament and as
sheriff and justice of the peace under the new administration set up by the Acts of Union (1536-43). He
extended the landed power of Gwydir in the upper
Conwy valley and beyond, rebuilt and enlarged the
mansion-like house originally erected by his father and
bequeathed to Morus, his eldest son and heir (the first
of the family to assume the surname Wynn), a substantial territorial inheritance. He, in turn, continued
the estate-building activities of his father and served in
local affairs. He was a squire in the ascendant and was
to become one of the most trusted supporters in north
Wales of Robert Dudley, earl of Leicester, and Chief
Ranger of the Forest of Snowdon.

It was Morus Wynn's son John (later Sir John) who dominated public affairs in north Wales for nearly half a century and who concerns us here as author of the *History* and the *Memoirs*. He succeeded to his inheritance as head of a Tudor gentry family descended from ancient Welsh stock. Although he took great pride in ancestry and lineage he was opportunist and materialistic. He has been described as 'a man of great abilities and an eccentric genius, haughty in his views and austere in his measures'. Sir John's presence was felt at all times in matters affecting the counties of Gwynedd. He was an overbearing personality, cultivated and ambitious, who was acknowledged equally as an able administrator, as an astute landowner and as the generous patron of traditional Welsh poetry. On the one hand typical of the Tudor gentleman who had built up his power on the achievements of his predecessors, he was exceptional in the way he strengthened his personal position. The Wynn family were *parvenu*, inasmuch as they rose to a position of authority largely through Maredudd ab Ieuan's determination to break loose from the stranglehold of family feuding that had ruined the fortunes of his own clan in Eifionydd. In establishing the nucleus of an estate in a remote and lawless region of north Wales, the opportunity and achievement was to create law and order where none before existed. It was upon these achievements that Sir John Wynn was able to build and exercise his power as one of the principal squires in Gwynedd.

The author of the *History* was accorded the same upbringing and education as the more affluent gentry of his day. He was entered for All Souls, Oxford, though he did not graduate. He enrolled at Furnival's Inn and at the Inner Temple for a short period but did not complete his studies. His legal background, however, enabled him, on his return, to manage the estate efficiently on his father's death in 1580 and to deal with his property affairs with remarkable adroitness. He married Sidney, daughter of Sir William Gerard, Lord Chancellor of Ireland and Vice-President of the Council in the Marches, and established influential contacts with other north Wales gentry. His interests were varied. As industrialist, he managed his lead mines and drew up plans for land reclamation in Traeth Mawr near Porthmadog, and his ambitions included the exploitation of Anglesey copper mines and the establishment of a Welsh frieze industry in the Conwy valley. As an administrator and office-holder he cut an impressive figure on the magistrates' bench in three counties and was equally active as sheriff, deputy-lieutenant and, later, as member of the Council in the Marches. He was at pains to grasp at any means that might help to increase his personal importance and stature. He provided education for his sons in the chief seats of learning and was probably donor of the free grammar school at Llanrwst. Wynn was also a keen and percipient assessor of men and a skilled commentator on events and developments in his day. He was knighted in 1606 and elevated to a baronetcy in 1611. His voice was always forthright among his colleagues, and at Gwydir and elsewhere he was constantly engaged with county business and the cares of a growing estate.

In the past, historians and antiquarians alike have tended to lean too heavily on unfounded traditions in assessing the character of Sir John Wynn. He has been described as a 'selfish and arrogant man' and a 'ruthless tyrant' totally indifferent to the well-being and affairs of others. He was doubtless a strong-willed man, intent on maintaining and strengthening his power and influence, but was no more ambitious than some of his equally jealous, cunning and grasping neighbours and kinsmen who sought every opportunity to defame and even destroy him. The extant portraits appear to depict a significantly proud and ostentatious man in later life. In his younger days he was described as a tall, dark person—well-set and broad in the shoulders—an impressive and formidable figure to behold but also a man who represented what was considered most appealing and virtuous in the Tudor gentlemen of his day. He managed his property affairs well and planned to present his son, Sir Richard Wynn, with a handsome estate, worthy of his standing in society. As far as land tenure was concerned, he did not regret the passing of a tribal society. On the contrary, he was a capitalist landowner anxious to extend profitable investments on his lands and, in so doing, he came into violent conflict with fellow gentry, tenantry and leading churchmen.

The Wynns of Gwydir were prominent patrons of the bardic order—as is shown in the many manuscript sources that survive. Sir John Wynn was eulogised by Simwnt Fychan, Siôn Tudur and Huw Machno, among others, and was himself knowledgeable in the mechanics of the poetic craft. The *Booke of Sir John Wynn*, which includes the original autograph copy of the *History*, also contains a large selection of panegyrics addressed to the Wynns and some of their forbears, most of them in the hand of Huw Machno, Sir John's household poet. It also provides transcripts of a series of administrative records, all of which were used to assist in composing the chronicle. Wynn was keen to expedite the publication of the immense Latin-Welsh dictionary compiled by his kinsman, Sir Thomas Wiliems of Trefriw, scholar and lexicographer, and corresponded with Dr John Davies, rector of Mallwyd, the most eminent Welsh scholar of his day, with a view to seeking his aid in revising and preparing the text. It eventually appeared as the second part of Davies's monumental *Dictionarium Duplex* (1632). Further-more, Wynn reminded Richard Parry, Bishop of St Asaph (1604-23), of the urgent need for a rendering of the Psalms in Welsh for use in parish churches. Judging by his own correspondence and the testimony of others, he owned a valuable library at Gwydir which contained William Camden's *Britannia* and Sir Walter Raleigh's *Chronicles* among other notable works. He had established close contacts with intellectual circles in London and had encouraged his sons to cultivate influential relationships in the city. The expense involved doubtless imposed a very severe strain on his material resources, but he strove to keep up appearances in clothes, fashions and social contacts. He extended his house at Caernarfon and added to the buildings at Gwydir where Crown officials and dignitaries enjoyed exceptional hospitality. At Gwydir too, the best food, wine, fruit, spices and even tobacco were amply provided. A more gracious Tudor gentleman it would have been hard to find: nevertheless, he was a man, to some extent, a captive in his own environment. Essentially Sir John Wynn was the rural squire, conscious of his obligations to society, and a home-loving landowner devoted to his growing estate. Within him were the elements of the *uchelwr*, the nobleman, who combined the attributes of both the Welsh country gentlemen and the urbane courtier. This unique blend added distinction to his appeal as the author of the *History* and the *Memoirs*.

It is not known when exactly Sir John Wynn wrote the *History*. It seems likely, however, that he took some considerable time to accumulate and prepare his source material. As a man busily involved in local government he used what leisure time he had to seek new evidence to supplement his narrative and add factual details. From internal evidence the *History* would appear to have been put together sometime between 1580, the year when he settled as owner at Gwydir, and 1616, two years after the death—while on his Grand Tour of Italy—of his eldest son and namesake. At that time he had intended to complete the chronicle. It may well be that the *Memoirs* were written between c.1621 and 1624 and designed as an addendum to the larger work. The narrative contained in the *History* is frustratingly obscure in places and the manuscript is brought abruptly to a close. Historians would fondly have wished for more detailed information about Maredudd ab Ieuan's career, especially in his latter days at Dolwyddelan and at Gwydir. It appears that Wynn had been hindered in his task by the lack of any system in the archive of official documents in the Tower of London. The legal actions commenced against him in Star Chamber and elsewhere from the

1590s onwards must surely have irritated him especially when suspicions about the authenticity of his pedigree were aroused. Such hindrances, however, did not seem to have prevented him in his progress with the work and in all likelihood fortified him in his resolve to defend his family honour and refute charges of bastardy brought against him by vindictive neighbours, among them William Williams of Cochwillan and Thomas Prys of Plas Iolyn.

If it was the case that Wynn had become sensitive to attacks made on his lineage, he may well have written most of his chronicle before 1592. In that year William Williams accused him in Star Chamber of having sprung from an illegitimate line. It seems unlikely that Wynn would have revealed for publication passages relating to the marriage of Maredudd ab Ieuan to a bastard daughter of William Gruffudd ap Robin of Cochwillan after such an indictment. It seems altogether inconceivable, however, that only as few as the last five manuscript leaves were completed between that year and 1627. Embarrassment, if it entered into things, would most certainly have been caused before 1592, but Wynn appears to have made the conscious effort to conceal the matter of the illegitimacy. It appears that accusations of this sort would have had no damaging effect on his standing as a landed gentleman. That this is so is deducible from the assiduous manner in which he set about writing the chronicle. Twelve years or so after the Star Chamber suit—in 1604—Thomas Prys of Plas Iolyn also went to law against Wynn and accused him, among other things, of falsely claiming descent from Owain Gwynedd. By then Wynn had probably completed most of his work and had it in mind to use it to strengthen his hand against his adversaries. His advice to his eldest son in 1604 was distinctly cautious: 'you must learne to know yo'r frendes from yo'r enymyes ... as I shall leave you frendes so also enymyes whose cheife motive ys that I prosper'. Early seventeenth-century society bore within it new stresses that undermined the traditional social order which Sir John sought so vigorously to preserve. The death of his heir in 1614, combined with increasing ill-health and thwarted political ambition, may have dampened his enthusiasm for completing his family history.

In discovering the sources that were made available to the author in the course of writing the *History* we discover that his friend and relative, Sir Thomas Wiliems of Trefriw, an industrious copyist of manuscripts, had placed at his disposal a considerable amount of material, such as his own *Prif Acheu Holl Gymru Benbaladr*, a genealogical work of considerable magnitude, and a copy of *Brut y Tywysogion*. Wynn also thought highly of Richard Broughton, Salop, who copied for him some administrative documents in London. In addition, he made extensive use of the genealogical material compiled by Siôn Tudur and may have consulted John Speed, the cartographer, for some finer points of detail. Individual members of his family as well, such as his uncles Gruffudd Wynn of Berthddu, Owen Wynn of Cae'r Milwr and Robert Wynn of Plas Mawr, Conwy, could have added substantially to his reminiscences. His main guide to the early history of Wales was undoubtedly Dr David Powel's *Historie of Cambria* (1584), a work which may well have prompted the writing of the *History* in the first instance. What is certain is that Wynn had relied heavily on Powel's narrative supplemented by the use made of Matthew Paris's *Chronica Majora*, the *Itinerarium Kambriae* by Gerald of Wales, and a version of the *Historia Gruffud vab Kenan*. He readily informed his readers that a Welsh copy of the *Historia* was available at Gwydir 'in a most ancient book' and that Nicholas Robinson, Bishop of Bangor (1566-85), a scholar of considerable repute, had translated it into Latin at Morus Wynn's request. Wynn also consulted the *Annales Cambriae* together with a large corpus of official documentation uncovered at Caernarfon and London.

The main purpose of the *History*, then, is to account for the rise of Sir John Wynn's early ancestors from obscurity in twelfth-century Gwynedd. The scene is set principally in the commote of Eifionydd, particularly in the free townships of Pennant and Penyfed. Wynn claimed descent from Rhodri, second son of Owain Gwynedd by his second incestuous marriage to his cousin Christina. Gruffudd ap Rhodri had settled with his family near Denbigh in Gwynedd below the Conwy but had established branches in both parts of the Kingdom. It was a late thirteenth-century descendant, Gruffudd ap Caradog, who continued the line. His son Dafydd, who lived in Cantref Rhos, had married into the clan of *Gwely Wyrion Gruffudd* in Penyfed in Eifionydd where he settled. Wynn endeavoured to trace the fortunes of this Dafydd's descendants, especially the line of Hywel, his youngest son, from whom the Wynn line ultimately sprang. The author's main task in the *History* was to explain how this particular branch of the family had overcome social and economic obstacles, in particular the disabilities of partible inheritance, and had emerged in the early sixteenth century as a strong and resilient gentry house at Gwydir. Wynn's ancestors in the lordship of Denbigh had been forced by Henry Lacy, earl of Lincoln and lord of Denbigh, to move to the western parts of that region bordering on the Conwy river. This was not an uncommon practice at that time since it facilitated the settlement of English families in the more advantageously situated areas around the borough. Wynn, however, appeared to be more critical of the system of divided inheritance which he considered to have been the main cause of his ancestors' ineptitude and relative obscurity. His marked lack of evidence to boost the family reputation in the fourteenth century may well have accounted for the tale attributed to him about the supposed massacre of the Welsh bards by Edward I after the conquest and settlement of Wales in 1282-84. The King's decision to hang all bards by martial law 'as stirrers of the people to sedition', in his view, accounted for the dearth of bardic output during that century and consequently for the loss of evidence about his forbears. This story of the massacre of the bards, spurious though it is, was to have far-reaching international ramifications and became later an important motif in other literatures.

It was against a background of turmoil and change that Sir John Wynn described family circumstances in the two centuries before the accession of Henry Tudor. The deteriorating social and economic structure in the Principality and the March exacerbated the confusion in which rival clan groupings found themselves. The kindred system maintained its strength and the old Welsh law of inheritance, the law of Hywel Dda, had provided all male heirs with a portion of the patrimony. This custom, in certain circumstances, could and did intensify petty jealousies and cause financial distress. The inbred tribal elements, together with racial animosity near the English boroughs, did contribute significantly to the general economic *malaise*. Furthermore, as old methods of land tenure were gradually disintegrating and new economic practices were gaining hold, a visible decline in communal patterns was coming about. Welsh land law was slowly giving way to the more flexible English system of property law. Its adoption advantaged the more forward-looking among the Welsh *uchelwyr:* plague, war and revolt equally took their toll on population and on the maintenance of law and order. Rival ambitions within clans competed furiously for ascendancy in local politics. They also strove to acquire and retain office and sought to build up freehold estates at the expense of those who failed to survive the economic *débâcle*. While legal practices declined shrewd speculators prospered, often through ruthless scheming.

Robert ap Maredudd (grandson of the Hywel mentioned above) had lived and won through these conditions in the early fifteenth century. His direct descendant, Sir John Wynn, was concerned to identify his stock with this Robert whom he considered to be the elder of two blood-brothers. Robert lived at Y Gesail Gyfarch in Penyfed township in Eifionydd, and the

History relates in some considerable detail the cleavage
that occurred between him and his brother Ieuan, the
one taking sides with Owain Glyndŵr and the other
remaining loyal to Henry IV and defending Caernarfon
castle in the King's cause. So anxious was Wynn to link
his family with Robert that he quoted in his text a
portion of a *cywydd* supposedly composed by Rhys
Goch Eryri in honour of this rebel supporter of
Glyndŵr. Although he is not mentioned by name, for
obvious reasons, the poet depicts him as an aged and
respected *uchelwr*, one who, in his younger days, was
typical of the warrior-clansman class who displayed his
valour on the battlefield and prided himself on the
nobility of his forbears. The author then proceeded to
show how Robert's son, Ieuan, also a man of considerable standing and influence in his native Eifionydd, was
embroiled in a bitter clash with his kinsman, Hywel ap
Rhys of Bron-y-foel, in the township of Treflys in the
same commote. He was tall and robust and, according
to Wynn, a man of immense physical stature. He cut an
imposing figure of martial grandeur among his less
spectacular kinsmen, his career adding a heroic touch
as well as an element of crude reality. His kinsman, the
intrepid John ap Maredudd of Ystumcegid, is depicted
similarly as a stalwart of the older order in medieval
Welsh clan life, a rugged leader of men who overtly
displayed his chivalry and fearless spirit in combat. He
also demonstrated his complete mastery of the
traditional twenty-four feats of nobility in contest with
fellow *uchelwyr*.

Hywel ap Rhys sustained a protracted feud against
Ieuan ap Robert, and the most vivid episodes are
delineated in the *History*, albeit in the most tedious and
repetitive manner! The root cause of the conflict is not
easily determined, but it appears that personal prestige
and landed interests had much to do with it. The strife
originated in the middle years of the fifteenth century
at the time when the dynastic wars between York and
Lancaster broke out in England. The often gory details
of these violent internecine clashes obviously amused

Sir John who dramatically recalled that the redoubtable Ieuan had 'sustained deadly feud . . . at home in his door, a war more dangerous than the other'. In 1463 an agreement was reached between him and his protector, John ap Maredudd, concerning the division of the inheritance between them. Ieuan acquired substantial lands in Eifionydd, including Y Gesail Gyfarch, and upon his untimely death in 1469 he left a son, Maredudd, to inherit. He was Wynn's great-grand-father, a person who, according to the *History*, abandoned his disreputable clansmen ruined by their subjection to partible inheritance and also set up for himself a new and exciting career. It is hardly surprising that Wynn stressed the importance of a man's 'good descent' and the 'propagation of his seed'. It was by means of Maredudd's career that he was able to identify these features most clearly. Circumstances had favoured him in his youth. He was fostered by a free-holder (probably a scion of Cochwillan) from Crug in Llanfair-is-gaer near Caernarfon and was well brought up. In a school within the town he learnt Latin and English. He later married Alice, daughter of William ap Gruffudd ap Robin of Cochwillan. Eventually he decided to move with his growing family to the desolate southern fringes of the commote of Nanconwy where he settled upon bond lands that had become depopu-lated. In order to protect his property and establish peace he trained a private army, accoutred in his own livery, to combat the notorious brigands and outlaws of Ysbyty Ifan, and gradually made himself master of the region. It was a tough and exacting task in an untamed part of the Principality. It is at that point that the chronicle comes to an abrupt end. It omits any reference to Maredudd's settlement at Gwydir and to his achievements in his latter years. The closing section, however, does emphasize his complete mastery of his adopted region and his success in establishing law and order. It was a supremacy that brought peace and security in its trail and that, in time, paved the way for a more outstanding ascendancy at Gwydir.

Clearly, Sir John Wynn was the product of his age, a man who strove for recognition, an aspiring country gentleman and one who wished to enhance the fortunes of his family. The chronicle was intended to be read by his heir when he was preparing himself to become the inheritor of Gwydir. Though the reasons that lie behind the concept of the *History* go much deeper, Wynn's cultural interests compare with those of his social equals in England. Elizabethan writers wrote history to provide future instruction for 'wise administrators'. They perceived in the study of history a moral function, and sources of all kinds were researched and read to deepen a sense of regional identity. Wynn was conscious of the need to write history according to accepted conventions. He laid stress on an antiquarian interpretation of past events. He was at pains to establish as his hero Maredudd ab Ieuan, his great-grandfather, in his determination to succeed and prosper despite the encumbrance of bastard pedigree.

Contemporary writers believed that all family and regional histories should depict their protagonists as Renaissance gentlemen of integrity and gracious conduct. Within that context Maredudd does indeed emerge as an astute leader of men. An eminent lineal descent, Wynn observed, entailed many abstract qualities—divine providence, continuing pre-eminence and a man's wise control over his own actions—as exemplified in Maredudd's decision to cultivate peace rather than perpetuate anarchy in Nanconwy. These civilising elements recognisably emerge with the advent of Maredudd ab Ieuan.

Wynn was eager, as was the fashion, to establish and maintain the organic unity of society while emphasizing its hierarchical structure. In his view, such solidarity could never be achieved without a knowledge of the origin of one's social roots. This sense of destiny pervades Wynn's chronicle in its entirety—the belief that God's providence had led one particular branch of the family to greatness and had provided for it a secure future. Like others of his generation Wynn also took seriously to the study of history as a prime means of administering wise and just government. A sober consideration of the past, it was believed, enabled the Tudor gentleman to understand the differences between the good, the evil and the unproductive life and instructed him on how to cultivate the principal virtues. In its role as a civilizing influence history should reveal the conquest of good over evil. In Wynn's estimation his great-grandfather represented what was considered best in the individual leader. He combined the qualities of military leadership necessary for survival in his age together with the virtues of the cultured gentleman. He possessed foresight, integrity and loyalty to the Crown—vital prerequisites of the ideal gentleman. To serve any lasting purpose the chronicle would need to place on record the virtues of so exemplary a forebear at the appropriate time in order to perpetuate those virtues.

The *History* also stressed hierarchy and social unity. Obedience to authority was regarded as a quality that would resist any form of instability and would, in a family-orientated society, act as a stabilising factor. The author of the *History* was intent on asserting his natural superiority over 'upstarts and gent[lemen] of the first head'—the *nouveaux riches*—whose lineage was considered to be inferior. To him writing a family history was an offensive as well as a defensive exercise. Identifying a common forefather strengthened the bonds of kindred, and where property rights were concerned took in the freeholders of lesser descent. Landownership in the Middle Ages under the clan system was restrictive and any attempt to alienate property required the consent of kindred as far as the second cousin. It is hardly surprising, therefore, that property disputes were usually the underlying cause of local unrest and even hostilities in late medieval Wales. Following the Act of Union (1536), however, primo-genitural inheritance became general and men like Sir

John Wynn welcomed it as a stabilising measure and one which could only serve the general cause of aggrandizement among the landed classes.

In a patrilinear-structured society individuals were obliged to defend this status. Wynn was able proudly to record the advice given to him by his kinsman Ellis ap Cadwaladr who counselled him to follow the course of his antecedents 'w'ch with wisdome, longanimity and temperance from tyme to tyme' had raised their fortunes and deepened a sense of justice that bound men together in unity. Dynastic ambition was their driving force; longevity enabled them to enjoy the fruits of their achievements; and their temperance and self-denial strengthened their resolve for the future. Much of the self-confidence displayed by Sir John Wynn was a clear manifestation of his belief in 'dynasticism'. He stressed continuously the intrinsic morality associated with 'good' families and individuals of aristocratic stock. The *History* was intended as a safeguard for the reputation of the Wynn family of Gwydir.

The *History of the Gwydir Family* provides us with a lively picture of social conditions in the Principality of North Wales and part of the northern March in the century before the Acts of Union. The distinct impression that emerges is one of extreme lawlessness when justice and peaceful administration were hopelessly at a discount. The revolt of Owain Glyndŵr and the wars between York and Lancaster, in Wynn's opinion, had exacerbated the already tense situation in Eifionydd and adjacent regions. The colourful descriptions of the desolations which followed these events, however, markedly exaggerate the distress. The author's principal weakness seems to have been that he attributed much of the economic *malaise* to the revolt and the ensuing war without any attention to the deeper causes of economic contraction.

To some extent Wynn cannot be blamed for adopting a shortsighted view of the not too distant past. His approach is purely typical of the Tudor interpretation of history. He began to put together his material at a time when it was increasingly evident that the new system of government that extended over Wales was serving its purpose. Contemporary views maintained that it had rescued the realm from the turmoils of civil war, creating a degree of national unity and a sense of security that men like Wynn and his contemporaries welcomed and valued. George Owen, the Pembrokeshire historian, and Dr David Powel of Rhiwabon both displayed their adulation with greater enthusiasm, perhaps, but Sir John Wynn was an equally strong supporter and beneficiary of good order as they had been. The benefits of Tudor rule were emphasized by describing the background in anarchic terms but the consequences of kindred feuds, even at their most violent, were probably not as devastating and widespread as Wynn purports them to be. They usually involved small groups of men and had little lasting impact on local community life. The degree of lawlessness in any period or area is, of course, very difficult to assess but it is clear that the Glyndŵr revolt did not so severely damage all parts of the country as it had the backward regions of Eifionydd and Nanconwy. Indeed, some areas in Wales, such as the coastal areas of south Wales, were hardly affected at all. If anything, they benefited by a period of prosperity following the revolt. Sir John Wynn exaggerates for a specific purpose when he attributes all ills to disruptive factors that have since become considered the symptoms rather than causes of social cleavage. Neither did the revolt result in the wholesale desertion of towns. The economic *malaise*, as illustrated in the familiar reference to the reduced condition of the borough of Llanrwst, was more likely caused by the impact of plague and consequential fall in population rather than by the ravages of Glyndŵr's followers. There were flourishing boroughs in the fifteenth century and aspiring Welshmen did acquire key offices in the Principality and the March—on an increasing scale. They were men who either abandoned Glyndŵr or had, from the start, decided not to support his cause. Wynn's reference to the racial hatred between the Welsh and the English that ensued was only partly correct since the phenomenon of Welsh gentry participation in English affairs was a significant feature of fifteenth-century daily life.

Nor can it be said either that law and order had been totally neglected. In spite of the inefficiency and self-interest that often marred the effective administration of justice, legal records—particularly plea rolls—reveal that the King's Sessions in the Principality had not ceased to function and were, in fact, in reasonably satisfactory working order. The structure of local government likewise appears to have operated smoothly despite periodic outbreaks of lawlessness that are referred to in the official sources. Furthermore, economic recovery in the later fifteenth century had brought about a revival in architecture and the arts as well as in popular religious culture. Churches were being rebuilt and refurbished and provided with impressive towers and screens. Indeed, a new spirit took possession of lay and ecclesiastical life alike. A revival of Welsh poetry had occurred as a result of the increase in lay patronage, and poetic tributes herald improved standards of living being enjoyed by the *uchelwyr* in their sumptuous halls. Tudur Aled, in his *cywydd* to the Abbot of Aberconwy, described the sophistication and bounty of his hospitality:

> A lord who gives feasts gladly,
> Twice the custom, at his board . . .
> Wine-rich house, shrine of honey
> Passage and pantry below:
> In choosing his wines at once
> He was the best of all nations.*

The traditional military features of their abodes were being gradually replaced by a more highly sophisticated domestic architectural design that betrayed the impact of a broader European culture. In commerce and trade likewise the growth of a small but influential merchant

*G Jones (Ed) *The Oxford Book of Welsh Verse in English* (1977) p. 67.

class led to the appearance of landed estates owned by a spirited group of new monied gentry families eager to claim and enjoy the privileges which had hitherto been the preserve of their more traditional landed counterparts.

The fifteenth century in Wales, it seems, was far more progressive than Sir John Wynn would have us believe. It enjoyed a marked degree of economic resurgence and stability. His account of strife-torn Eifionydd and Nanconwy should not be taken as a valid description of the condition of Wales as a whole. Recent research has shown that cultural and material standards were not as depressingly low as the text makes them out to be. In those respects the *History* is distortive and of little practical value.

The chronicle, however, does have its uses. It does indicate significant trends in the social life of the fifteenth century. Wynn affords us a glimpse of this sort of life that was becoming more fashionable when he relates how his great-grandfather was given education at Caernarfon, the centre of 'civility and learning', as part of his 'good breeding'. Laymen were making successful livings for themselves in law and government and demanding formal education to enable them to prosper and to be of service. Favoured individuals were now able to adopt new and exciting ways of life. Such a trend in urban areas caused the gradual spread of anglicisation among a new breed of gentry. Together with the desire to acquire office, it proved to be a remarkable source of social aggrandizement.

New methods of landholding that led to the growth of freehold estates are also a point of discussion. Wynn, however, oversimplified the situation when he described Maredudd's move from Crug to Nanconwy. It was more than a matter of allowing himself and his growing family additional living space and a way of avoiding the constant unrest in Eifionydd. There were many vacant bond townships in Nanconwy and, like so many of his generation, Maredudd seized the opportunity to occupy them and apportion them among his followers. This method of encroachment at the time became one of the ways adopted to exploit Crown lands in a period when the ravages of war, plague and eonomic dislocation led to drastic depopulation. By this process Maredudd was, in fact, undermining this structure upon which the Welsh economy had been partly built. It was a result of his jealous holding on to lands by fighting off robbers on his eastern flank, by his establishing good order among his tenants and by his seeking the opportunities eventually to purchase lands outright that the decay of old property customs in Nanconwy took place. It also gave him personally a more lasting prominence than his less motivated kindred elsewhere.

In general, however, the *History* does not give the impression of alienation from the traditional ways of life. On the contrary, it only hints at new tendencies. It indicates a marked slackening off, as it were, from established conventions. Social changes were hastened and made more acute: the 'dislike and variance' that was revealed in the relations between John ap Maredudd and William Gruffudd of Penrhyn, for instance, were typical of the rivalries that occurred everywhere on a local scale over land and authority. Although the policy of the Crown during and after the Glyndŵr revolt had been to curb the advancement of ambitious Welshmen, the wars of York and Lancaster and the ineffectiveness of the anti-Welsh legislation by mid-century had given them further opportunity to assert themselves and flaunt officaldom that was, as Wynn remarked, 'great to them that held that room'. Individuals who managed to acquire office and cling on to it often became subject to jealousy and opposition. There existed in Wales not only a hatred of alien officials but also a deep resentment of Welshmen who themselves made the grade and prospered. Progressive families in the Principality and March hardly regarded the imposition of an English system as a burden; they disliked far more their exclusion from participating in it and benefiting from it. This is a point that Sir John Wynn vaguely describes but fails significantly to grasp.

The situation was similar in the March lordships. Old methods of rough justice, abused social customs and the use of faction are demonstrated clearly in the *History*. The spectacular expedition pursued by Ieuan ap Robert into the lordship of Chirk to seek out and bring to justice the criminals who had murdered the vicar of Llanfrothen in Merioneth was a military incursion into perilous territory. Only a proven warrior would have ventured as he did to recapture men harboured by equally notorious masters who were 'at continual strife one with another' in the lordships of Chirk and Oswestry. Their rivalry and cupidity, however, symbolised far more than squabbling between the Trefor and Kyffin houses; they were at odds with each other over sovereign rights within the lordships. Since their overlords were absentee, it was only to be expected that prominent family groups of this kind should be tempted to compete for the superior power vested in the privilege of office.

The *History* offers an attempt at a dramatic and sensational insight into the problems of the fifteenth century and into the inadequacy of the means available to deal with them. The author's main task was accomplished in his recording the triumph of men of affairs over adverse conditions and the superiority of cautious tactics over interminable feud and vendetta. To that extent Wynn's *History* is most useful as a social commentary on pre-Tudor Wales but its prime importance lies in reflection of the attitudes of Tudor historians, within a local context, to the century preceding their own. It excels as a flesh-and-blood source and breathes some life into the dry bones of chronicle history by acquainting us with the features of an age as expressed in human behaviour. Observable within its pages is a degree of primitive arrogance combined with magnanimity. There is also an unshakeable adherence to the principles of honour and family loyalty. Uncouth though sections of the work may be, there is always, however, a remarkably refreshing appeal about the events described and the circumstances that led to them. The wife of Thomas ap Robin of Cochwillan, a Lancastrian supporter who, according to tradition, carried away his blood-stained head in her apron after his execution near Conwy castle, illustrates vividly the reality of life in those days. Furthermore, when Ieuan ap Robert, on another occasion, ordered one of his men to execute two criminals captured in the lordship of Chirk he found himself both judge and executioner. When the appointed executioner failed in his office and struck too light a blow Ieuan stepped forward and boldly decapitated both fellows himself. Dramatic glimpses of gore and glory such as these with all their savagery and defiance, albeit sometimes exaggerated, are preserved for posterity in the chronicle history left to us by the redoubtable squire of Gwydir.

NOTE

Several variations of the placename 'Gwydir', such as 'Gwyder', 'Gwedyr', 'Gwydyr' and 'Gwaedir', appear in a large corpus of sources relating to the Wynn family and its successors, the dukes of Ancaster, who acquired the estate in 1678 on the marriage of Robert Bertie, baron Willoughby de Eresby to Mary Wynn, heiress of Sir Richard Wynn, 4th baronet, the grandson of Sir John Wynn. Various attempts have been made to explain it but it is now accepted that the name derives from 'gwedir' (lowlying land) as opposed to 'gorthir' (upland). The Welsh professional poets consistently use the correct form 'Gwedir'. In this edition of the *History of the Gwydir Family* and *Memoirs*, however, 'Gwydir', the modern and most commonly accepted name, is used.

FURTHER READING

B G Charles   *George Owen of Henllys* (1973).

R R Davies   *Conquest, Co-existence and Change: Wales 1063-1415* (1987).

A H Dodd   *A History of Caernarvonshire 1284-1900* (1968).

C A Gresham   *Eifionydd: a Study in Landownership from the Medieval Period to the Present Day* (1973).

J G Jones   '*The Wynn Estate of Gwydir: Aspects of its Growth and Development c. 1500-1580*', *NLWJ, xxii (Pt. ii)* (1981).

G D Owen   *Elizabethan Wales: the Social Scene* (1962).

G Roberts   *Aspects of Welsh History* (1969).

G Williams   *The Welsh Church from Conquest to Reformation* (1962).

G Williams   *Recovery, Reorientation and Reformation: Wales c. 1415-1642* (1987).

W O Williams   *Tudor Gwynedd* (1958).

Notes on Manuscript and Printed Versions of the
HISTORY OF THE GWYDIR FAMILY and the MEMOIRS.

A. *Manuscript Copies of the History.*

1.—Ca. MS. 83.89-106 'The Booke of Sir John Wynn' [now catalogued as Ca. MS. 4.101]. Reputed to be the autograph manuscript by Sir John Wynn of Gwydir. *RWM*, ii (Pt. ii), pp. 783-9; *DNB*, lxxi, p. 257. A few editorial corrections and additions were made in the author's hand. It probably came into the possession of John Williams, agent of Lord Ancaster of Gwydir, and his son, the Rev. John Williams (1760-1826), rector of Llanbedr-y-cennin and Caerhun in the Conwy valley, who preserved most of the Wynn of Gwydir papers. *DWB*, p. 1050. It was later owned by Richard Cyffin Kenrick of Nantclwyd, Denbighshire, and from 1826 onwards by Sir Thomas Phillipps, Bart. (1792-1872), of Cheltenham, a renowned collector of manuscripts and antiquities. It was purchased, together with many of the Welsh manuscripts in the Phillipps Collection, for the Cardiff Public Library in 1896. *DWB*, p. 756; *CWP*, ix-xiii for further details. Several transcripts were made of the chronicle *History* but were often marred by mistranscription, bad punctuation and indifferent renderings into modern English.

2.—Peniarth MS. 120. Late seventeenth century c. 1672. *RWM*, i (Pt. ii), p. 731.

3.—NLW. MS. 3075 (Gloddaith—Mostyn MS.) c. 1674. A copy made by Sir Thomas Mostyn of Gloddaith (1651-1700), son of Sir Roger Mostyn, first baronet, by his second wife Mary Bulkeley of Baron Hill. The copy was compared with the original which, as Mostyn recalled in 1683, 'was in many places corrected and interlin'd and much of it writ with the hand of Sir John Wynn himselfe the Author'. *HGF* (1927), ix; *DWB*, p. 674.

4.—NLW. MS. 3061 (Mostyn MS. 165). Early eighteenth-century copy referred to by the Rev. Evan Evans (Ieuan Fardd) (1731-88), antiquary and priest, in his major work *Some Specimens of the Poetry of the Antient Welsh Bards* (1764), pp. 45-6, 155-61; *DWB*, pp. 229-31; *RWM*, i (Pt. i), p. 273.

5.—NLW. MS. 2025 (Panton MS. 58). Eighteenth-century copy, a transcription of no. 3 above by Ieuan Fardd. *RWM*, ii (Pt. iii), pp. 867-8.

6.—NLW. MS. 2035 (Panton MS. 69). Eighteenth-century copy of Sir Thomas Mostyn's transcript (no. 3 above), *RWM*, ii (Pt. iii), p. 864.

7.—NLW. Add. MS. 27B (Sir John Williams MS. 231), pp. 29-111. J. H. Davies (ed.), *Catalogue of Manuscripts*, i (1921), pp. 73-4. Early eighteenth-century copy in the hand of the Rev. David Lloyd, a native of Llanrwst and incumbent of Llan-ddoged (1720-35) and Eglwysbach (1735-8), later Canon Cursal of St. Asaph (1748). *H.St.A.* i, p. 354. It was from this copy, later owned by the Rev. John Jones (Tegid) (1792-1852), a Welsh scholar of some repute, that Angharad Llwyd copied the *Memoirs* which she printed in her 1827 version of the *History of the Gwydir Family. DWB*, p. 478. The manuscript also contains notes 'to be observed before you let your Survay Pass your hands' (pp. 115-37). They were subsequently published (from a copy belonging to Thomas Wright, the antiquary) under the misleading title *An Ancient Survey of Penmaenmawr* (1859) (J. O. Halliwell, ed.) and later printed by W. Bezant Lowe in 1906.

8.—NLW. Brogyntyn MS. (1st sequence), 13. It was probably a copy that appeared in the third quarter of the seventeenth century. This was the earliest copy W. W. E. Wynne of Peniarth (1801-80) knew of as he himself testifies. He was another celebrated antiquary and genealogist. *DWB*, pp. 1103-4; E. D. Jones (ed.), *Catalogue of Brogyntyn Manuscripts and Documents*, ii (1937), p. 23.

9.—NLW. Wynnstay MS. 120. A collation by W. W. E. Wynne of Angharad Llwyd's copy with nos. 2 and 8 above. It had probably been in the possession of Humphrey Humphreys, Bishop of Bangor (1689-1701), who annotated the text. *DWB*, pp. 395-6.

10.—NLW. MS. 21253D. Early eighteenth century, a text which originally formed part of the muniments at Mostyn and seemed to have derived from Add. MS. 27B and Wynnstay MS. 120. It is annotated, probably by Bishop Humphreys.

11.—NLW. MS. 12854D. Late eighteenth century. See *Handlist of Manuscripts in the National Library of Wales*, xxviii, p. 328.

12.—NLW. MS. 8427B. Late eighteenth century. Copy by John Thomas (1736-69), cleric, antiquary and a scholar of some reputation, from one of Ieuan Fardd's manuscripts (possibly NLW. MS. 2025:see no. 5 above).

13.—NLW. MS. 16969B. Dated 1766.

14.—NLW. MS. 1206 (Deposit), Tanybwlch MS. pp. 416-48. Early eighteenth century, almost a complete copy.

15. NLW. Bodewryd MS. 11D. Late eighteenth-century copy of MS. 3075 (No. 3 above). See NLW *Schedule of Bodewryd Manuscripts and Documents* (1932), 3.

Other copies are known to have existed but their present location is unknown.

B. *Printed Versions*

(i) *The History of the Gwydir Family* (1770) edited by the Honourable Daines Barrington (1722-1800), judge and antiquary, with introduction; notes and geneological tables were supplied by Dr. Thomas Percy (1768-1808). *DNB*, xliv, p. 437. Daines Barrington was Second Judge of the Anglesey Circuit of Great Sessions and became acquainted with Welsh antiquities. *DNB*, iii, p. 286; W. R. Williams, *The History of the Great Sessions in Wales 1542-1830 together with the Lives of the Welsh Judges* (1899), p. 67.

(ii) *Miscellanies by the Honourable Daines Barrington* (1781). A copy of the *History* is included with introduction, notes and tables etc. as above.

(iii) *The History of the Gwydir Family* (1827), edited by Angharad Llwyd (1779-1866) and published at Ruthin by the editor and her father, the Rev. John Lloyd (1733-93), rector of Caerwys, who was a scholar and antiquary of considerable renown, and a friend of Peter Yorke. *DWB*, pp. 582-3, 593, 1111. This edition contains an introduction, genealogical tables, notes and other details. M. Ellis, 'Angharad Llwyd, 1780-1866', *Flintshire Historical Society Publications*, xxvi, 1973-4, 80-4.

(iv) *The History of the Gwydir Family* (1878), edited by J. Askew Roberts (1826-84), and published at Oswestry, pp. 12-84. He was a well-known antiquary and journalist and the author of the famous *The Gossiping Guide to Wales* (1872).

The edition reproduces the notes of Daines Barrington together with additions obtained from W. W. E. Wynne of Peniarth whose annotated copy of the *History* (1827 ed.) is found in NLW. Peniarth MS. 420C. *DWB*, pp. 869-70; F. Boase (ed.), *Modern English Biography, 1851-1900* (1965) iii, p. 199.

(v) *The History of the Gwydir Family* (1927), edited by John Ballinger, then National Librarian of Wales, and published by the University of Wales Press to commemorate the tercentenary of Sir John Wynn's death. He reproduces (but not without some minor errors) the original autograph manuscript (Ca. MS. 83 [MS. 4.101] above). Since all earlier transcripts had departed from the autograph manuscript the editor considered it 'desirable to produce a text following the original in all its details and omitting all notes'. He supplies a comparatively short but inadequate introduction on the Wynn family and the social background to the chronicle but is considered more useful on manuscript and printed sources. Some of the details supplied about copies of the manuscripts, however, are now out of date. The non-inclusion of notes on the text is considered a serious deficiency in this edition.

C. *Manuscript Copies of the Memoirs*

The original manuscript is lost and only four transcripts survive.

(a) NLW. Add. MS. 27B, pp. 5-28. Transcribed by the Rev. David Lloyd c. 1720 (See no. 7 above).

(b) NLW. 21253D. Early eighteenth century. This version contains a prologue as follows: 'Now haveing taken View and Survey of the Soils and Situation of the County of Caernarvon it would be considered and remembered what Witts and Worthy Members to the Common wealth from time to time this poor County brought forth'. It is not included in other copies, which suggests that the author had intended the *Memoirs* to be part of a larger work on Caernarfonshire. The manuscript also contains the notes, later to be published under the title *An Ancient Survey of Penmaenmawr*, appended to the Add. MS. 27B version *of the History of the Gwydir Family* (see no. 7 above).

(c) NLW. MS. 1577 and (d) NLW. MS. 1592, both of which were transcribed by Angharad Llwyd from the transcripts of the Rev. David Lloyd which she had borrowed from the Rev. John Jones (Tegid). The first copy contains a short preamble and notes which were to be published in the 1827 printed edition of the *History*. M. Ellis, op. cit., 80-2.

D. *Printed Versions of the Memoirs.*

(i) *The History of the Gwydir Family* (1827), edited by Angharad Llwyd with the *Memoirs* attached, pp. 102-21 [incomplete].

(ii) *The History of the Gwydir Family* (1878), edited by J. Askew Roberts with the *Memoirs* (and notes) attached, pp. 90-109.

(iii) *The History of the Gwydir Family* (1927), edited by John Ballinger with the *Memoirs* attached, pp. 61-75.

Gruffudd ap Cynan, prince of Wales, had by his wife Angharad, the daughter of Owain ab Edwin, lord of Englefield, Owain Gwynedd, Cadwaladr and Cadwallon, who was slain before his father's death. He reigned over Wales fifty years. His troublesome life and famous acts are compiled by a most ancient friar or monk of Wales, and was found among the posterity of the said Gruffudd ap Cynan in the house of Gwydir in north Wales, and at the request of Maurice Wynn, esquire (who had the same in a most ancient book written, and was lineally descended from him) was translated into Latin by Nicholas Robinson, Bishop of Bangor, and are extant.

> Let it be known to those now living and to those yet to come that I Gruffudd son of Cynan have granted, given and ratified to God and to the church of Saint John the Evangelist, Haughmond, and to the canons serving God in that place for their church of Nefyn three acres in Nefyn and Abraham son of Aldred the cobbler and the two sons of Serenna, namely Wasdewi and John, as a perpetual almsdeed, and may it, by perpetual right, belong without let or hindrance to the church of Saint Mary at Nefyn and the aforesaid canons of Haughmond.

Owain Gwynedd was prince after his father. He married as his first wife Gwladys, the daughter of Llywarch ap Trahaearn, lord of Dyfed, by whom he had only Iorwerth or Edward with the broken nose. And by his second wife called Christina, the daughter of Goronwy ab Owain ab Edwin, lord of Englefield, being his cousin, he had Dafydd (who after him was Prince), Rhodri, lord of Anglesey, and Cadwallon, who was Abbot of Bardsey. This Prince Owain, with his brother Cadwaladr, as the Welsh chronicle makes mention, in his father's time made many victorious voyages into south Wales against the Normans who encroached mightily on that country, and in a pitched field slew

3,000 men and put the rest to flight. Being prince after his father's death he overthrew the earl of Chester and a number of marcher lords and, as Giraldus Cambrensis has in his history entitled *Itinerarium Kambriae*,
5   repulsed King Henry the Second who made three royal voyages against Wales with all the power of England, Normandy and Aquitaine together with the succours of Flanders and Brittany. In one of which voyages, at Colshill Wood, the whole army of the King was put to
10 flight, as the French Chronicle says, the King's person endangered and the great standard of England overthrown and forsaken. This caused Robert Montfort, a noble baron, to apeach Henry of Essex, the standard bearer (who held that office by inheritance) for
15 beginning the flight of treason which, being tried by battle, the standard bearer was overthrown, his office, lands and goods confiscated and himself shaven a monk in the abbey of Reading. After this prince had reigned most victoriously thirty two years, he died. It is written
20 of him that he was so fortunate that he never attempted that enterprise which he achieved not.

Cadwaladr, brother to prince Owain, was married to Alice, daughter to Richard, earl Clare, and was lord of Ceredigion or Cardiganshire.

25   Cadwaladr brother of Owain the Great greetings in the Lord. Be it known to all that I Cadwaladr, for the salvation of my own soul and of my ancestors and my heirs have given and granted to God and to the church of Saint John the Evangelist, Haughmond, and to the
30   canons serving God in that place the church at Nefyn as a pure and perpetual almsdeed. Witness Alice de Clare my wife.
            To Ranulf, earl of Chester etc. I decree that the Abbot of Shrewsbury and his community are to have the
35   whole tenure (of land) between the Ribble and the Mersey (rivers). Witness Richard de Clare and Cadwaladr ap Gruffudd ap Cynan, King of Wales, and Robert Basset and Geoffrey Despenser at Chester.

Although this record calls this Cadwaladr King of
40 Wales because he had kingly authority in this country,

he was ever a subject to his brother by whom he was banished and lost his land till, by composition, the same was restored. The Welsh chronicle calls him Prince of Wales: he dwelt mostly at the castle of Aberystwyth and he was murdered by the English soldiers 5 which the King sent to conduct him to his country.

After the death of Owain, Iorwerth or Edward, his son, being thought unfit to govern by reason of the deformity of his face, Dafydd, his brother, became prince in his father's room. 10

I find that Iorwerth Drwyndwn or Edward with the broken nose, being put from the government of the Principality, had assigned him for his part of his father's inheritance the hundreds of Nanconwy and Ardudwy. He dwelt at the castle of Dolwyddelan where it is 15 thought credibly his son, Llywelyn the Great or Prince Llywelyn, was born whose mother was Mared, the daughter of Madog ap Maredudd, Prince of Powys. Cynan ab Owain Gwynedd's sons had, for their part, the country of Meirionnydd. 20

Dafydd married Emma, sister to King Henry the second and had by her a son called Owain; and, upon confidence of that match, he banished his base brothers and imprisoned his brother Rhodri because he desired his portion of inheritance. But Rhodri, breaking his 25 brother's prison, entered the isle of Anglesey and was received of the people as sovereign lord thereof, and within a while recovered all that part of Wales which lies above the river of Conwy. At such time as Giraldus Cambrensis, in the company of Baldwin, Archbishop of 30 Canterbury, travelled through Wales preaching the Cross against the infidels, Dafydd held no other part of the Principality of Wales save Rhuddlan castle and the territory adjacent which he held with a garrison of English where the Archbishop lodged one night to visit 35 the King's sister. The same Giraldus does testify in his book entitled his Journey through Wales.

Giraldus Cambrensis makes mention that Rhodri was prince at such time as the Archbishop preached the Cross in Anglesey, and that he had in his court 40

Llywelyn, the son of Iorwerth or Edward, his nephew. Though he was overborn by his uncle Dafydd (who married the King of England's sister and had by her issue male, as also his uncle Rhodri who, to strengthen himself with the power of south Wales, had married his own cousin, the daughter of the Lord Rhys ap Gruffudd ap Rhys ap Tewdwr Mawr, and by her had issue Gruffudd and Thomas) yet God so advanced the right of the young Prince Llywelyn that in time he put down both his uncles from the princely sceptre and their posterity.

Yet may be imagined considering what place they held in their country and what friends they had abroad, not without an honourable composition and provision for themselves and their posterity first had:

To all the sons of God's holy church both now living and to come, greetings from King Dafydd, son of Owain. Be it known to you that I have granted to the abbot and canons of Haughmond the land that he has had in the town of Nefyn free of all local customs, and I likewise grant to the aforesaid canons the tithes of my mill in Nefyn as a perpetual almsdeed. Witness John de Burchelton, Radulf of Leigh, Einion Sais etc.

Dafydd, son of Owain, prince of North Wales to all Christ's faithful in France and England greetings in the Lord always. Know that this is with the consent of Emma my wife and Owain my heir. To this witness bishop Reiner, Radulf of Leigh.

Lady Emma, sister of King Henry, wife of King Dafydd, son of Owain prince of North Wales etc. Know that this is with the consent of Dafydd, my husband and Owain my heir etc. Witness Einion Sais, Radulf of Leigh.

It appears by the records in King John's time remaining in the Tower that the King gave to Owain, the son of Dafydd (being his cousin german) and to Gruffudd, the son of Rhodri, three *cantrefi*, Rhos, Rhufoniog and Dyffryn Clwyd excepting the castle of Deganwy and the territory of Creuddyn wherein the said castle did stand, and also gave them three other *cantrefi* if they could win them. The record follows in these words.

John by the Grace of God, etc. Know that we have
granted and by this our charter confirmed to Owain, son
of Dafydd and Gruffudd, son of Rhodri three *cantrefi*,
that is Rhos, saving to us the camp of Deganwy with
Creuddyn, where that camp is situated, Rhufoniog and   5
Dyffryn Clwyd with their appurtenances, to hold in full
for the said Owain and Gruffudd and their heirs from us
and our heirs to pay to us and to our heirs the services
undermentioned, that is, each year 12 *dextrarii* [war-
horses], at their cost from each cantref 4 *dextrarii*, and   10
in addition from these three *cantrefi* one pack of hounds
each year and ten greyhounds and hawks and falcons
and sparrow hawks from the said *cantrefi* paying them
to us and our heirs each year at Salop on the feast of St.
Peter *ad Vincula*; in addition they shall both go on our   15
service with the people of the said *cantrefi* and another
shall remain if we wish it: the said Owain and Gruffudd
shall give sureties to us for their loyal service if Owain,
son of Dafydd, gives his son from his wife or betroths
etc.   20
And if by their own efforts and by our approval they are
able to win Arfon, Arllechwedd and Llŷn they shall do
the same service for these aforementioned *cantrefi* as
for the other three *cantrefi* mentioned earlier. Witnesses. Lord Peter, Bishop of Winchester; William, earl of   25
Salisbury, our brother; Geoffrey, son of Peter, earl of
Essex; William, earl of Arundel; William, earl of Warenne;
Saher, earl of Winchester; William, earl Ferrars;
William Briwer; Peter, son of Herbert; Thomas of
Ardinton; Philip of Orby, Justice of Chester. Dated by   30
the hand of Master Richard Marsk, Archdeacon of
Northumberland, at Southwark 3 October in the 14th
year of our reign.

By this record, as also by the Welsh history which
mentions that Dafydd ab Owain often attempted by the   35
power of the King of England to recover the Principality
against Prince Llywelyn, his nephew, it may appear
that the cousins Owain, the son of Dafydd, and
Gruffudd, the son of Rhodri, joined with the King of
England against their prince, Llywelyn. But all in vain   40
for Giraldus makes mention that they got no other
portion but what they had by composition in what
place it was in Wales the sons of Rhodri had possessions

granted them. Whether it was in diverse places (as is most likely it should be) to weaken men of their alliance, friends and authority among the commons, it does not appear by certain record.

5   Whether Dafydd ab Owain had any more children by the King's sister but Owain, and whether any, or who, be descended either by male or female of them, I can yet find no certainty thereof.

In a fragment of a Welsh chronicle I copied by Sir
10   Thomas Wiliems I find that in [the] end Llywelyn killed his uncle Dafydd and all his posterity at Conwy, so that I think there is none descended from the said Dafydd and the Lady Emma, his wife, either by male or female.

The posterity of Rhodri were large possessors in
15   Denbighland called Rhos and Rhufoniog, near and about Denbigh castle in the chiefest and best part of the same as shall hereafter in this History appear (whereby it may seem that King John's grant of that country was not wholly frustrate unto them or whether they had
20   that land given them by the last Prince Llywelyn, it is uncertain). They were also lords of diverse lordships in the county of Caernarfon, especially in the hundred of Eifionydd. The Eifionydd men have it among them by tradition that Llywelyn the Great gave the lands in
25   Eifionydd unto the posterity of Rhodri.

I find in a fragment of a Welsh chronicle, copied by my kinsman Sir Thomas Wiliems, that Rhodri had another son called Einion, as is afore specified, by the daughter of Lord Rhys, prince of south Wales, besides
30   Gruffudd (before mentioned) and Thomas.

Rhodri's second wife was the daughter [of] Godred, King of Man. In Anno Domini 1243 Rhodri ab Owain, by the help of Godred, King of Man, invaded Anglesey but within one year was thence repulsed by the sons of
35   Cynan ab Owain Gwynedd who held the isle to themselves. Query: who are descended of this Cynan? There is in the township of Pennant, Eifionydd, a Gwely called Gwely Wyrion Cynan held very freely; men suppose that there part of this Cynan's inheritance was.
40   I remember the words of Giraldus Cambrensis who says

so. I will advisedly omit the cruel and unnatural wars
that were for ambition of government between prince
Owain's children and offspring in the time of the said
Giraldus. Rhodri lies buried in the College of Caergybi.
This I had out of the Welsh chronicle copied by Sir   5
Thomas Wiliems.

Thomas married Mared, the daughter of Einion ap
Seisyllt and had by her Caradog ap Thomas who
married Efa, the daughter of Gwyn ap Gruffudd, lord of
Cegidfa. He had by her Einion ap Caradog, lord of   10
Penychen (where his manor is called to this day viz.
Llys Einion ap Caradog), Baladeulyn and Pen-y-berth
and of many places more as may be imagined by his
greatness in his time; and Gruffudd ap Caradog, lord of
Ffriwlwyd (where the ruins of his manor house do   15
also appear), Ystrad Ysgeibion and of other great possessions in Rhos and Rhufoniog; and Syna married to
Gruffudd ap Llywelyn ab Iorwerth, eldest son to the
great Prince Llywelyn by whom the said Gruffudd begat
Llywelyn ap Gruffudd ap Llywelyn, last Prince of Wales   20
of the British race who was slain at Buellt.

Llywelyn, the son of Iorwerth, the son of Owain
Gwynedd (having, by the help of his cousins Cynan ab
Owain Gwynedd's sons, deposed his uncles) began to
reign the year of our Lord 1194. He achieved so many   25
noble enterprises that he obtained the name Llywelyn
the Great among all posterity and writers. His works
and worthy deeds, being remembered by so many
writers, do make me the less to dwell upon the
rehearsal of them, seeing my purpose is no more than   30
cursoriwise to touch the reign of the princes to the end
to make the History. I write more easy to be understood
when, as it shall appear, in the reign of what prince
everything was done. Only I have thought good to
insert here a copy of one of King Henry the Third's   35
letters unto the said Prince Llywelyn, which is extant
in the record of the Treasury at Westminster (because it
is extant in no chronicle that I have seen), and thence
brought to light by Richard Broughton, esquire, Justice
of North Wales, the chief antiquary of England, a man   40

to whom his country is most beholding. He preferred
nothing more than the honour thereof which he most
carefully rakes out of the ashes of oblivion in searching,
quoting and copying to his great charge all the ancient
5   records he can come by.

Henry King of England etc. To Llywelyn, prince of Aber-
ffraw, lord of Snowdon greetings. Since because of
floods and damage to the roads our messengers are not
able to reach you we have sent these present letters to
10   you by a courier by which we indicate to your majesty
that we for us and our people have kept peace with you
and your people and will keep it in future and have given
this in orders to our bailiffs that they keep peace firmly
with their fellow-marchers and observe it wherefore we
15   ask your serenity that you will please give in orders to
your bailiffs who live in the march that they should
keep the peace inviolate with our men: if this is pleasing
to you that you will signify to us, may your excellency
be well.
20   Llywelyn, prince of North Wales to all his faithful both
present and future who see this present writing
greetings. Know all of you that we have granted to God
and to the church of St. John the Evangelist at Haughmond and to the canons who serve God there for the
25   salvation of our soul and that of our father and Dafydd,
son of Owain our uncle etc. as the charter of the said
Dafydd, son of Owain testifies. Witnesses Reiner,
Bishop of St. Asaph and Radulf of Leigh etc.

In Anno Domini 1253 one Gruffudd ap Cynan ab
30   Owain Gwynedd was buried in a monk's cowl in the
abbey of Conwy as says the Welsh chronicle. Anno 1201
Prince Llywelyn banished Maredudd, the son of Cynan
ab Owain Gwynedd, suspected of treason, and seized
the *cantrefi* of Llŷn and Eifionydd, which were Cynan's
35   lands, into his own hands. Giraldus Cambrensis, in his
Itinerarium Kambriae says that the *cantrefi* of Llŷn and
Eifionydd were the possessions of Owain Gwynedd's
children when he passed through Wales, and that they
had two castles, the one in Carnfadryn in Llŷn, the
40   other called Deudraeth *juxta Montana Borealia de
Eryri*; which confirms that Ardudwy and Eifionydd

made but one *cantref* for Penrhyndeudraeth, where that
castle stood, is in Ardudwy.

I am of opinion that the *cantrefi* of Llŷn and Eifionydd
were the possessions of Rhodri and given by this Prince
Llywelyn upon the expulsion of Rhodri from the Princi-   5
pality of this Maredudd ap Cynan. Howsoever it was,
the posterity of Rhodri held it till the conquest of Wales
by the King of England and then, how they lost what
remained as principal undivided into small portions
shall hereafter be shown in this History.   10

Prince Llywelyn married Joan, the daughter of King
John, begotten by his wife Agatha, daughter of Robert
Ferrers, earl of Derby. The King, in marriage, gave with
his daughter the lordship of Ellesmere in the marches of
Wales. Some will affirm that Agatha was not the King's   15
wife but a paramour, but that is most untrue for he
married her long before he was King, and because she
bore no issue male (as some affirm) divorced himself
from her. Others think she died anon after he was King.

Prince Llywelyn in youth, long before this recited   20
marriage, had married Tangwystl ferch Llywarch Goch
of Rhos by whom he begot a most valiant son called
Gruffudd ap Llywelyn who, as heir apparent in his
father's time, after many wars between him and his
father, had the *cantrefi* of Englefield, Rhos, Rhufoniog   25
and Dyffryn Clwyd given him by his father, [they] being
countries next adjoining unto England, to the end he
might defend his country from the English.

This Gruffudd, in his father's [life]time, married Syna
or Senena (as the Latin book calls her), daughter to   30
Caradog ap Thomas ap Rhodri ab Owain Gwynedd.
Some of our Welsh pedigrees say she was the daughter
of the King of Man, but it is an untruth. There are other
most ancient records to the contrary verifying as here is
laid down.   35

Also, it was evident that her brothers Einion ap
Caradog and Gruffudd ap Caradog lost their land in the
quarrel of her son, Llywelyn ap Gruffudd, last Prince of
Wales, when his uncle Dafydd held the Principality
against him, as shall hereafter appear. In Prince   40

Llywelyn ab Iorwerth's time you shall find mention made of Hywel ap Gruffudd ap Cynan ab Owain Gwynedd whom the Prince does banish in Anno 1211, and after in Anno 1215 you shall find him first remembered in the honourable voyage Prince Llywelyn made into south Wales when he razed Carmarthen. Query: where his possessions were and who are come of him?

Hywel ap Gruffudd ap Cynan died and is buried at Conwy. I find not during Prince Llywelyn ab Iorwerth's reign any mention made of anything done by the posterity of Rhodri ab Owain Gwynedd. A man may easily guess the reason for that he held them under and suspected lest they should aspire to the princely dignity which their ancestors sometimes had held.

In the reign of Dafydd ap Llywelyn, son of the said Prince Llywelyn by Joan, King John's daughter, who began to reign Anno [1240], Einion and Gruffudd ap Caradog took part with their sister's son, Llywelyn ap Gruffudd, the last Prince of Wales of that line, after slain at Buellt.

We receive it by tradition from father to son in Eifionydd that Dafydd ap Llywelyn, being prince by the aid of his uncle, the King, came to the town of Pwllheli in Llŷn to parley with the brothers Einion and Gruffudd, whom the brothers met with such a force at that meeting or day of truce that the Prince told them they were too strong to be subjects. Whereof they answered that he was rather too weak to be a prince, and so parted without any conclusion of agreement. In the end they were forced by long war to forgo that country and to lose their land there, and to join themselves to their nephew, Llywelyn ap Gruffydd, who then had his court at Maesmynan in Flintshire. [He] held, as afore is mentioned, the *cantrefi* of Englefield, Dyffryn Clwyd, Rhos and Rhufoniog against his uncle Dafydd, [he] having war on the one side with the King, on the other side with his uncle, who gave them great possessions, as some think, as afore is remembered about Denbigh castle.

Original MS. of part of the *History of the Gwydir Family* in Sir John Wynn's hand

MS. copy of part of Rhys Goch Eryri's *cywydd*
to Robert ap Maredudd

Llywelyn, the son of Gruffudd, their nephew, after
the death of his uncle Dafydd, attaining the government of Wales, restored to his uncles their lands and
possessions in the county of Caernarfon. I find no
record of anything done by them in the time of the same   5
prince.

Einion ap Caradog had a son of whom mention shall
be made hereafter, called Tudur, lord of Penychen, Pen-
y-berth and Baladeulyn, and whether he had any more
sons is to me uncertain.   10

Gruffudd ap Caradog married Lleucu ferch Llywarch
Fychan ap Llywarch Goch ap Llywarch Howlbwrch,
and had but one son to my knowledge called Dafydd ap
Gruffudd. [This] Dafydd married Efa, the sole heir of
Gruffudd Fychan ap Gruffudd ap Moreiddig of Penyfed   15
in Eifionydd by whom he had three sons viz., Dafydd,
Maredudd and Hywel, as may appear by the record of
the extent made of Denbighland in the time of Edward
the First by Henry Lacy, earl of Lincoln, to whom the
King gave that land upon the conquest of Wales. For   20
Henry Lacy, minding to make a princely seat of the
castle of Denbigh, perforce compelled the children of
the said Dafydd ap Gruffudd to exchange their possessions about Denbigh castle (which were great) with
him for other land of less value in the said lordship in   25
the furthest part from him, the words of the record do
follow in these words.

How they lost the lordship of Ffriwlwyd and other
their lands in the county of Caernarfon I can find no
record of but only have it by tradition that it was taken   30
from them by the King's officers. For to this day it is
part of the possessions of the Principality of Wales,
which is not unlike, considering what befell the other
cousins, the heirs of Einion ap Caradog, lord of Penychen, Pen-y-berth and Baladeulyn, whereof there is a   35
very good and certain record remaining in the Prince's
Treasury in Caernarfon.

Einion ap Caradog had one son called Tudur ab Einion
and one daughter called Gwerfyl, whereof the record
ensuing after makes mention. You are to understand   40

that, after the conquest of Wales, the country in general
as well as in particular found themselves aggrieved for
the wrongs offered them by the English officers and,
therefore, sent certain men with their general and
private griefs to the Prince lying at Kennington near
London in the time of the parliament in Anno 29 of
Edward the First, among the which these are.

Petitions of Kennington made at Kennington for the
men of North Wales alike for counts as for individual
persons presented to our lord the prince, son of King
Edward, conqueror of Wales, and to his council at
Kennington outside London in the time of the parliament of the aforesaid king held at Westminster on the
first Sunday of Lent in the 33rd year of the reign of the
aforesaid king; and the responses to these same
petitions made and delivered to the Justice of North
Wales under the private seal of the said lord the Prince,
for the execution of the aforesaid responses and for
firmly observing them in the parts of North Wales.

To the petition of Llywelyn and Gruffudd, sons of
Owain ap Llywelyn, concerning the fact that Tudur ab
Einion, their uncle, was lord of Baladeulyn, Penychen
and Pen-y-berth in the county of Caernarvon and was
seized after the proclamation of the peace almost for
one year, after whose death the aforesaid holding should
have descended to Gwerfyl, sister of the said Tudur, as
to the nearest related heir of the same Tudur, but the
lady queen, mother of the Prince, laid claim to the
holding and obtained it from its lord, which holdings are
now in the hand of the Prince, and by right of inheritance look to them, wherefore they seek a remedy. It was
responded that the Justice should inform himself
concerning what was contained in the aforesaid
petition, and at what time the said Tudur died and
whether he paid forfeit or not, and concerning all the
other circumstances, and inform his lord of this.

To the petition of the said Llywelyn and Gruffudd that
the lord should be willing to grant to them certain
bailiffs in the county of Caernarvon for a due rent to be
paid for them until such time as it shall be decided what
is to be done concerning their inheritance, it was
responded that it should pertain to the Justice to make
such arrangements concerning these bailiffs as seemed
best fitting for the interest of the lord.

It is necessary for the understanding of this record, and the sense thereof, that you first understand that, after the death of Prince Llywelyn in Buellt, the King made a proclamation of peace to all the inhabitants of Wales receiving therein all that would come in and yield themselves to him into his protection, granting them the use and fruition of their lands, liberties and privileges they held before in their country under the Prince of Wales. This is the peace specified in this record after the which Tudur ab Einion had held his lands almost one year. To whom or to what family this Gwerfyl was married I cannot as yet learn. This land so taken is part of the possessions of the Principality of Wales to this day. It is to be noted here that, at the self same time in the reign of Edward the First, the Queen, his wife, took perforce the land of Einion ap Caradog's offspring in the county of Caernarfon and Henry Lacy exchanged perforce with Gruffudd ap Caradog's offspring in Denbighland, and that the cousins stood in equal degree of kindred one to another (viz. cousin germans removed): which hard dealing must needs pull down a kindred. It cannot be otherwise also but that Ffriwlwyd was, by the same Queen or by the Justice, William Sutton or others (who dealt hardly with the gentry of these parts in those days), taken from the posterity of Gruffudd for that it is part of the Principality to these days although the record happened not into my hands.

But to return to the offspring of Gruffudd ap Caradog of whose succession, with the state and condition they lived in from time to time to this day, being my purpose to entreat. Of the three brothers, Dafydd, Maredudd and Hywel, who exchanged land, as above is remembered, with the earl of Lincoln, the posterity only of Hywel does remain in credit and show in their country, the posterity of the other two being, by the division and subdivision of gavelkind (the destruction of Wales) brought to the estate of mean freeholders and so, having forgotten their descents and pedigree, are become as if they never had been. If you ask the question why the

succession of Hywel sped better than the posterity of
the other two brothers I can yield you no other reason
but God's mercy and goodness towards the one more
than the other (as God said in the book of Moses: 'I will
5   have mercy on whom I will have mercy'). For they lived
in the same commonwealth and under the same storm
of oppression so as if God had not left us a seed we had
been like Sodom or compared to Gomorra. Nevertheless, by the goodness of God we are and continue in the
10   reputation of gentlemen from time to time since unto
this day as shall appear by the discourse following. The
offspring of Dafydd and Maredudd hold the land
exchanged by the earl of Lincoln with their ancestors
viz. the township of Esgair Ebrill in Eglwysbach and
15   half Mathebrwd in Llanrwst, and are reputed as
descended from Gruffudd ap Cynan in that quarter
where they dwell but yet, as afore, are not able to lay
down the certainty of their pedigree.

      Dafydd ap Gruffudd ap Caradog, as afore, married Efa,
20   the daughter and heir of Gruffudd Fychan ap Gruffudd
ap Moreiddig and by her had that land which, in the
Extent of North Wales, is called Gwely Gruffudd in
Penyfed in Eifionydd in the county of Caernarfon. The
quit rent of the Prince of this *Gwely* is three pounds
25   nineteen shillings. Which Moreiddig the grandfather of
this woman was I am uncertain for there were of that
name two; one in north Wales is descended of Sandde
Hardd of Fortyn (of whom the chief men in Yale and
Maelor derive their descent) and another in south
30   Wales called Moreiddig Warwyn of whom are come all
the Vaughans. It was not extant in the Welsh pedigrees
that this Gruffudd was descended of Moreiddig till I
found the record thereof in the Exchequer of Caernarfon. If a man list to be curious which of both
35   Moreiddig's this was, let him find [which one] of them
lived nearest this time, and that sure was he.

      Hywel ap Dafydd married Efa, the daughter and heir
of Ieuan ap Hywel ap Maredudd of Eifionydd (by some
cards of pedigree she is called Myfanwy) and had by her
40   large possessions in Eifionydd which, to this day,

remain to the posterity of the said Hywel, yet mangled
with division and subdivision of gavelkind.

Memorandum: that Ieuan ap Hywel ap Maredudd had
another daughter and co-heir married to one of Penllyn,
of the stock of Rhirid Flaidd of Penllyn. Her name was 5
Gwenllïan and she married Ieuan ap Gruffudd ap
Madog ap Rhys ap Madog ap Rhirid Flaidd of Penllyn.
And the said Ieuan ap Hywel ap Maredudd had a third
daughter and coparcener who married Hywel ap
Goronwy ab Ieuan ap Goronwy ap Hywel of Maelor and 10
by him she had two daughters, to wit Gwerfyl, married
to Tudur Hobydili, the other was Alicine, married to
Puleston and brought Hafod-y-wern to the Pulestons.
Ieuan ap Hywel ap Maredudd, father to this Efa, was
brother to Gruffudd ap Hywel ap Maredudd who was 15
father to Einion ap Gruffudd and Hywel ap Gruffudd.
This Hywel was knighted at the field of Poitiers and, by
our countrymen, is reported to have taken the French
King, but, howsoever it was, he did such service there
that the Prince bestowed a mess of meat to be served up 20
daily during his life before his battle-axe which after
was bestowed on the poor; whereof he was called Sir
Hywel 'Y Fwyall'. Also, he was Constable of Chester
and Cricieth castle, had the mills to farm and other
many great offices and places of profit. Of Einion, his 25
brother, are descended very many gentlemen of
principal account in this county of Caernarfon. Hywel
begat Maredudd and Dafydd. Maredudd ap Hywel dwelt
in Eifionydd at his houses Cefn-y-fan and Y Gesail
Gyfarch, and Dafydd in Llanrwst in Denbighland at his 30
house called Yr Henblas in Mathebrwd. Maredudd ap
Hywel married Morfudd, the daughter of Ieuan ap
Dafydd ap Trahaearn Goch of Llŷn, who [was] descended of the house of Rhys ap Tewdwr. In the Extent of
North Wales, made in the 26th year of Edward the Third 35
you shall find that Maredudd ap Hywel and others are
the heirs of Gwely Gruffudd. Dafydd ap Hywel, his
brother, married [   ] ferch Ieuan ap Hywel ap
Maredudd. The daughter of Gwenllïan and Ieuan ap
Gruffudd ap Madog ab Iorwerth was wife to Rheinallt ap 40

Bleddyn and had by her issue Robin Fychan ap Dafydd
ap Hywel. He married Angharad, the daughter of Rhys
ap Gruffudd ap Rhys ab Ednyfed Fychan and had no
issue male but one daughter called Catherine ferch
5 Robin Fychan who married Rhys ab Einion Fychan of
Llanrwst, a gentleman of the house of Penwyn of
Nanconwy and Denbighland. He, having no issue male
by her but daughters, the greatest part of the possessions of that house, which were now worth a thousand
10 marks a year, came to the Salusburys for Robert
Salusbury the elder, fourth son of Thomas Salusbury of
Llyweni in the county of Denbigh, esquire, married
Gwenhwyfar, the daughter of Rhys ab Einion and
Catherine, the daughter and heir of Robin Fychan ap
15 Dafydd ap Hywel. Rhys ab Einion had one other
daughter by her called Lleucu (to whom he gave fair
possessions but nothing comparable to the other) who
was married to Gruffudd ap Madog Fychan in Abergele.
All the inheritance of this Robin Fychan ap Dafydd ap
20 Hywel held after the Welsh tenure within the lordship
of Denbigh was, by the custom of the country, to
descend to his heir male, and so descended to Ieuan, the
son of Robert ap Maredudd, his cousin, as hereafter
shall be laid down in the life of the said Ieuan. I have in
25 my house the probate of the testament of Morfudd, the
wife of Maredudd ap Hywel as fair to behold as at the
first day bearing date in anno 1416. The probate of the
will is dated at Cricieth before one Robert Swathen,
official of the archdeacon of Meirionydd. Maredudd ap
30 Hywel had by her two sons, Robert and Ieuan, and a
daughter called Marsli (married to Jenkin Conway of
Rhuddlan), mother to Hen John Aer y Conwy, of whom
all the Conways of Rhuddlan and Botryddan and lords of
Prestatyn are descended. She was the first Welsh
35 woman who was married into that house as John
Conway, esquire, my cousin, now lord thereof, often
told me. Siôn Tudur, one of our Welsh heralds, says that
there was a third brother called Robin whose daughter
and heir married Ithel Fychan and so all the Bithels,

being descended of him, do quarter Owain Gwynedd's eaglets.

1461 -1471

I find an obligation, bearing date 20 July 2 Edward IV, *1463* wherein John ap Maredudd stands bound to Ieuan ap Robert ap Maredudd to stand to the award of Gruffudd   5 ap Robin ap Gruffudd and Lewis ap Hywel ap Llywelyn, arbitrators elect, for the said John ap Maredudd, and Maredudd ap Rhys and Ieuan ap Hywel ap Rhys ab Einion, arbitrators elect for the said Ieuan ap Robert to part certain tenements between them in Eifionydd and,   10 in case they could not agree, then was Hywel ab Einion ap Hywel Coetmor named umpire.

Memorandum that, during Robert ap Maredudd's time, the inheritance descended to him and to his brother, Ieuan, was not parted after the custom of the   15 country being gavelkind but Ieuan, being married, enjoyed both their houses viz. Cefn-y-fan and Y Gesail Gyfarch, and for that Ieuan, then constable of Cricieth, clave fast to the King. Owain Glyndŵr burnt them both to cold ashes, neither was the inheritance between   20 their posterity divided until such time as Ieuan, the son of this Robert, was married and had many children as may appear by the indentures of partition between Ieuan, the son of this Robert, and John ap Maredudd ab Ieuan, grandchild to the other brother Ieuan (the one   25 part of which indentures I have), and those that made partition between them were Thomas ap Robin of Cochwillan, who married Gwenhwyfar ferch Ieuan ap Maredudd [and] . . .

This Thomas ap Robin was after beheaded near the   30 castle of Conwy by the Lord Herbert for that he was a follower of the house of Lancaster, and his wife is reported to carry away his head in her apron. Some affirm Ieuan ap Maredudd to be the elder brother and so does all the race that are of him contend. Myself, and   35 those that are come of Robert, have this reason to think him to be the elder. Robert had issue Ieuan; Ieuan, his brother, had issue Maredudd; Maredudd had issue John. John, being of man's estate, had the tuition of his uncle, Ieuan ap Robert, my ancestor, and yet Robin Fychan ap   40

Dafydd ap Hywel's land in Denbighland, being cousin
to them both, descended to Ieuan ap Robert, my
ancestor, and not to John ap Maredudd which I hold for
an invincible argument that Ieuan is come of the elder.

5   Also, I have the King's writ directed to Robert ap
Maredudd, Maredudd ab Ieuan ap Maredudd, and to the
principal gentlemen of Eifionydd for the apprehension
of Ieuan ap Robin 'herwr', a notable rebel and outlaw
and others of his quality. The writ does place Robert ap

10   Maredudd first before his nephew, which also may
fortify the opinion of them who hold him to be the elder
brother to Ieuan ap Maredudd. The words of which writ
follow in these words.

15   Henry by the grace of God king of England and France
       and lord of Ireland to his beloved Robert ap Maredudd,
       Maredudd ab Ieuan ap Maredudd, Rhys ap Tudur,
       Hywel ap Madog ab Ieuan, John ap Goronwy and Hywel
       ab Ieuan Fychan greetings. Since we are for certain
       informed that Ieuan ap Robin and other various

20   notorious outlaws and others unknown, from day to day
       and by force of arms, with various felons in their county
       have, it is said, made raids against various of our faithful
       subjects in our county of Caernarvon, and have despoil-
       ed and ill-treated various of our faithful subjects, to the

25   clear destruction and impoverishment of our liegemen
       and against the form of the statutes of our ancestors
       provided in these parts. We assign you and each of you
       jointly and severally to arrest and capture the aforesaid
       Ieuan ap Robin and any associated with his company

30   wherever they shall be found within the commote of
       Eifionydd and to bring them safe and sound to our castle
       at Caernarvon without delay, to deliver them to our
       constable there and let them stay in the said castle until
       we shall have seen fit to order otherwise regarding their

35   deliverance. And therefore we command you that you
       strive diligently concerning this task and so carry it out
       that you would be willing to answer to us in person
       concerning it. And we firmly enjoin all and sundry of
       our faithful subjects, by means of these presents, that to

40   you and to any of your men in all matters which pertain
       to the arrest and capture of the said Ieuan ap Robin and
       the others they shall strive and give assistance by force
       of arms and by responding in all ways. In testimony of

which matter we have had these our letters patent to be made, with myself as witness at Caernarvon the 28th day of August in the 20th year of our reign.

But howsoever it be the gavelkind and custom of the country, not yielding to the elder any prerogative or superiority more than to the younger, it is not a matter to be stood upon. 5

Indeed, Ieuan ap Maredudd married in his youth Lleucu, the daughter of Hywel Sele ap Meurig of the house of Nannau in Merionethshire and begat by her Maredudd ab Ieuan (whom, in his youth, he matched with Margaret, the daughter and heir of Einion ab Ithel of Rhiwedog in Penllyn in the county of Merioneth, esquire, of the tribe of Rhirid Flaidd), and Hywel ab Ieuan ap Maredudd. 10 15

Query: whether any males descended of this Hywel be living now. Owen Holland of Berw and Rhydderch ap Richard of Myfyrian in Anglesey be descended by females of him as Richard Gruffudd ap Hugh affirms. Also, it would be known how his land is gone from his posterity. 20

This Einion ab Ithel was esquire to John of Gaunt, duke of Lancaster, to whom, for his service as well in the time of war as peace, he gave a pension of twenty marks per annum issuing out of his manor of Halton. The charter I have seen, being in French with the duke's seal and arms, and remains in the custody of John Owen of Ystumcegid, esquire, the heir of Owain ap John ap Maredudd. 25

Maredudd ab Ieuan begat by the daughter of Einion ab Ithel, John ap Maredudd ab Ieuan (who married and was at man's estate before his grandfather's brother, Robert ap Maredudd, my ancestor, ever married) and Robert ap Maredudd, Abbot of Bardsey. For we have it by certain tradition that Robert was almost four score years old before he ever married and then in his dotage fancied and married Angharad, the daughter of Dafydd ap Llywelyn ap Dafydd of Cefnmelgoed in the county of Cardigan, whose wife was the daughter of Rhydderch ab Ieuan Llwyd of that country. 30 35 40

By her he had issue Ieuan ap Robert and [several?] daughters viz. Of this Robert, abbot, are descended my three *Pencenedl* because they are descended of church nobility viz. Gruffudd ap Richard of Madryn Isaf, Robert
5   ap Richard of Llecheiddior and Owain ap John ab Ieuan ap Robert of Bron-y-foel in Eifionydd.

The cause why this Robert ap Maredudd was so long unmarried may appear partly by record and partly by tradition.   *1399– 1413*

10   It is certain that as in the time of Henry the Fourth Ieuan ap Maredudd, having matched his son, as is aforesaid, to Einion ab Ithel's daughter (who belonged to the house of Lancaster) so he clave fast to that house in that time when Owain Glyndŵr rebelled in Wales. In the
15   time of that war he and Maredudd ap Hwlcyn Llwyd of Glynllifon had the charge of the town of Caernarfon and an English captain was over the castle; in revenge whereof Owain burnt his two houses, Cefn-y-fan and Y Gesail Gyfarch in Eifionydd.

20   In the process of continuance of this war died Ieuan at Caernarfon, and was brought by sea (for the passages by land were shut up by Owain's forces) to Penmorfa, his parish church, to be buried. Robert, his brother, taking
     1408 –   a clear contrary course, was out with Owain Glyndŵr,
25   as may be gathered by a pardon granted him in the ninth
     1399   year of Henry the Fourth by Henry the Fifth, then
     – 1413   Prince of Wales, which I have to show, whereof the true copy ensues.

30   Henry, illustrious firstborn of the king of England and France, Prince of Wales, Duke of Aquitaine and Lancaster and Cornwall and Earl of Chester, representative of our most revered Lord king and father in the parts of South and North Wales. To all and sundry who read these our present letters greeting. Know that we, by the
35   authority and power entrusted to us by the said most revered Lord the king and father, have taken a decision concerning Robert ap Maredudd ap Hywel, lately a rebel of the said our Lord king and father in the parts of Wales, in return for a fine paid to the coffers on behalf of our
40   said Lord our father the King. We have received and admitted the said Robert into the favour of the said our

Lord king and father and have pardoned him in the name of the same our lord king and father and restore to him of the peace which pertains to the same our Lord king and father for all and every the aforesaid insurrections, rebellions, fires, felonies, associations, trespasses, errors and ill deeds whatsoever committed and perpetrated by the said Robert in the parts and marches of Wales before this time, for which he has been charged, indicted, or summoned. And also if any outlawries were promulgated against him on these occasions, we grant the firm peace of our aforesaid king and father, and his goods and chattels, whatever was forfeited to the aforesaid our Lord king and father on past occasions in the name and by the authority of the aforesaid we grant by these presents. On these terms, however, that he should duely stand in the court of the aforesaid our Lord king and father, and in our own court, if anyone wishes to speak against him concerning these past things or any thing of the past. In witness of which matter we have caused these our letters patent to be made, given at London on the 20th day of September in the ninth year of the reign of the aforesaid most revered our Lord king and father Henry the Fourth after the conquest.

It is enrolled at the session held at Caernarvon on the next Monday after the Feast of the Assumption of the B.V.M. in the 11th year of the princeship of our lord Henry, Prince of Wales.

Rhys Goch Eryri, a bard of that time, made him a song showing what noble qualities he had and yet dared not name him therein for that, as it seems, he was an outlaw at that time the song was made, but shows in the song his descent from Gruffudd ap Cynan and that he was the hope of that stock. The song thus begins:

Long did our Kinsman Gruffudd ap Cynan, with his bloody spear, fiery lance, shield and flaming sword lie dormant like a grey headed lion, while this country was all ablaze by the hands of the enemy who heaped together dry wood to kindle the fire. Tremble not at the relation, he did not tremble. From him there grows a beautiful branch, an eminent heir worthy in battle and master of the ancient martial feats of the Britons. In my confusion if I am asked the Christian name of him who is called the descendant of the illustrious family on the throne of the province, it is Alexander, the beloved chief of the multitude with the golden crown of Trystan the Wise. I prophesy that he will deserve the title of a wise baron and withstand an army between the famous water of the Severn and the clear stream of Garthen. Dark envy and detraction will not suffer his praise to be celebrated. If it is his desert, timid caution avaunt. If any magnificent, eloquent and brave offspring of Cynan's lineage was ever bred, this must be he. Beware the scoff of those who have before detracted; if I speak of him it must be to his honour.

Composed by Rhys Goch Eryri.

This is the most ancient song that I can find extant to any of my ancestors since the reign of Edward the First who caused our bards all to be hanged by martial law as stirrers of the people to sedition; whose example, being followed by the governors of Wales, until Henry the Fourth's time, was the utter destruction of that sort of man. Then and since then this kind of people were at some further liberty to sing and to keep pedigrees as in ancient time they were wont. Since which time we have some light of antiquity by their songs and writings, and from the reign of Henry the Fourth to Edward the First there is no certainty or very little of things done other than what is to be found in the Prince's records which now, by tossing the same from the Exchequer at Caernarfon to the Tower and to the offices in the Exchequer at London, as also by ill-keeping and ordering of late days, are become a chaos and confusion for any man to find things in order as were needful for him to have who would be ascertained of the truth of things done from time to time. I have, to my charge, done what I could but for my travail have reaped little or nothing as you see.

You shall find in the ministers accounts in Henry the Fourth's time Robert ap Maredudd, farmer of Dolbenmaen, the King's weir of Aberglaslyn, the mill of Dwyfor and of other the King's things about his dwelling.

Ieuan, the son of Robert ap Maredudd, being a child of tender age at the death of his father, was put in the tuition of his cousin german's son, John ap Maredudd ab Ieuan, his next Kinsman, who cross-married him and his sister with Hywel ap Rhys ap Hywel Fychan of the house of Bron-y-foel in Eifionydd which, in those days, was of great possessions and ability and was then accounted the chief house descended of Collwyn 5 whereof there be many of great account in that country.

The widow of Robert ap Maredudd [was] married to Maredudd ap Rhys ab Ieuan Llwyd of the hundred of [Arllechwedd] Uchaf, without the consent of her ally, John ap Maredudd, and therefore was fain to flee the day 10 she was married and to go to her husband's house before she dined 24 miles off and that of rough way.

At this time or near about it fell a dislike and variance between William Gruffudd, esquire, Chamberlain of North Wales, and John ap Maredudd who, that 15 time, bore chief rule and credit in the quarters where he dwelt. The one by reason of his authority (which, in those days, was great to them who held that room) expecting that all should reverence and obey him: the other, in regard of his descent, kindred and ability in his 20 country, acknowledging none but his Prince his superior. Here hence grew the debate (*Nec Caesar ferre maiorem; Pompeius vel parem*) which continued long. To John ap Maredudd, his kindred and friends clave like burrs so that then it began to be a proverb or a phrase to 25 call the sect and family of Owain Gwynedd *Tylwyth John ap Maredudd* (which Englished is) the kindred of John ap Maredudd. This beginning of division bred in the posterity a conceit of mislike long after in the kindred the one towards the other, but with matches 30 and continuance of time it is worn out.

This John ap Maredudd was cousin to Owen Tudor and went with a hundred gentlemen of north Wales, his kinsmen, to visit the said Owen, being in trouble at Usk castle called Brynbuga. In his return, being beset 35 with enemies, favourers of the house of York, he made an oration to comfort his people willing them to remember at that time the defence of the honour and credit of their ancestors and concluding that it should never in time to come be reported that there was the 40

place a hundred north Wales gentlemen fled but that
the place should carry the name and memory that there
a hundred of north Wales gentlemen were slain. And for
that some of his kinsmen there had brought with them
5   all their sons; some others had but one son to succeed
them in their name and inheritance, as Hywel
Llywelyn ap Hywel and others. He placed all those in
the rearward, out of the fury of the fight, placing all his
sons in the vanward which he himself led, where he
10   was sorely wounded in his face whereof he was called
Sgweier y Graith to his dying day. But God gave his
enemies the overthrow, he opening the passage with
his sword.

Queen Katherine, being a Frenchwoman born, knew
15   no difference between the English and Welsh nation.
Until her marriage being published, Owen Tudor's
kindred and country were objected to disgrace him as
most vile and barbarous, which made her desirous to
see some of his kinsmen. Whereupon, he brought to her
20   presence John ap Maredudd and Hywel Llywelyn ap
Hywel, his near cousins, men of goodly stature and
personage but wholly destitute of bringing up and
nurture, for when the Queen had spoken to them in
diverse languages and they were not able to answer her,
25   she said they were the goodliest dumb creatures that
ever she saw! This being not impertinent to the matter
I treat of and reserved by tradition, I thought fit to insert
here.

John ap Maredudd had, by his wife, five sons, Morus,
30   Gruffudd, Robert, Owain and Ieuan; whereof Robert, in
his father's time, was slain without issue near Ruthin
in this manner. The rest survived their father and have
many descended of them.

The Thelwalls of Ruthin, being ancient gentlemen of
35   that country who came into that country with the Lord
Grey, to whom King Edward the First bestowed the
country of Dyffryn Clwyd, being at contention with a
sect or kindred of that country called the family of
Gruffudd Goch. These, being more in number than the
40   Thelwalls (although the Thelwalls carried the whole

offices of the country under the lord thereof, the lord of
Kent, then Treasurer of England) drove the Thelwalls to
take the castle of Ruthin for their defence where they
besieged them until the siege was raised by John ap
Maredudd's sons and kindred to whom the Thelwalls   5
sent for aid. In that exploit Robert, the son of John ap
Maredudd, was slain with an arrow in a wood within
view of the castle of Ruthin called Coed Marchan, in
revenge whereof many of the other side were slain both
at that time and after.   10

Some affirm John ap Maredudd to have been at a field
in Pennal for Thomas Gruffudd, which field was fought
between Thomas Gruffudd ap Nicholas and Henry ap
Gwilym and the earl of Pembroke's captains; where
Thomas ap Gruffudd got the field but received there his   15
death wound.

Henry the Seventh, minding his entry into England
to claim the Crown against the tyrant Richard the
Third, wrote this letter, which is extant, to John ap
Maredudd in these words.   20

Henry 7: letter to John ap Maredudd. By the King.
Right trusty and well-beloved, we greet you well: and
where it is so that through the help of Almighty God,
the assistance of our loving friends and true subjects,
and the great confidence that we have to the nobles and   25
commons of this our Principality of Wales, we be
entered into the same purposing by the help above
rehearsed, in all haste possible to descend into our
realm of England, not only for the adoption of the
Crown unto us of right appertaining, but also for the   30
oppression of that odious tyrant Richard, late duke of
Gloucester, usurper of our said right; and, moreover, to
reduce as well our said realm of England into its ancient
estate, honour and prosperity, as this our said Principality of Wales, and the people of the same to their   35
former liberties, delivering them of such miserable
servitudes as they have piteously long stood in. We
desire and pray you, upon your allegiance, strictly
charge and command you that, immediately upon the
sight hereof, with all such power as you may make   40
defensibly arrayed for the war, you address yourself
towards us without any tarrying upon the way until

such time as you be with us, wheresoever we shall be, to
our aid for the effect above rehearsed wherein you shall
cause us in time to come to be your singular good lord;
and that you fail not hereof as you will avoid our
5   grievous displeasure and answer unto at your peril.
Given under our signet at our . . .

　　To our trusty and well-beloved John ap Maredudd ab
Ieuan ap Maredudd.

Ieuan ap Robert ap Maredudd, my ancestor, having,
10   as before is remembered, married cross with the house
of Bron-y-foel in Eifionydd had, by his wife called
Catherine, three sons, Maredudd, Robert and John, and
after her death he married Gwenhwyfar ferch Madog
Fychan of the house of Llwyndyrus, descended of Sir
15   Gruffudd Llwyd, by whom he had two sons, Gruffudd
Fychan and Ieuan, and a daughter.

　　Ieuan died being but one and thirty years old of the
plague at Y Gesail Gyfarch, his house.

　　In the wars between the houses of York and Lancaster
20   he (as all his kin) were Lancastrians and he was one of
the captains of them that burnt the duke of York's lands
of Denbighland, in revenge whereof the King sent
William Herbert, earl of Pembroke, in Edward the
Fourth's time, who came with a great army to recover
25   the castle of Harlech held by Dafydd ab Ieuan ab Einion
for Jasper, earl of Pembroke, then beyond the seas, and
wasted with fire and sword all Nanconwy and all the
country lying between Conwy and Dyfi. He granted the
same time a protection or safe-conduct to Ieuan ap
30   Robert ap Maredudd and to his followers to come to
parley with him which I have to show, under his seal of
arms, in these words.

To all the faithful of Christ to whom this present
writing shall come William, Earl of Pembroke, Justice
35   of our lord the king in the parts of North Wales
greetings. Know that we have given and by this present
granted to Ieuan ap Robert of the commote of Eifionydd
in the county of Caernarfon safe and secure conduct of
entering and approaching, travelling, waiting and
40   staying, and going and coming through and within the
counties of Caernarfon and Merioneth for himself and

his goods and chattels without arrest, molestation,
impeachment, forceful dispossession, apprehension,
disturbance or any other harrassment, alike on the part
of our Lord the king as on the part of any other person,
from the day of the completion of these presents until   5
he shall have through us a warning of six days. Given
under our seal on the fourth day of the month of
November in the fourth year of the reign of king
Edward, the eighth after the conquest.

He was a most goodly man of personage, of great   10
stature, as may appear by the Welsh songs made unto
him, and most valiant withal. Besides the turmoils
abroad he sustained deadly feud (as the northern man
terms it) at home in his door, a war far more dangerous
than the other.   15
His sister, married to Hywel ap Rhys, died within few
years after the marriage leaving no issue male, and
Hywel ap Rhys married Tudur Gruffudd ab Einion's
daughter of Ardudwy, a courageous stirring woman
who never gave over to make debate between her   20
husband and his next neighbours and brother-in-law,
my ancestor. Many bickerings passed between them,
either making as many friends as they could, and many
men were slain, but commonly the loss fell on Hywel
ap Rhys's side.   25
Dafydd ap Siencyn, being a near kinsman to Hywel ap
Rhys and then an outlaw, a man of great valour, came to
aid his cousin against my ancestor, but prevailed
though they came upon the sudden on my ancestor's
house and although he was from home. Thereupon, as   30
we have it by credible tradition, Dafydd ap Siencyn
wished his cousin to keep friendship with his brother-
in-law for, said he, 'I will not come with you to invade
this man's house when he is at home since I find such
hot resistance in his absence'!   35
This woman caused the parson of Llanfrothen to be
murdered because he had fostered to my ancestor. But
God so wrought that the murderers, being three
brothers, were all slain after by my ancestor in revenge
of the parson's unworthy death.   40

I have a number of obligations wherein Hywel ap
Rhys stands bound for the observation of the peace and
awards touching that controversy but the plague,
taking away my ancestor, ended the strife between
5   them which was likely, if he had lived, to have been
ended with the death of one of them or both. So bloody
and ireful were quarrels in those days and the revenge of
the sword at such liberty as almost nothing was punished by law whatsoever happened.

10   The cause of this mortal hatred between them grew,
as it is credibly reported, in this sort. John ap Maredudd
and Hywel ap Rhys were ever lightly at variance. My
ancestor (having had his bringing up with his cousin
John ap Maredudd) affected him best, though allied
15   nearly together, which was taken so heinously by
Hywel ap Rhys that he converted the sum of his rancour
upon his brother-in-law and next neighbour. Which
quarrels, my ancestor being dead, never ended till, in
assaulting the house of the said Hywel by the sons of
20   John ap Maredudd with their cousin Gruffudd ap John
ap Goronwy (a gentleman of great account who had
been captain, as is reputed, of a company of lancers in
Aquitaine), the said Gruffudd ap John ap Goronwy was
slain, being shot into the beaver with an arrow out of
25   the house. Whereupon, the said Hywel was fain to leave
the country to avoid the fury of the revengement of
blood.

In the partition of the inheritance of Ieuan ap Robert
ap Maredudd between his five sons, according to the
30   custom of Wales, the Henblas in Mathebrwd and all the
land in Llanrwst in Denbighland descended upon him
(as afore is mentioned, as cousin and next heir to Robin
Fychan ap Dafydd ap Hywel [ap Dafydd] ap Gruffudd) fell
to be the part and portion of Gruffudd Fychan, his son,
35   who married the daughter of Gruffudd ap Madog
Fychan who was a grandchild to Rhys ab Einion Fychan
viz. his daughter's daughter.

You are to understand that though Robin Fychan did
not defeat his cousin and next heir, Ieuan ap Robert ap
40   Maredudd, of the land held in the Welsh tenure, yet

minding the preferment of his daughter as much as law
would suffer him, he charged the land with a mortgage
of £12 to Rhys ab Einion Fychan, his son-in-law, which
the said Rhys ab Einion did release to Gruffudd ab Ieuan
ap Robert in part of his marriage goods with his cousin,   5
the daughter of Owain ap Gruffudd ap Madog, the very
release I have in my custody, the copy whereof follows
in these words.

To all the faithful of Christ to whom this present
writing shall come Rhys ab Einion Fychan greetings in   10
the lord everlasting. Know that I, the aforesaid Rhys,
have remitted and relaxed the twelve pounds of *prid*
which I have over the land of Robin Fychan ap Dafydd ap
Hywel with its appurtenances lying and existing in the
commote of Uwchdulas in the Lordship of Denbigh to   15
Gruffudd ab Ieuan ap Robert, his heirs and assigns in
perpetuity. Thus see that I the aforesaid Rhys nor my
heirs nor executors nor anyone else through us for us or
in our name shall in the aforesaid twelve pounds nor in
the aforesaid land and holding with its appurtenances as   20
is aforesaid lying and existing in the aforesaid commote
and the aforesaid lordship be able to claim, exact, or
demand any right, statute, title, claim, interest or
demand, nor in any other parcel there, nor shall we in
any manner in the future, but from all accession, right,   25
statute, title, claim, interest and demand of it we shall
in the future be utterly excluded for ever by these
presents. In witness of which matter I have affixed my
seal to this present writing in the presence of these
witnesses. Maredudd ap Dafydd ab Einion, Dafydd ap   30
Maredudd ap Dafydd Llwyd, Sir Robert Cowsyth,
Cleric, Thomas Cowsyth and Ieuan ap Dafydd ap
Llywelyn with many others. Given the twentieth day of
the month of October in the 11th year of the reign of
king Henry the Seventh.   35

God has shown mercy to our kind that, ever since the
time of Rhodri, the son of Owain Gwynedd, lord of
Anglesey, our common ancestor, there lived in the
commonwealth in eminent sort one or other of our
name and many together at times. I have in my mind, in   40
the perusal of the whole course of the history of our
name and kindred, compared or likened God's work in

that to a man striking fire into a tinder-box for, by the beating of the flint upon the steel, there are a number of sparkles of fire raised. Whereof but one or two takes fire the rest vanishing away. As, for example, in Einion ap
5   Caradog, Gruffudd Caradog and Sir William Caradog alias Wilcocke Caradog, brothers; Einion ap Caradog, as [it] should seem the elder brother, lord of Penychen, Pen-y-berth and Baladeulyn. His son, Tudur ab Einion, died without issue of his body and his lands were begged
10   by the Queen, King Edward the First's wife, as appears in this History. Gruffudd [was] lord of Ffriwlwyd, Ystrad and Ysgeibion: he had issue Dafydd, which Dafydd had three sons, Dafydd Chwith ap Dafydd, Maredudd and Hywel who are mentioned before to have exchanged
15   their living at Denbigh with Henry Lacy, earl of Lincoln. William alias Wilcocke Caradog, married an inheritrix in Pembrokeshire where his posterity remained ever since.

Having by the house called Newton named them-
20   selves Newton Cradock, both in Pembrokeshire and Somersetshire. Note among these three brothers the posterity of the one remains; of the other two the one being vanished and the other gone out of the country.

Of Gruffudd's grandchildren only the posterity of
25   Hywel are extant who seems to be the youngest of the three. Lastly, of Ieuan ap Robert ap Maredudd's children, being five, only the posterity of Maredudd are extant and of account. Whereupon, comparing things past with things that are to come I presage God's mercy
30   to the kindred hereafter as heretofore.

Now, after this large digression, to return to the course of the former history. Rhys ab Einion Fychan, having had warning (as aforesaid) that the Henblas should be redeemed, hastened to build Brynsyllty
35   before that Michaelmas appointed. I have seen an old man in my time called Ieuan ap John Dafydd Fychan, at least ninety years old: this man's mother served Rhys ab Einion Fychan at that time and she was wont to report that corn, failing them to build the house, they

reaped the corn that grew in the rain to serve that turn whereas the corn in the ridge was not ready.

The wars of Lancaster and York, beginning this summer, made Ieuan ap Robert ap Maredudd forgetful of his promise to redeem the lands for, in the time of that 5 civil war, land was not ought worth; neither was it redeemed during his life. In those wars Ieuan ap Robert ap Maredudd, even in the sixth year of Edward the Fourth, with Dafydd ap Siencyn and other captains of the Lancastrian faction, wasted with fire and sword the 10 suburbs of the town of Denbigh and all the lordship of Denbigh. In revenge whereof Edward the Fourth sent William, earl of Pembroke, with a great army to waste the mountain countries of Caernarfonshire and Merionethshire and to take into the castle of Harlech, 15 held then by Dafydd ab Ieuan ab Einion for the two earls, Edmund, earl of Richmond, and Jasper, earl of Pembroke, the remains of the Lancastrian faction; which earl did execute his charge to the full, as witnesses this Welsh rhyme. 20

> Harlech a Dinbech, pob dôr—yn cynnau
>   Nanconwy yn farwor;
>   Mil a phedwarcant i'm Iôr,
>   A thrugain ag wyth rhagor.

In that expedition Ieuan ap Robert lay one night at the 25 house of Rhys ab Einion at Henblas, married to his cousin Catherine ferch Robin Fychan. Setting forth very early before day he unwittingly carried upon his finger the wrest of his cousin's harp whereon, as it seems, he had played over night, as the manner was in 30 those days, to bring himself to sleep. Which he returned by a messenger unto his cousin with this message withal, that he came not into Denbighland to take from his cousin as much as the wrest of her harp, whereby it appears that by his means neither her house nor any of 35 her goods were burnt, wasted, hurt or spoilt. Both her houses, Henblas and Brynsyllty, escaped the earl of Herbert's desolation though the same consumed the whole borough of Llanrwst and all the vale of Conwy besides to cold coals whereof the print is yet extant, the very stones of the ruins of many habitations in and along my demesnes carrying yet the colour of the fire. [John] ap Maredudd, being cousin german to Ieuan ap

5   Robert ap Maredudd, notwithstanding he was so much older than he, so that the one was in man's estate and the other was but a youth, and had the government of his uncle and of his living. During which time of his nonage Robin Fychan ap Dafydd ap Hywel dying, as

10   aforesaid, John ap Maredudd came over with his uncle to Llanrwst, to the Lordship of Denbigh, to take possession of the inheritance lately befallen him called the Henblas in Mathebrwd where Rhys ab Einion Fychan and Catherine ferch Robin Fychan, his wife, then

15   dwelt.

Having surveyed the land they gave Rhys ab Einion Fychan then warning that he should avoid the land at Michaelmas following for then he should have the twelve pounds mortgage money paid him. He requested

20   to be tenant and was answered by Ieuan ap Robert ap Maredudd that he would lie there at times himself and therefore would not set it.

Whereupon, Rhys ab Einion Fychan built Brynsyllty house upon part of that land which land Henry Lacy,

25   earl of Lincoln, lord of Denbigh exchanged with our ancestors and which he had bought of some of our kinsmen who had the same by gavelkind whose name is forgotten, as is the pedigree of two other freeholders in Mathebrwd besides who held land in my time in that

30   township lineally from that grant and exchange. The one was called Rhys Llywelyn ap Dafydd, whose posterity does yet inherit a parcel of this land; the other, the wife of one Lancellet, a weaver, whose inheritance my uncle Gruffudd Wynn bought, being a matter but of

35   three pounds a year, into so little parts did the gavelkind by many descents chop our inheritance, being at first large.

Conferring often with the freeholders of the parish of Llanrwst, my neighbours, how they held their lands

40   and from what common ancestor they were descended,

most of them are descended lineally from Ednyfed Fychan in the township of Tybrith and Garthgarmon.

And enquiring of them whence the freeholders of Mathebrwd, Rhys Llywelyn ap Dafydd and Lancellet's wife were descended, they said that they were foreigners and came from the castle of Denbigh as though the castle of Denbigh did procreate men, which shows that the tradition is not yet forgotten from whence they came. The most part of that town of Mathebrwd is in our blood, blessed be God.

Robin Achwr, the greatest antiquary of our country, being at Gwydir with my great-grandfather, was going one day to a *chwaraefa gampau* where the country was assembled at a place called Gardd-y-felin in the parish of Llanrwst. He asked him whether he would command him any service thither: 'nothing', said he, having a nosegay in his hand by chance, 'but deliver this nosegay to the best gentleman you see in the company upon the credit of your skill'. He delivered the same, with protestation of his charge in the presence of all the company, to Llywelyn ap Dafydd (Rhys Llywelyn ap Dafydd's father) but I cannot get neither his pedigree nor Lancellet's wife's pedigree in any certainty to join them to ours. The reason is that poverty soon forgets whence it be descended, for it is an ancient received saying that there is no poverty but is descended of nobility nor no nobility but is descended of beggary.

> When Adam delved and Eve span
> Who was then a gentleman?
> Then came the churl and gathered good,
> And thence arose the gentle blood.

Yet a great temporal blessing it is, and a great heart's ease to a man to find that he is well descended and a greater grief it is for upstarts and gentlemen of the first head to look back unto their descents, being base in such sort, as I have known many such hate gentlemen in their hearts for no other cause but that they were gentlemen.

The conditional promise by God to David was that, if his children would keep his laws, he should not want a man of his loins to sit on his seat for evermore. Whereby he had two things promised him; propagation of his
5   seed and eminence of continuance in the world.

The Rechabites, for their obedience to their father's commandment not to drink wine, have the like promise of God.

During the time the earl of Pembroke's army lay in
10   Snowdon Ieuan ap Robert was fain to leave his own house and lodge at night in the rock called Ogo'r Filan, standing at Meillionen in the parish of Beddgelert, and all the day with the Lancastrians, his friends and followers, skirted the army and skirmished with them in the
15   straight and rough passage of Nanhwynan until, at last, being sent for by the earl under his protection and received into grace as may appear by the earl's deed under his hand and seal. The like he did not grant to any in north Wales as far as I can hear.
20   The beginning of the quarrel and unkindness between Ieuan ap Robert and Hywel ap Rhys ap Hywel Fychan grew in this sort. Ieuan ap Robert, after his sister's death, upon some mislike left the company of Hywel ap Rhys and accompanied John ap Maredudd, his
25   nephew, and his children who were at continual debate with Hywel ap Rhys.

The fashion was in those days that the gentlemen and their retinues met commonly every day to shoot matches and to try masteries. There was no gentleman
30   of worth in the country but had a wine-cellar of his own where wine was sold to his profit. Thither came his friends to meet him and there spent the day in shooting, wrestling, throwing the sledge and other acts of activity, and drinking very moderately withal, not
35   according to the healthing and gluttonous manner of our days.

Hywel ap Rhys did draw a draft upon Ieuan ap Robert ap Maredudd [and] sent a brother of his to lodge overnight at Y Gesail Gyfarch to understand which way
40   Ieuan ap Robert ap Maredudd meant to go the next day.

He was determined to shoot a match with John ap
Maredudd's children at Llanfihangel-y-Pennant, not far
from John ap Maredudd's house. This understood, the
spy (Hywel ap Rhys's brother) slips away in the night to
his brother and lets him know where he should lie for
him.

Now had Hywel ap Rhys provided a butcher for the
purpose that [he] should have murdered him; for he had
direction by Hywel to keep himself free, not to undertake any of the company until he saw them in the
meddle and every man fighting. Then was his charge to
come behind the tallest man in the company (for otherwise he knew him not, being a stranger), and to knock
him down, for Hywel ap Rhys said: 'You shall soon
discern him from the rest by his stature, and he will
make way before him: there is a foster-brother of his,
one Robin ab Inco, a little fellow, who uses to watch
him behind. Take heed of him, be the encounter never
so hot. His eye is ever on his foster-brother.'

Ieuan ap Robert, according as he was appointed, went
that morning with his ordinary company towards Llanfihangel to meet John ap Maredudd. You are to understand that in those days and in that wild world every
man stood upon his guard and went not abroad but in
sort and so armed as if he went to the field to encounter
with his enemies.

Hywel ap Rhys ap Hywel Fychan's sister, being Ieuan
ap Robert's wife, went a mile or thereabouts with her
husband and the company, talking with them, and so
parted with them; and on her way homewards she met
her brother on horseback with a great company of
people, armed, riding after her husband as fast as they
could. She cried out upon her brother and desires him,
for the love of God, not to harm her husband who meant
him no harm. And withal steps to his horse, meaning to
have caught him by the bridle which he, seeing, turned
his horse about. She caught the horse by the tail and,
hanging upon him so long, crying upon her brother, that
in the end he drew out his short sword and struck at her
arm. She, perceiving [this], was fain to let slip her hold

and, running before him to a narrow passage whereby he must pass through a brook where there was a foot-bridge near the ford, she steps to the footbridge and takes away the *canllaw* or handstay of the bridge and,

5   with the same lets fly at her brother. If he had not avoided the blow she had struck him off his horse— *Furor arma ministrat.*

Hywel ap Rhys and his company, within a while, overtook Ieuan ap Robert and his company who turned

10 head upon him though greatly over-matched. The bickering grew very hot and many knocked down of either side. In the end, when that should be performed [for] which they came, for the murdering butcher (having not struck one stroke all day, but watching

15 opportunity and finding the company more scattered than at first from Ieuan ap Robert) thrust himself among Ieuan ap Robert's people behind and making a blow at him was prevented by Robin ab Inco, his foster brother, and knocked down, God bringing upon his

20 head the destruction that be meant for another: which Hywel ap Rhys perceiving, cried upon his people: 'Let us away and be gone, for I had given charge that Robin ab Inco should have been better looked unto.' And so that bickering broke with the hurt of many and the

25 death of that one man.

It fortuned anon after that the parson of Llanfrothen took a child of Ieuan ap Robert to foster which sore grieved Hywel ap Rhys ap Hywel Fychan's wife, her husband having then more land in that parish than

30 Ieuan ap Robert had. In revenge whereof she plotted the death of the said parson in this manner. She sent a woman to ask lodging to the parson who used not to deny any. The woman, being in bed, after midnight began to strike and to rave whereupon the parson,

35 thinking that she had been distracted, awakening out of his sleep and wondering at so sudden a cry in the night, made towards her and his household also. Then, she said, that he would have ravished her and so got out of doors threatening revenge to the parson. This woman

40 had to her brothers, three notable rogues of the damned

crew, fit for any mischief (being followers to Hywel ap Rhys). In a morning these brothers watched the parson as he went to look to his cattle in a place in that parish called Ogo'r Llychwin (being now a tenement of mine) and there murdered him; and two fled to Chirkland in   5 Denbighshire to some of the Trefors, friends or of a kin to Hywel ap Rhys or his wife.

It was the manner in those days that the murderer only and he that gave the death wound should only fly, which was called in Welsh a *llawrudd*, which is a 'red   10 hand' because he had blooded his hand. The accessories and abettors to the murder, they were never hearkened after.

In those days in Chirkland and in Oswestryland two sects or kindreds contended for the sovereignty of the   15 country and were at continual strife one with another, the Kyffins and Trefors. They had their alliance, partisans and friends in all countries round thereabouts to whom, as the manner of that time was, they sent such of their followers as committed murder or man-   20 slaughter, who were safely kept as very precious jewels, and they received the like from their friends. This kind of people were stowed in the daytime in chambers in their houses and in the night they went to the next winehouse that belonged to the gentleman or to his   25 tenants' houses not far off to make merry and to wench.

Maredudd ap Hywel ap Morus, in those days chief and leader of the sect of the Kyffins, was a kin to Ieuan ap Robert and in league with him; to whom he sent to desire him to draw him a draft to catch those   30 murderers. [He] sent him word that he should come privately into Chirkland only accompanied but with six, and he made no doubt to deliver the murderers into his hands.

As Ieuan ap Robert was on his way going thither   35 passing by Tŷ-yn-Rhos (being a winehouse standing in Penrhyndeudraeth), Hywel ap Rhys ap Hywel Fychan's wife, being in the house, said to the people that were with her: 'Yonder goes Ieuan ap Robert: *Hwyr y dial fo*

i dadmaeth', which is as much [as] to say that he would
not in haste be revenged of the wrong done to his foster.

Being come to Chirkland he abode there many days
in secret and, unseen, sleeping in the day and watching
5   all night. In the end, with the help of his friends, he
caught the two murderers which he had no sooner in
hand but the cry arose. The Trefors to their friends and
the Kyffins to their leader, Maredudd ap Hywel ap
Morus, resorted, who told Ieuan ap Robert that it was
10   impossible for him to carry them out of the country to
any place to have judicial proceeding against them by
reason of the faction of the Trefors [which] would lay
the way and narrow passages of the country, and if they
were brought to Chirk castle gate to receive the trial of
15   that country's laws it was lawful for the offenders'
friends (whosoever they were) to bring five pounds for
every man for a fine to the lord and to acquit them, so it
were not in cases of treason. A damnable custom used
in those days in the lordships marchers which was used
20   also in Mawddwy until the new ordinance of Wales
made in [the] twenty seventh [year] of Henry the
Eighth. Hereupon, Ieuan ap Robert ap Maredudd
commanded one of his men to strike off their heads
which, the fellow doing faintly, the offender told him
25   that if he had his [i.e. the executioner's] neck under his
sword he would make his sword take better edge than
he did, so resolute were they in those days and in
contempt of death. Whereupon Ieuan [ap] Robert, in a
rage, stepping to them struck off their heads.

30   Dafydd Llwyd ap Gruffudd Fychan, grandchild to
Ieuan ap Robert ap Maredudd, in his youth waited upon
Hugh, son to Mr. Robert ap Rhys, at Cambridge, elected
abbot of Conwy, by his father's procurement, in his
minority. He, being at Plas Iolyn, at the house of the
35   said Mr. Robert ap Rhys, an old woman who dwelt there
in Rhys ap Maredudd's time told him that she had seen
his grandfather, Ieuan ap Robert, at that house both in
going and coming from his voyage into Chirkland, and
that he was the tallest and the goodliest man that ever
40   she had seen, for sitting at the fire upon the spur, the

hinder part of his head was to be seen over the spur which she never saw to any other man. Also, she said that, in his return from Chirkland she saw Lowri ferch Hywel, viz Rhys ap Maredudd's wife, his kinswoman, wash his eyes with white wine, being bloodshot by long watching.

Ieuan ap Robert, on his return from Chirkland, riding home to his house by Gallt y Morfa Hir by moonlight (the tide in Traeth Mawr giving him no sooner passage), talking with his men carelessly and out of danger, as he imagined, suddenly lighted an arrow shot among them from the hillside which was then full of wood. Whereupon, they made a stand and shot wholly all seven towards the place from whence the other arrow came. With one of which arrows of theirs shot so at random they killed him that shot at them, being the third brother of the murderers, God revenging that wicked murder by the death of the three brothers. Hywel ap Rhys ap Hywel Fychan and especially his wife, boiling in revenge, drew another draft against Ieuan ap Robert in this manner. Ieuan ap Robert's mother was of the house of Cefnmelgoed in the county of Cardigan, whose mother was sister to Rhydderch ab Ieuan Llwyd, then and yet the greatest family in that county. His kinsmen and friends in that county and in Chirkland and elsewhere were wont to send unto them their *llawrudds*, whereof there were very many and his house continually full, which he kept very choicely.

Hywel ap Rhys, understanding that Ieuan ap Robert and his people had occasion to go to Caernarfon to the assizes, thought it a fit time by force to enter upon his house in his absence and to apprehend all these and to bring them to Caernarfon to be hanged, for there was none of them but was outlawed of murder or felony in the country where he dwelt. To this end, to strengthen himself in this purpose, he sent for his trustiest friends about him, and among the rest procured Dafydd ap Siencyn, his cousin german, then a famous outlaw in the rock of Carreg-y-gwalch, with his crew and followers to assist him. And so suddenly came in a morning to the

hall of Ieuan ap Robert's house where there were not
many men to be seen for the outlaws were in outhouses
about and upper chambers in the lower end of the hall
stowed and none to be seen. Those people of Ieuan ap
5 Robert that were in the hall raised a cry and took
themselves to their weapons whereupon the outlaws
awakened, arose, betook themselves to their weapons
and bestirred themselves handsomely. It happened the
same time that Ieuan ap Robert's wife stood at the
10 fireside looking on her maid boiling of wort to make
metheglin, which seething wort was bestowed liberally
among the assailants and did help the defendants to
thrust back them that were entered and afterwards to
defend the house.

15 The house was assaulted with all force and pierced in
diverse places, and was well defended by those who
were within for, having made diverse breaches, they
dared not enter, few resolute men being able to make a
breach good against many. Upon the cry the country did
20 rise and Ieuan ap Robert's tenants and friends
assembled in great numbers, whereof Robin ab Inco was
captain who fought with the besiegers who, in the end,
with their arrows did drive the besiegers from the one
side of the house who continually assaulted the other
25 side.

After they had continued all that day and all night in
that manner, the next morning, seeing they could
prevail little to enter the house, they came to a parley
with Robin ab Inco who advised them to be gone in time
30 for, said he, 'as soon as the water at Traeth Mawr will
give leave Ieuan Grach, my master's kinsman, will be
here with Ardudwy men, and then you shall be all
slain'.

This Ieuan Grach was a man of great account in those
35 days at Ardudwy and dwelt at Y Gellilydan in the parish
of Maentwrog. Whereupon they gave over their
enterprise and returned to Bron-y-foel to Hywel ap Rhys
ap Hywel Fychan's house where Dafydd ap Siencyn
advised his cousin, Hywel ap Rhys, to take Ieuan ap
40 Robert for his brother-in-law, neighbour and friend for,

Vera effigies Chriss Do.ni Iohanis Wynn de Gwedur in
Com. Carnarvon Equitis et Baronetti &c.
Obijt primo die Martij 1626. Ætat: 73.

Sir John Wynn (engraving by Robert Vaughan)

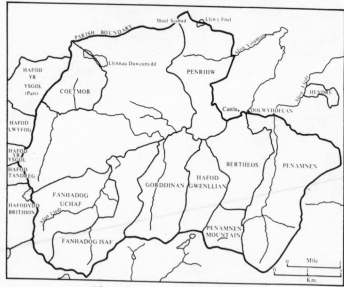

Brass effigy of Maredudd ab Ieuan ap Robert
in St. Gwyddelan's church, Dolwyddelan

(Crown Copyright Royal Commission on Ancient and Historical Monuments in Wales)

The *Ffriddoedd* of Dolwyddelan

(by permission of the late Dr. Elwyn Davies)

said he, 'I will not be one with you to assault his house when he is at home seeing I find such hot resistance in his absence'!

Daily bickerings too long to be written passed between so near and hateful neighbours. In [the] end the plague, which commonly follows war and desolation after the earl of Pembroke's expedition, took away Ieuan ap Robert at his house in Y Gesail Gyfarch in the flower of his age being but one and thirty years old. Whose death ended the strife of those houses for his three eldest sons were sister sons to Hywel ap Rhys ap Hywel Fychan.

Enmity did continue between Hywel ap Rhys and the sons of John ap Maredudd after the death of Ieuan ap Robert.

Gruffudd ap John ap Goronwy (cousin to John ap Maredudd's sons, of Gwynfryn, who had long served in France and had charge there), coming home to live in the country, it happened that a servant of his, coming to fish in Ystumllyn, his fish was taken away and the fellow beaten by Hywel ap Rhys ap Hywel Fychan's servants and by his commandment.

Gruffudd ap John ap Goronwy took [the] matter in such dudgeon that he challenged Hywel ap Rhys to the field which he refusing, and assembling his cousins, John ap Maredudd's sons and his friends together assaulted Hywel in his own house after the manner he had seen in the French wars, consumed with fire his barns and his outhouses. Afterwards [while] assaulting the hall which Hywel ap Rhys and many other people kept, being a very strong house, [he] was shot out at a crevice of the house through the sight of his beaver into his head, and slain outright, being otherwise armed at all points.

Notwithstanding his death, the assault of the house was continued with great vehemency, the doors fired with great burdens of straw, besides the smoke of the outhouses and barns not far distant annoyed greatly the defendants so that most of them lay under boards and benches upon the floor in the hall: the better to avoid

the smoke. Only the old man, Hywel ap Rhys, never stooped but stood valiantly in the middle of the floor armed with a glaive in his hand, and called unto them and bid them arise like men for shame for he had known
5   there as great a smoke in that hall upon a Christmas evening.

In [the] end, seeing the house could no longer defend them, being overlaid with a multitude, upon parley between them, Hywel ap Rhys was content to yield
10 himself prisoner to Morus ap John ap Maredudd, John ap Maredudd's eldest son, so as he would swear unto him to bring himself to Caernarfon castle to abide the trial by law, for the death of Gruffudd ap John ap Goronwy, who was cousin german removed to the said
15 Hywel and of the very same house he was of. Morus ap John ap Maredudd, undertaking [this duty], did put a guard about the said Hywel of his trustiest friends and servants which kept and defended him from the rage of the kindred, and especially of Owain ap John ap
20 Maredudd, his brother, who was very eager upon him.

They passed by leisure thence, like a camp, to Caernarfon. The whole country being assembled Hywel's friends posted a horseback from one place or other by the way, that brought word that he was come thither
25 safe for they were in great fear lest he should be murdered and that Morus ap John should not be able to defend him, neither dared any of Hywel's friends be there for fear of the kindred.

In the end, being delivered by Morus ap John ap
30 Maredudd to the constable of Caernarfon castle and there kept safely in ward until the assizes, it fell out by law that the burning of Hywel's houses and assaulting him in his own house was a more heinous offence in Morus ap John ap Maredudd and the rest than the death
35 of Gruffudd ap John ap Goronwy in Hywel who did it in his own defence. Whereupon, Morus ap John ap Maredudd and five and thirty more were indicted of felony, as appears by the copy of the indictment which I had from the records.
40 Hywel, delivered out of prison, never dared come to

his own house to Eifionydd but came to Penmachno, to his mother's kindred Rhys Gethin's sons, and there died.

Yet is a note worth observation that the house decayed by little and little ever since. Neither has any of his posterity been buried in his own sepulchre, being four descents besides himself.

Rhys ap Hywel ap Rhys, his son, cousin german to my great-grandfather, Maredudd ab Ieuan ap Robert, married to his first wife an inheritrix of the Trefors by whom he had great possessions in Hopesland. After-wards, by the procurement of my great-grandfather, married Margaret, daughter of Hugh Conway the elder, Rheinallt ap Meurig's widow (his next neighbour in Gwydir) and was overseer of his works when he built Gwydir house, as William Dafydd ab Elis Eyton, his cousin who lived then with him in those days, told me. He was buried at the right side in the chancel in Llanrwst and his bones, which were very great, were taken up at the burying of Cadwaladr ap Robert Wyn of Hafod-y-maidd, as my uncle Owen Wynn guessed by the greatness of the same.

Thomas ap Rhys ap Hywel sold all his mother's living in Hopesland and a part of his own, and was buried in Hopesdale. Cadwaladr ap Thomas, his son and heir, lying in Chester at physic, died there.

Ellis ap Cadwaladr, who had married my cousin german (my uncle Owen Wynn's daughter), my kind cousin and friend, a man endowed with many good parts, [being] sick of an impostume went to one Doctor Davies, near Brecknock, and there died.

This man's name I am bound to make an honourable mention of, for diverse kindness he showed unto me, and especially for the wise advice and counsel he was wont to give me among many, one especially of me and my posterity to be remembered, which I think worthy to be recorded in writing.

Unkindness and variance befalling between myself and my uncle Owen Wynn, being neighbours, for ways across my grounds for the carrying of his hay from the

King's meadow in Trefriw to his house at Cae'r Milwr,
grew to a great heat, and said that he should not pass
that way without the loss of men's lives. Whereupon,
he being present and wishing well unto us both,
5   reproved me sharply willing me to follow the course of
my ancestors which, with wisdom, longanimity and
temperance from time to time had raised their fortunes,
assuring his ancestors might be an example unto me of
the contrary, that with headiness and rashness, did
10   diminish and impair their estate from time to time.
Which counsel of his took deep root in me and ever
after, and to my great good bridled my choler
whereunto I was much subject.

It may be a question here and a doubt to the reader
15   wherefore the land of Robin Fychan [ap] Dafydd ap
Hywel should descend to Ieuan ap Robert ap Maredudd,
his cousin and next heir, he having a daughter and heir
of his own lawfully begotten.

To answer this question you are to understand that
20   Henry Lacy, earl of Lincoln, upon the conquest of
Wales, having received of Edward the First's gift the
countries of Rhos and Rhufoniog, now Denbighland,
and planted the same with diverse Englishmen which
held their land and their posterity in the English tenure,
25   the rest, the Welshmen, loaded with many bad
customs, were said to hold their land in Welsh tenure.
One condition whereof was that the inheritance should
not descend to daughters but should go to the heir male
of the house if there were any such within three degrees
30   to the dead man. If not [it] should escheat to the lord.
Yet, in respect of the possibility of issue male, which
the owners of the land might have while he was alive,
the custom of the country did permit him to mortgage
the land to serve his need without the lord's leave. You
35   see hereby that Robin Fychan did what he could,
according to the custom of the country, towards the
preferment of his daughter, and the reason why Ieuan
ap Robert ap Maredudd, his next kinsman and heir, had
the land which proves also that Robert ap Maredudd
40   was eldest brother to Ieuan ap Maredudd, John ap

Maredudd's grandfather, which his posterity greatly gainsaid, for if Ieuan ap Maredudd had not been the elder brother then John ap Maredudd should have inherited this land and not Ieuan ap Robert, his father's cousin. 5

Maredudd, son to Ieuan ap Robert, his eldest son, in the time of his father was taken to nurse by an honest freeholder in the hundred of Is Gwyrfai who was owner of Crug in Llanfair, and the best man in the parish; and, having no children of his own, gave his inheritance to 10 his fosterchild. Crug stands some sixteen miles off from Y Gesail Gyfarch whereby it may appear how desirous men were in those days to have a patron who could defend them from wrong, though they sought him never so far off. 15

Crug stands between Caernarfon and Bangor, two miles off from Caernarfon. In those days Caernarfon flourished as well by trade of merchandise as also for that the King's Exchequer, Chancery and common law courts for all north Wales were there continually 20 residing, the way to London and to the marches little frequented whereby civility and learning flourished in that town: so as they were called the lawyers of Caernarfon, the merchants of Beaumaris and the gentlemen of Conwy. 25

I heard diverse of judgement and learned in the laws to report that the records of the King's courts kept in Caernarfon in those days were as orderly and as formally kept as those in Westminster. Thither did his foster-father send my great-grandfather to school, 30 where he learnt the English tongue, to read, to write and to understand Latin, a matter of great moment in those days, for his other brothers, losing their father young and nursed in Eifonydd near their father's house, wanted all this. To the honest man, his foster and his 35 second father (for he gave him with breeding also his inheritance) may be attributed his good fortune (God's providence always excepted) which sometimes works by secondary means whereof this man was the instrument. 40

Having lived there until the age of twenty years or thereabouts, his foster-father being dead, he fell in liking with a young woman in that town who was daughter-in-law to one Spicer, the reputed daughter of
5 William Gruffudd ap Robin, sheriff of the county of Caernarfon. This Spicer was a landed man of some fifty pounds per annum, as his posterity yet are, had an office in the Exchequer and dealt with trade of merchandise also: so as he was a great wealthy man. His son, John
10 Spicer, was a justice of the peace in the first commissions after the new ordinance of Wales, and was brother by the mother to Alice ferch William, the wife of Maredudd ab Ieuan ap Robert. Their mother is said to be of the Bangors whom I have known often to have
15 claimed kindred of me by that woman.

At Crug he began the world with his wife; and begat there by her two daughters, Janet, first married to Edmund Gruffudd and afterwards to Sir John Puleston, and another called Catherine, married to Rowland
20 Gruffudd of Plasnewydd. Then, finding he was likely to have more children and that the place would prove narrow and straight for him, he was minded to have returned to his inheritance in Eifionydd where there was nothing but killing and fighting, whereupon he did
25 purchase a lease of the castle and *ffriddoedd* of Dolwyddelan of the executors of Sir Ralph Birkenhead. I find in the records of the Exchequer of Caernarfon, in the transcript of an act of resumption enrolled, made in 3 Henry 7th, by which act all King Richard's gifts are
30 resumed excepting one lease of the *ffridd* of Dolwyddelan granted to Sir Ralph Birkenhead of the county of Chester, Knight, Chamberlain of North Wales. Having purchased this lease he removes his dwelling to the castle of Dolwyddelan which, at that time, was in part
35 thereof habitable, where one Hywel ab Ieuan ap Rhys Gethin, a base son of Ieuan ap Rhys in the beginning of Edward the Fourth's time, captain of the country, an outlaw, had dwelt.

Against this man Dafydd ap Siencyn rose and
40 contended with him for the sovereignty of the country,

and being supported by the English officers, for the
other was too hard for him, in the end drew a draft for
him and took him in his bed at Penamnen with his
concubine, performing by craft what he could not by
force, [and] brought him to Conwy castle. 5

For after many bickerings between Hywel and
Dafydd ap Siencyn, Dafydd ap Siencyn, being too weak,
was fain to fly the country and go to Ireland where he
was a year or thereabouts. In the end [he] returned in a
summer time, having himself and all his followers clad 10
in green, which, being come into the country, he
dispersed here and there among his friends lurking by
day and walking in the night for fear of his adversaries.

Such of the country as happened to have sight of him
and of his followers said they were fairies and so ran 15
away. All the whole country then was but a forest,
rough and spacious as it is still, but then waste of
inhabitants and all overgrown with woods, for Owain
Glyndŵr's wars, beginning in Anno 1400, continued
fifteen years, which brought such a desolation that 20
green grass grew on the market-place in Llanrwst called
Bryn-y-boten and the deer fed in the churchyard of
Llanrwst, as it is reported, for it was Owain Glyndŵr's
policy to bring all things to waste, that the English
should find not strength nor resting-place in the 25
country. The country, being brought to such a
desolation, could not be replanted in haste, and the
wars of York and Lancaster, happening some fifteen
years after, this country, being the chiefest fastness of
north Wales, was kept by Dafydd ap Siencyn, a captain 30
of the Lancastrian faction fifteen years in Edward 4th's
time, who sent diverse captains to besiege him, who
wasted the country while he kept his rock of Carreg-y-
gwalch, and lastly by the earl Herbert, who brought it to
utter desolation. You are to understand that in those 35
days the country of Nanconwy was not only wooded but
also all Caernarfonshire, Merionethshire and Denbighshire seemed to be but one forest and wood, having few
inhabitants over that it has this day: though, of all
others, Nanconwy had the fewest, being the worst then 40

and the seat of the wars, to whom the countries about paid contribution from the town of Conwy to Bala, and from Nanconwy to Denbigh.

5   When wars did happen to cease in Hiraethog, the country adjoining to Nanconwy, there was continually fostered a wasp's nest which troubled the whole country. I mean a lordship belonging to St. John's of Jerusalem, called Ysbyty Ifan; a large thing which had privilege of sanctuary, a peculiar jurisdiction not

10   governed by the King's laws. [It was] a receptacle of thieves and murderers who (safely being warranted there by law) made the place thoroughly peopled; no place within twenty mile[s] about was safe from their incursions and robbery. What they got within their

15   limits was their own: they had to their backstay friends and receptors, all the county of Merioneth and Powysland. These, helping the former desolations of Nanconwy and preying upon that country as their next neighbours, kept most part of that country all waste

20   and without inhabitant.

In this state stood the hundred of Nanconwy when Maredudd removed his dwelling thither, being, as I guess, about the four and twentieth year of his age, and in the beginning of Henry 7th's time.

25   Being questioned by his friends what he meant to leave his ancient house and habitation and to go to dwell to Nanconwy, swarming with thieves and bondmen (whereof there are many in the King's lordship and towns in that hundred), he answered that

30   he should find elbow room in that waste country among the bondmen and that he had rather fight with outlaws and thieves than with his own blood and kindred: 'for if I live in my own house in Eifionydd I must either kill my own kinsmen or be killed by them'. Wherein he said

35   very truly for the people were such in those days there; for John Owen ap John ap Maredudd, in his father's time killed Hywel ap Madog Fychan of Abercain for no other quarrel but for the mastery of the country and for the first good morrow. In which tragedy he had likely been

40   an actor if he had lived there, for the reason aforesaid.

He and his cousin, the heir of Bron-y-foel, were both out of the country. Morus ap John ap Maredudd and Owen ap John ap Maredudd were grown old men, so as there was no one in the country who dared strive with John Owen ap John ap Maredudd but Hywel ap Madog   5 Fychan of Abercain, which cost him his life.

Hywel ap Madog Fychan's grandmother was Ieuan ap Robert ap Maredudd's sister; therefore, he was cousin german to Maredudd. John Owen, who killed him, was cousin german to my grandmother, daughter to Morus   10 ap John ap Maredudd. In respect of that feud my grand-mother could not abide any descended of Owen ap John ap Maredudd's house, neither could she abide any of his kindred of Abercain.

I write it but to show the manifold divisions in those   15 days among so private friends.

Hywel ap Madog Fychan, having valiantly fought it out with his people, received his deadly wound in the head. Being down, his mother being present, clapt her hand on his head, meaning to ward the blow and had   20 half her hand and three of her fingers cut off at that blow.

Dafydd Llwyd [ap] Gruffudd Fychan, my uncle, did tell me that his father, dwelling at Cwm Ystradllyn in Eifionydd, hearing of the affray, but not of his cousin's   25 death (for Hywel ap Madog Fychan outlived the affray certain days), sent him, being a child, to see how his cousin did, and coming to Abercain, found him laid in his bed and his wounded men in a great number lying in a *cocherie* above the degree near the high table all the   30 breadth of this hall all gored and wallowing in their own blood, and saw the gentleman's milch kine brought to the hall door and there milked. And their milk carried hot from the kine to the wounded men by them to [be] drunk for the restoring of their blood.   35

Hywel Fychan, upon his deathbed, did say that that quarrel should never be ended while his mother lived, and looked upon her hand. Which was true indeed for she prosecuted eagerly all her time (and John Owen was kept prisoner seven years in Caernarfon castle) for so   40

long she survived her son, and his life saved with much
ado. After her death the feud was compounded for.

John Owen and his followers were exceedingly sore
hurt in that bickering; so that returning to his father's
5   house from the affray, and his aged father sitting or
walking before the door of his house, and seeing his son
and his company all hacked, wounded and besmeared
with their own blood, he said to them: 'Drwg yw'r drefn
yna: a wnaethoch chi eich gwerth?', which is as much
10   [as] to say: 'you are in an ill-favoured pickle; have you
done nothing worthy yourselves?' Said the son: 'I fear
me we have done too much'. 'If that be so', said Owen
ap John ap Maredudd, 'I was this morning the best man
in my country (meaning Eifionydd), but now I know not
15   who is'.

You are to understand that in Eifionydd of old there
be two sects or kindreds, the one lineally descended of
Owain Gwynedd, prince of Wales, consisting then and
now of four houses viz. Y Gesail Gyfarch, Y Llys yng
20   Nghefn-y-fan (now called Ystumcegid), Clenennau and
Bryncir, Glasfryn or Cwm Ystradllyn; the other sect
descended of Collwyn, whereof are five houses or more
viz. Chwilog, Bron-y-foel, Abercain, Gwynfryn,
Talhenbont and the house of Huw Gwyn ap John Wyn
25   ab William called Pennarth, all descended of their
common ancestor, Ieuan ab Einion ap Gruffudd, whose
brother was Hywel ap Gruffudd, that worthy gentleman called Syr Hywel y Fwyall who behaved himself so
worthily at the field of Poitiers (where John, the French
30   King, was taken by the Black Prince) that he received of
the Prince in gift the constableship of Cricieth castle
and other great things in north Wales: also, the rent of
Dee mills in Chester and, which more, was a mess of
meat to be served before his battle-axe or partisan
35   forever in perpetual memory of his good service, which
mess of meat was afterwards carried down to be given to
the poor for his soul's health. [This] mess had eight
yeomen attendants, found at the King's charge, which
were after called Yeomen of the Crown, which Yeomen
40   of the Crown had eight pence a day and lasted till the

beginning of Queen Elizabeth's time. Sergeant Roberts
of Hafod-y-bwch near Wrexham was, at his beginning,
Yeoman of the Crown. He married Sir William Gerard's
half-sister by the mother, as did Robert Turbridge of
Caerfallen near Ruthin, esquire, another to whom he   5
told that, being Yeoman of the Crown, he heard it by
tradition in the King's house that the beginning of their
order was upon that occasion as is afore remembered—
which Robert Turbridge related to me upon the credit of
the other man. The country people, grounding upon the   10
songs made to him in those days, which say that he
bridled the French King, will needs have it that he took
the French King prisoner, a matter unlikely seeing the
one served afoot and the King ahorseback: but the foot
captain is the brazen wall of the army and may be said   15
truly to win the field.

After Maredudd had lived certain years at Dolwyddelan castle he built his house in Penamnen, being the
principal best ground in Dolwyddelan, and also within
certain years after he removed the church of Dolwydd-   20
elan from a place called Bryn-y-bedd to the place where
now it is, being part of the possessions of the priory of
Beddgelert, and there new built the same as it is now,
one cross-chapel excepted which my uncle, Robert
Wynn, built. It should seem by the glass window there   25
that it was built in the year 1512, but whether it was in
that year glazed (which might be long after the building
of the church) I am uncertain. The church, which is
very strongly built, the castle and his house of Penamnen stand three square like a trivet, either a mile   30
distant from another.

Questioning with my uncles what should move him
to demolish the old church which stood in a thicket and
to build it in a plain stronger and greater than it was
before, their opinion was [that] he had reason for the   35
same because the country was wild and he might be
oppressed by his enemies on the sudden. In that woody
country it stood him in policy to have diverse places of
retreat. Certain it was that he dared not go to church on
a Sunday from his house of Penamnen but that he must   40

leave the same guarded with men and have the doors
sure barred and bolted and a watchman to stand at Y
Garreg Big during divine service (being a rock whence
he might see both the church and the house and raise
5   the cry if the house were assaulted). He dared not,
although he were guarded with twenty tall archers,
make known when he went to church or elsewhere or
go and come the same way through the woods and
narrow places least he should be laid for. This was in
10   the beginning of his time.

To strengthen himself in the country he provided out
of all countries adjacent the tallest and most able men
he could hear of. Of them he placed colonies in the
country, filling every empty tenement with a tenant or
15   two whereof most was the King's land whereof many of
their posterity remain until this day. One, William ap
Robert of Is Gwyrfai (being one of his followers), he
placed in a tenement of the township of Gwydir called
Pencraig Inco, now worth £30 per annum, who paid for
20   the same only a relief to the King which was 10s. 4d.

Such were the laws in those days and are still that if
the King's tenant holding in freehold or any other
tenant of [a] lord in fee cease for two years to do his
service to the King or lord, the lord may re-enter. The
25   writ is called *cessavit per biennium*. The exactions
were, in those days, so manifold that not only the
bondmen ran away and forsook the King's land but also
freeholders their own land. Here, to lay down in particular the Welsh customs, would make the volume too
30   great.

Owen ap Hugh ab Ieuan ab William, great grandchild
to the said William, enjoys the land to this day though,
in my grandfather's time, it was in suit by the countenance of John ap Madog ap Hywel but not recovered by
35   the means of my grandfather.

Einion Gruffudd ab Iocos, a freeholder of Ffestiniog
and Llanfrothen, he placed in the King's *ffridd* at
Bryntyrch, of whom are descended many in Nanconwy,
Ffestiniog and Llanfrothen. Hywel ab Ieuan ap Pellyn, a
40   Denbighshire man and a tall archer, of whom are

descended the race of the Pellyns, he placed in the tenement of Garth. One Gruffudd ap Tudur, a Denbighshire man, in Rhiwgoch; Ieuan Dafydd ab Edward, an Abergele man who felled in one day eighteen oaks towards the building of a part of Penamnen house, he placed in Bwlch Cynnud. Robert ap Maredudd he placed in Bertheos, of whom are descended many, whereof his son, John ap Robert, was dairyman there until the beginning of my time; and many others too long to be repeated. In Fynhadog, he found Rhys ap Robert, a tall stout man who, being originally (as they say) a Faenol Bangor man born, and a freeholder, having killed a man there, forsook his land and fled thither, of whom lineally is descended Humphrey Jones of Craflwyn, gentleman. Rhydderch and Richard ap Rhys ap Robert, sons to the said Rhys ap Robert, were my father's fosters and of the said Richard ap Rhys ap Robert is lineally descended Humphrey Jones of Craflwyn, gentleman.

Diverse other tall and able men dwelt in the country which drew to him as to their defender and captain of the country, so as within the space of certain years he was able to make seven score tall bowmen of his followers in the country arrayed, as I have credibly heard, in this manner. Every of them had a jacket or armolet coat, a good steel cap, a short sword and a dagger, his bows and arrows; and most of them had horses and chasing staves, all of which were to answer the cry upon all events.

Whereby he grew so strong that he began to put back and to curb the sanctuary of thieves and robbers which, at times, were wont to be above a hundred and fifty well horsed and well appointed.

It is to be noted also that certain gentlemen and freeholders dwelt in the country but not many who were to answer the cry and to come in also upon the like distress.

This country in Queen Elizabeth's time produced six that were bishops in sundry places. And the last in order and first to be remembered (as the course of this History leadeth), was Henry Rowlands, Bishop of Bangor, born at Mellteyrn in Llŷn (son to one Rowland ap Robert, an ancient esquire) who sat in that see eighteen years. He was sufficiently learned, for he preached twice with approbation before King James and was a good and provident governor of his church and diocese, a great repairer of his decayed cathedral church, and a great builder upon the glebe of diverse other churches which he had *in commendam*; in housekeeping and hospitality, both to rich and poor, the greatest that has been in our time, and yet died rich. And though he was in the commission of the peace continually and in other commissions that came into the country, yet he would put them off as much as in him lay, having no will to deal but in his own element. He left an almshouse for six poor men in the town of Bangor. He has left lands for two Fellowships in Jesus College in Oxford, and other lands for the maintenance of a free school in Llŷn at Botwnnog, being the place that he was brought up himself at school, and liberally left money to build it. He, with the voluntary contribution of his clergy (whereof he had the command in good will more than any before him), bought three fair bells for the steeple of the cathedral church of Bangor, they having but one before. He erected a monument there in the church with fair statues of himself and of his cousin, the next precedent bishop, Doctor Richard Vaughan, with the following inscription:

In pious memory of two bishops in this church succeeding one another, who were born close to one another, of like age, mutually beloved fellow pupils and blood relations, from the illustrious family of the Vaughans of Talhenbont in Eifionydd. The first: the son of Thomas ap Robert Vaughan, gentleman, of Nyffryn in Llŷn, who held this see for two years, then Chester for seven years,

5

10

15

20

25

30

35

and afterwards held the see of London for three years,
where he finally ended his life by an untimely death in
the month of March, the year of our Lord 1607; whose
virtue lived on after his death. The second: Henry, son
5 of Roland ap Robert, Esquire, of Mellteyrn in Llŷn by his
wife Elizabeth, daughter of Gruffudd ap Robert Fychan,
Esquire, of Talhenbont, who now passes the eighteenth
year of his consecration and leads many faithfully to the
honour of God and the propagation of the gospel. In
10 mutual love one for the two constructed this monument
in the month of May, the year of our Lord 1616.

> We are born, and in our turn we die,
> They follow who have not gone before.

Next to him in that see preceded Richard Vaughan,
15 D.D., born also in Llŷn, descended of the Vaughans of
Talhenbont, an ancient house of esquires. He sat there
two years but never was at the bishopric in all that time
for that the means and domains of the bishopric were
not able to find him, being a worthy housekeeper and a
20 liberal minded man, as the proof did manifest, while he
lived at Chester whereto he was translated. He was an
excellent and rare scholar, a discreet and temperate
man and very industrious and painful in his vocation,
which shortened his days. He was translated from
25 Chester to London by King James in whose good grace
and favour he lived as any other bishop whatsoever. He
died a poor man for he respected a good name more than
wealth.

Next before him was Nicholas Robinson D.D., born
30 in the town of Conwy in Caernarfonshire. [He] was of
honest parents and wealthy, whose father I knew,
bailiff of the town, being chief officer (having by their
charter authority to keep courts with sergeants and
under officers). He was an excellent scholar and would
35 have preached exceeding[ly] well, especially when he
did it without premeditation, for then he exceeded
himself; but, upon meditation (in my conceit), not so
well for I have heard him at both, at St. Paul's in London
in time of parliament once and in the country often—
40 whereof I can attribute no occasion but that he was
extreme[ly] choleric and fearful withal which, in my

judgement, put him out of his natural bias. Withal, he was a very wise man. He died rich and left many hopeful children for whom he had well provided.

Thomas Davies LL.B., and Chancellor of the diocese of Bangor, born within three miles of the town of   5 Conwy. Some say that he was born within the town, son to [Dafydd ap Robert ap Dafydd] of Caerhun, gentleman. He was, after Richard Davies's translation, elected Bishop of St. Asaph where he sat many years. He had at one time one brother called Gruffudd Davies,   10 high sheriff of the county of Caernarfon, and another brother of his, coroner, and another brother escheator in the said county.

This county anon, after the beginning of Queen Elizabeth's reign, produced three that were bishops at once,   15 born within or near the town of Conwy. The one, Richard Davies, first of St. Asaph, after translated to St. David's where he governed like himself and for the honour of our nation (loving entirely the north Wales men) whom he placed in great numbers there, having   20 ever this saying in his mouth: 'Myn y Wyry Faglog! (his familiar oath), I will plant you north Wales men, grow if you list'. He kept an exceeding[ly] great post, having in his service younger brothers of most of the best houses in that country to whom, with his own sons   25 Thomas, Peregrine and Gerson (whom I knew at Oxford) both born at Geneva, he gave them good maintenance and education. He did stoutly confront Sir John Perrot, Knight, in those days, an inward favourite of the earl of Leicester, who afterwards was Lord   30 Deputy of Ireland and one of the lords of the Privy Council. [He was] a man of great possessions in that country [who] would have wronged him.

He [Davies] called to him William Salesbury, esquire, of Plas Isa near Llanrwst in the county of   35 Denbigh, and diverse others, Welshmen, profound scholars and skilful linguists; and translated the New Testament, the Psalms and Book of Common Prayer into the Welsh tongue, and was very far onward with the Old Testment and had gone through with it if   40

variance had not happened between him and William Salesbury (who had lived almost two years with him in that business) for the general sense and etymology of one word which the Bishop would have to be one way
5 and William Salesbury another, to the great loss of the old British and mother tongue. For, being together, they drew homilies, books and diverse other tracts in the British tongue and had done far more if that unlucky division had not happened. For the Bishop
10 lived five or six years after and William Salesbury about twenty-four but gave over writing (more was the pity), for he was a rare scholar, and especially a Hebrician, whereof there were not many in those days. This worthy prelate, Richard Davies, was a poor curate's
15 son who served at y Gyffin within half a mile of the town of Conwy, born in a place called Plas-y-person. In Queen Mary's time he was fain to flee with his wife to Geneva where, being an exceeding[ly] poor man and living of[f] the contribution and alms of the fugitives
20 there, he was so industrious that in three years or somewhat more he attained the country language spoken in Geneva which I think to be French. He served a cure there and preached and, in the latter end, lived well thereby. Oh! how my heart does warm in recording the
25 memory of so worthy a man. He died poor having never had regard to riches.

In Queen Mary's time time sat William Glyn in Bangor—a great scholar and a great Hebrician, as by quotation of his books do appear, being rare in that
30 time. He was a good and religious man after the manner of that time. He was born at [Heneglwys, Anglesey] in this county of Caernarfon [sic]. He was a priest's son as I have heard. Query: of what kindred and house?

Another William Glynn, LL.D., of the house of Glyn-
35 llifon, being an ancient house of esquires, proceeded before him as suffragan to Bishop Skevington, being Abbot of Bermondsey, who never came into the country but yet bestowed great cost on the cathedral church of Bangor, for he built the body thereof and the
40 bell tower, and furnished the same with bells which

were sold by the Bishop, Dean and Prebends in King
Edward VI's time when it was expected that all the bells
of England should have rung in the courtiers' purses,
which likely had been so if the duke of Somerset had
stood longer. This man (viz. Glynn) was of a stirring   5
spirit and a great housekeeper, and spent all, and had a
hand in all the great temporal affairs of the country as
well as the spiritual.

Query: whether there were any before him of this
county who were Bishops of Bangor.   10

William Morgan, D.D., born in Dolwyddelan in the
commote of Nanconwy and county of Caernarfon,
descended of the race of the bondmen of that
town[ship], servants (both he and his ancestors) to the
house of Gwydir where he was brought up in learning.   15
His first preferment was with myself and by my means.
He was first made Bishop of Llandaff and afterwards
translated to St. Asaph where he died after he had sat
there some two or three years. He translated the Old
Testament into the Welsh tongue before he was bishop   20
wherein he had the benefit and help of Bishop Davies's
and William Salesbury's works who had done a great
part thereof, yet he carried the name of it all. He
repaired and slated the chancel of the cathedral church
of St. Asaph which was a great ruin. He died a poor man.   25
He was a good scholar, both a Grecian and a Hebrician.

This county also produced Sir William Jones, now
living, who was Chief Justice of the King's Bench in the
realm of Ireland and now is one of the Judges of the
Common Pleas at Westminster. He was born in Llŷn at   30
his own house called Castellmarch which is a very
ancient house of gentlemen.

In King Henry VI's time there was also a Judge of
Common Pleas, Jeffrey Coetmor, born in the hundred
of Nanconwy, in the county of Caernarfon, of the   35
Coetmors there which were very worthy gentlemen.
His grandfather, Hywel Coetmor, who lies buried in a
fair monument in Llanrwst church in the county of
Denbigh, was captain of a hundred Denbighshire men
with the Black Prince at the field of Poitiers where   40

John, King of France, was taken. He lived at Henley-upon-Thames.

William Thomas, son and heir to Rhys Thomas, esquire, born in Caernarfon, captain of two hundred
5 men out of north Wales, went with Robert, earl of Leicester, to the Low Countries where, finding Sir Thomas Morgan and Sir Roger Williams and Sir Martin Schenk, the most forward of that army, associated himself with them and especially with Sir Martin
10 Schenk. With him [he] put himself and his company into Berk-upon-Rhine whereas the Prince of Parma, with all his army, did invest him and besieged them for a great time, omitting nothing that was to be performed for the winning of the same, but in the end he was fain
15 to give it over. After which time both Sir Martin Schenk and he came to the earl of Leicester to the camp before Zutphen where, in that great skirmish Sir Philip Sidney, Knight, was hurt to the death and slain; a brave, courageous, wise gentleman as any in this country
20 produced in his time or for many ages before. He had been page to the duchess of Somerset and was brought up under the same tutors as her son, the Lord Edward Somerset was, who was not much older than he. He could speak Latin, Italian and French. It was thought
25 that his language was the occasion of his death for it is reported that he yielded himself in the Italian tongue. Envious that he should possess such, a prison[er] killed him in cold blood. These are reported and whether true or not I cannot say, but there he died.

30 Gruffudd Wynn, born at Gwydir in that said county, second son of John Wynn ap Maredudd, esquire, served in his youth Sir Edmund Knevett, Knight, lord of the castle of Bucknam in Norfolk, who, having a quarrel those days with the Lord Fitzwalter, son and heir to the
35 earl of Sussex (for his mother-in-law, the earl's wife with whom it was thought he was too familiar) retained a great many of our county gentlemen on whom it was thought he did most rely for his safety. There served him at one time four of the house of Gwydir viz. . . .
40 next Gruffudd Wynn, Cadwaladr ap Maredudd, John ap

Rhys Wynn and Dafydd Llwyd ap Rhys Wynn, brothers; Thomas Williams, father to Sir William Williams, Baronet, and of the younger sons of William Williams the elder of Cochwillan, esquire, and Edward Williams, his brother who after was a man of arms at Boulogne 5 and servant to Lord Paget. Query: whether he was his man or no? . . . Last high sheriff of this county, Robert ap Hugh of Creuddyn, esquire, after high sheriff of this county. [He] died a wealthy man.

Sir Edmund Knevett, being a very gallant, forward 10 gentleman, was the first that of the King's side did set upon the rebels of Norfolk. [He] lay in the neighbouring village five hundred strong with thirty horse of his own servants where he killed five or six of the rebels; but there he received a blow which afterwards was the 15 occasion of his untimely death. From thence he rode to the Court to advise the state of the rebellion and to get the King's pardon for those whom he had killed. From the Court he returned in great credit and authority with the marquess of Northampton, the Lord Sheffield and 20 diverse other noblemen.

Gruffudd Wynn was with Sir Edmund and was of his chamber and with him in all places; and at the battle that was fought within the city of North Norwich between the marquess of Northampton, General for the 25 King, and Ket, wherein the King's men were put to the worst, and the Lord Sheffield and many other gentlemen killed. I have heard himself often reported that his master and he were as forward as the Lord Sheffield: they were armed with white armour capapee and that 30 he received such a blow at that time on the head [that] he staggered and one of his horse's ears was cut off with a glaive and thrust through the withers. If it had not been for the goodness of his horse he had never come of[f] which [i.e. the horse] brought [him] to a park near 35 the city and there fell under him dead.

And he did verily believe that the cause of the Lord Sheffield's death was the reason that he was in gilt armour, and therefore they sought after him more than others. Sir Edmund Knevett's lady was fain to flee by 40

night from her house to Framlingham castle . . . where the King's daughter, the Lady Mary, then lay. The rebels came to Bucknam castle and burnt it and made havoc of all that they found therein for the people were
5   fled.

The marquess and Sir Edmund and the rest who survived, [having] return[ed] to the Court, the earl of Warwick and diverse other noblemen (as appeareth by the chronicle of that time) and Sir Edmund were sent
10 down against the rebels with a greater army where they fought with them and overthrew them, and Ket was slain. [His] nag and saddle (being of russet velvet) Gruffudd Wynn brought home with him to Gwydir, and the nag was called 'Glas Ket' by his former Master's
15 name while he lived. After Sir Edmund's death Gruffudd Wynn became servant to William, earl of Pembroke, with whom he served as a man at arms at Wyatt's field in rank that day with old William Mostyn, esquire, who served the earl also. His younger brother,
20 Doctor [John] Gwynn, made him his heir and thereby advanced his estate much. He was the most bountiful housekeeper both to rich and poor; a religious, stout and wise man, and was high sheriff of the two counties of Denbigh and Merioneth. I brought him a commission
25 to be justice of the peace in the counties of Caernarfon and Merioneth but he refused them. At the time of his death his living was worth a thousand pounds per annum and was wealthy withal.

Robert Wynn, born at Gwydir in the county, third son
30 to John Wyn ap Maredudd, serving Sir Philip Hoby, Knight, in his chamber (being one of the Council of King Henry VIII and a great Commander of his army) was with the King and his master at the siege of Boulogne where he received a shot in his leg whereof he
35 was long lame notwithstanding all the surgery the King's men could afford. It was strange that the surgeons could not find it at first and have it out, but it remained in that place for the time before mentioned. It was wont, sometimes in four years, sometimes in six
40 years, to grieve him, drawing an inflamation to his leg

which, by repercussives being driven back, he should be well again. First, he married Dorothy [daughter] of Sir William Gruffudd of Penrhyn, Knight, Chamberlain of North Wales, and widow to William Williams the younger of Cochwillan, esquire, who was past child-bearing, with whom he lived till he was past threescore and six years old. After, he married a young gentle-woman, daughter of Thomas Dymock of Willington in the county of Flint, esquire, who, in his old age brought him many children. Some six years after his last marriage his body, being stirred in getting children at those years (untimely for that purpose), his wonted inflation took him in the leg extraordinary vehemence so that he supposed it would endanger his life. In the end it grew to a heat and he, who was of his chamber, found with his probe a hard thing in the orifice which he supposed a great scale of his skin-bone. Fearing lest the same should rot (he being at my house at Gwydir) I brought him to his chamber desiring that I might see his man dress his leg afore he went to bed. Being unbound and the sore open I found with my nail a hard thing in the orifice and of a great length. So I called for the probe and with the same searched the wound deeper than his man dared for hurting him, and found it was no bone but the lead that had lain so long in his flesh, and so sent for a surgeon to cut the dead flesh and skin and pull it out, which he did; and he was well recovered and felt no pain at all while he lived. He was at the winning and burning of Edinburgh and Leith in Scotland and at the memorable journeys mentioned in the chronicles in King Henry VIII's and Edward VI's time excepting Musselburgh Field in Scotland where at I did hear him say he was. In the latter part of King Edward VI's reign his master was sent ambassador to the Emperor Charles V who was then in Hungary with the greatest army that the Christians ever had to confront Soleiman the Turk, who came with 500,000 men to conquer Christendom, at which service both his master and he were. His master, being revoked by Queen Mary and another placed in his stead by reason of his religion (being a

Protestant), found the Queen's countenance averse from him whereupon, after he had kept his house for a while very privately, he desired of the Queen licence to travel, which she granted, with this addition, that she would give him leave, and all of his opinion, to travel out of the land and never to return. He travelled not but within a while after died in his own house of melancholy and grief of mind.

Robert Wynn, his servant, returned home and anon after married, as aforesaid, and built a goodly house in the town of Conwy in this county where he kept a worthy plentiful house all his time. [He] lies buried in the church there, having two monuments, the one for himself and another for his first wife.

Hugh Gruffudd, son to Gruffudd ap John Gruffudd of Cefnamwlch, esquire, a very proper man of a comely tall personage, was by his father put an apprentice to a merchant adventurer in London whom he served very honestly and well until his years were out, and he became Factor, both for his master and others in the parts beyond the sea. [He], passing from London towards his place of trade with twelve hundred pounds which he had taken up upon his own credit, was taken by the Dunkirks and there imprisoned and thence delivered by the means of Hugh Owen, who was the private counsel to the Prince of Parma. This Hugh Owen was born in this county, a younger brother of an ancient gentleman's house called Plas Du. He served in great credit with the earl of Arundel and was a chief actor in the duke of Norfolk's action, and was thought [to] be the wisest man among them. When he saw that his counsel was not followed [he] traversed his ground in time into Brussels where he continued Privy Counsellor to that state forty years and until the end of his days. This Hugh Gruffudd, being by his means released, and having paid his ransom and having lost his credit irrevocably gets a letter of mark and furnished himself to sea and proves there the worthiest and the most valiant captain of any nation who was at sea. In the end, within the Straits, lighting upon the ship of

Cathedral church of Bangor

(Samuel and Nathaniel Buck)

Plas Mawr, Conwy

(Gwynedd Archives Service)

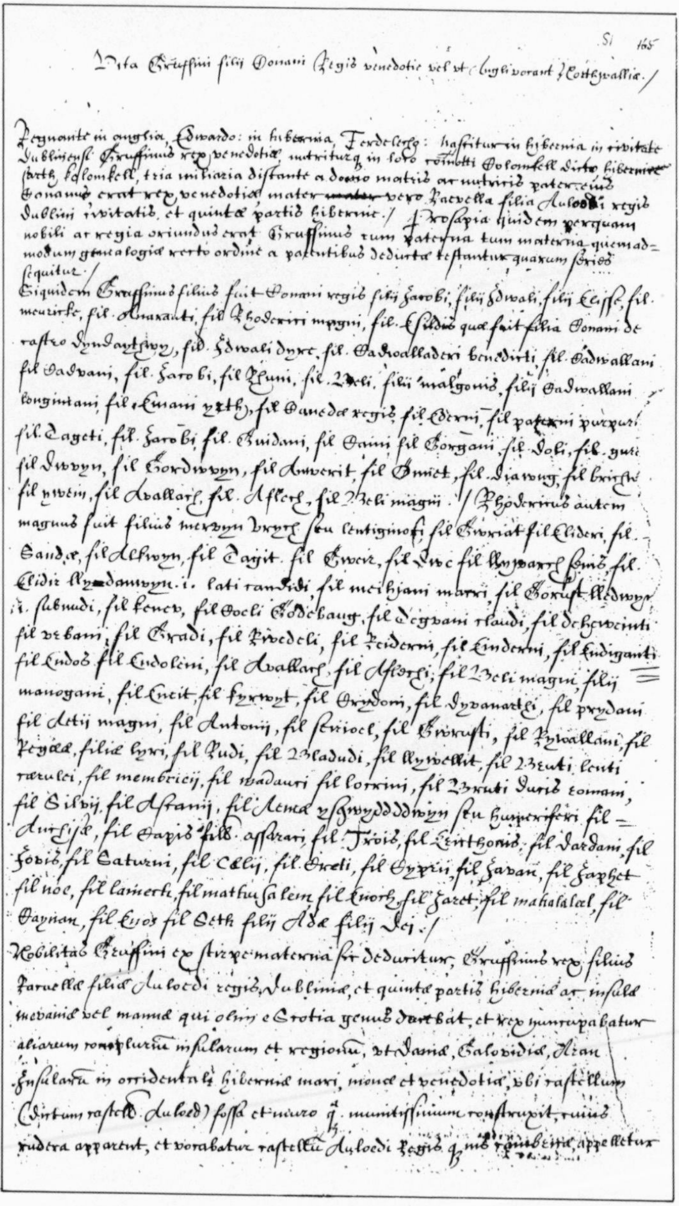
51 165

Vita Gruffini filii Conani Regis venedotie vel ut Angli vocant Northwallie.

Regnante in anglia, Edwardo: in hibernia, Terdelecho: nascitur in hibernia in civitate Dubliniensi Gruffinus rex venedotiae, nutriturque in loco Rorulli Colomkell dicto hibernice Surth Colomkell, tria milliaria distante a domo matris ac nutricis pater eius Conanus erat rex venedotiae mater mater vero Racvella filia Aulodi regis Dublini civitatis et quintae partis hiberniae. / Prosapia quidem perquam nobili ac regia oriundus erat Gruffinus tum paterna tum materna quemadmodum genealogiae certo ordine a parentibus deducta testantur quarum series sequitur. /
Siquidem Gruffinus filius fuit Conani regis filii Jacobi, filii Idwali, filii Elissé, fil. meurike, fil. Anaraudi, fil Rhoderici magni, fil. Essilus quae fuit filia Conani de castro Dyndaythwy, fil. Idwali dyrt, fil. Cadwalladeri benedicti, fil. Cadwallani fil Cadvani, fil. Jacobi, fil Rhuni, fil. Beli, filii malgonis, filii Cadwallani longimani, fil Enniani yrth, fil Cunedae regis, fil Ederni, fil paterni purpuri fil. Tageti, fil. Jacobi, fil. Guidani, fil Caini fil Gorgani, fil. Doli, fil. guir fil Dwyn, fil Gordwyn, fil Amerit, fil Amict, fil. Diaring, fil brithe fil yrwein, fil Avallach, fil. Afleth, fil Beli magni. / Rhodericus autem magnus fuit filius mervyn vrych seu lentiginosi fil Gwriat fil Elideri, fil. Sandae, fil Alcwyn, fil Tagit. fil Gwair, fil Doc fil llywarch hen, fil. Elidir llydanwyn .i. lati candidi, fil meirhiani macri, fil Gorust lledwm .i. seminudi, fil Ceneu, fil Coeli Godebaug, fil Tegvani claudi, fil dehewaint fil urbani, fil Gradi, fil Rivedeli, fil Rideric, fil Eudeyrn, fil Eudigant fil Eudos fil Eudolem, fil Avallach, fil Aflergi, fil Beli magni, filii manogani, fil Eneit, fil Kyrwyt, fil Crydoni, fil Dyvanarthi, fil prydani fil Aetii magni, fil Antonii, fil Serioel, fil Gorusti, fil Ryvallani, fil Regae, filiae Lyri, fil Rudi, fil Bladudi, fil llywellit, fil Bruti lenti caeruli, fil membricii, fil madauci fil locrini, fil Bruti ducis romani, fil Silvii, fil Ascanii, fil Aeneae ysgwyddddwyn seu humerisferi fil Anchisae, fil Capis fil assaraci, fil Trois, fil Erithonis, fil dardani, fil Jovis, fil Saturni, fil Caeli, fil Creti, fil Cyprii, fil Javan, fil Japhet fil noe, fil lamech, fil mathusalem fil Enoch, fil Jaret, fil mahalaleel, fil Caynan, fil Enos fil Seth filii Adae filii Dei. /
Nobilitas Gruffini ex stirpe materna sic deducitur, Gruffinus rex filius Racvellae filiae Aulocdi regis Dubliniae, et quintae partis hiberniae ac insulae mevaniae vel manniae qui olim e Scotia genus ducebat, et rex nuncupabatur aliarum complurium insularum et regionum, ut Daniae, Galovidiae, Ariae insularum in occidentali hibernica mari, moniae et venedotiae, ubi castellum (dictum castell Auloed) fossa et muro quam munitissimum construxit, cuius rudera apparent, et vocabatur castellum Auloedi Regis quamvis nunc Cambrice appellatur

MS. copy of part of *Vita Gruffini filii Conani*

(South Glamorgan County Library)

war of the King of Spain (that carried the King of Spain's
treasure out of Italy into Spain) resolved there either to
die or to win it which, in the end, he did after a most
admirable fight for four or five days continuance,
having slain the most valiant captain (being a most   5
valiant Dutchman) and a great number of the soldiers.
[He], having received a great loss by the other (himself
being sore hurt) and his company so weakened, he was
fain to be taken himself to Argier for refuge where
either he died of his hurts or was poisoned and his goods   10
seized upon to the Turks' use. Robert Powell, one of
[his] followers, returned home full of double pistoletts
and was searched, tortured and beaten with a bull's
pessel to make him confess, as he told me himself. He
also told me that in the fight, which was long, fierce and   15
admirable, both parties would rest at times and the
captains part and drink one to another.

Four martial men our age has produced out of this
country, Sir Maurice Gruffudd, Knight, born in the
town of Caernarfon, and one of the younger sons of   20
William Gruffudd, esquire. He served in the realm of
Ireland all his youth and was captain there, and for his
good services received his degree. [He] lives at this time
in Connaught castle which [he] himself built and is
called Balimerusk, and is one of the Council of the   25
province.

Captain Prichard, born at Madryn Isaf in Llŷn in the
said county, younger brother to Gruffudd ap Richard,
heir of that house, commanded with great credit a
hundred men under the states of the Low Countries in   30
Queen Elizabeth's time.

Sir Richard Wynn of Caernarfon, Knight, of the house
of Bryncir, captain of a hundred men in Ireland, Provost
Marshal of Flushing under Sir Philip Sidney. [He was]
sometime page to Captain Randall, who was slain in   35
the north of Ireland, whose armour he brought to Sir
Henry Sidney, then Lord Deputy of Ireland, whose
follower he was all his lifetime. After his death, for his
sundry good services, [he was] Knighted and after
having got the widow of Captain Thomas   40

(afore-mentioned) in the country, lived at Caernarfon all the rest of his time. He was one of the Council of the Marches, keeping a very worthy house, being a religious, honest and true-hearted man to his friend,

5   having always in his mouth this saying: 'Duw a diwedd da' which in English is: 'God and a good end': which, no question, God did here for he made [a] Christian and a good end, as Gruffudd Williams, Doctor in Divinity (now living), being his ghostly father at his end, did

10   respect; which also the Reverend Father Lewis, now Bishop of Bangor, preaching the funeral sermon of William Glynn of Glynllifon, Knight, did remember, persuading all to the imitation of him, John Wynn ap Hugh, esquire.

15   The memorable services of John Wynn ap Hugh, esquire, born at Bodfel in Llŷn in the said county, whereof he lived. He now, in this tract, is not to be forgotten. He was standard-bearer to John, earl of Warwick and afterwards duke of Northumberland in

20   the great field fought between him and Ket and the rebels of Norfolk and Suffolk near Norwich in Edward VI's time. His horse was slain under him and himself hurt, and yet he upheld the Great Standard of England. There is mention of this shot made at the Standard of

25   England in chronicles of that time. For the which service the duke of Northumberland bestowed upon him two fine things: in Llŷn viz. the Isle of Bardsey and the demesne house of the Abbot of Bardsey near Aberdaron, called the Court, with the honourable

30   mention of his good service in the grant, which I have seen and read, a rare matter to find so good a master.

In Queen Elizabeth's time lived John Wynn, Doctor of the Arches, born at Gwydir in the said county, youngest son to John Wyn ap Maredudd, esquire. In his

35   youth [he was] Fellow of St. John's College and Proctor of the University. He arrested John, duke of Northumberland, who yielded unto him. He died without issue and gathered a great estate which he left to Gruffudd Wynn, second brother of that house. He was learned

40   and a wise man and a bountiful housekeeper and never

married. He found two Fellowships and three Scholarships in St. John's College in Cambridge whereof he had
been Fellow. This small foundation has God so blessed, of
fifty years standing at the most, that it has produced in
our time the Right Honourable John Williams, Doctor   5
in Divinity, Bishop of Lincoln and Lord Keeper of the
Great Seal of England; Owen Wynn, Doctor of Divinity,
son to Gruffudd Wynn and brother to the said founder,
now Master of that college (God grant that his mercy
may follow the same society forever); James Ellis,   10
Doctor of the Civil Law and Chancellor of Peterborough, in Queen Elizabeth's time, son to Ellis
Maurice, esquire, born in Clenennau in the said
county; William Gruffudd, Doctor of the Arches, one of
the younger sons of William Gruffudd of Caernarfon,   15
esquire, born in Caernarfon, Judge of the Admiralty in
north Wales in Queen Elizabeth's time; Maurice
Glynn, Doctor of the Civil Law, son to Robert ap
Maredudd, esquire, born at Glynllifon in the said
county, a younger brother of that house, was Dean of   20
the Arches. [He] died without issue and what he had he
left to (a) religious house. He lived in King Henry VIII's
time before the ruin of the monasteries; Gruffudd
Williams, Doctor in Divinity, born at Treflan in the
said county of ancient freeholders, his mother   25
well-descended, being of the house of Penmynydd in
Anglesey; a great scholar and an industrious preacher of
God's words as appears by diverse of his sermons in
London preached at St. Paul's Cross and are extant in
print. Also, he was lecturer in [St.] Paul's for some eight   30
years together, now chaplain in [the] household of the
Right Honourable the earl of Montgomery; Owen
Meredith, sometime Fellow of All Souls in Oxford,
Bachelor in Divinity, an honest fellow and a good
scholar, son to Maredudd ap Thomas Gruffudd of   35
Clynnog in the said county, esquire; Edmund Gruffudd,
Bachelor in Divinity and now Dean of Bangor, born in
Llŷn in the said county and a younger son to Gruffudd
ap John Gruffudd of Cefnamwlch of an ancient house
and a worthy gentleman; William Bryncir, bachelor in   40

Divinity, born at Bryncir in the commote of Eifionydd in the said county, a younger son to Robert Bryncir, esquire.

SUPPLEMENT TO MEMOIRS

*An insert in NLW MS 21253D (f.32r-32v)—in Bishop Humphrey Humphreys's hand—following a copy of the *History*, may well have been intended as a preface to the *Memoirs* which are contained in this document (f. 32v et seq.). Wynn notes that he had surveyed the 'soile and situation' of Caernarfonshire (which has not survived) and proposes to supply details of the 'Witts and Worthy Members', other than major gentry, who had earned for themselves a good reputation by their activities. He intended to focus on 'such as by there own Industry have Advanced their fortunes and became Eminent'. According to his own testimony the work was written about forty-five years after Edmund Grindal's elevation to the Archbishopric of Canterbury (1575) and the year when Sir Thomas Ramsey, a London grocer, was appointed Lord Mayor of the city (1577). *DNB*, xxiii, p. 261; J. Stow, *A Survey of London* (1842), pp. 45, 195. This dates the *Memoirs* c.1620-2. It may well have been that John Speed, cartographer and antiquary, had prompted Wynn to undertake the work. J. G. Jones, 'Sir John Wynn and John Speed', 257-8; *CWP*, nos. 984-5, 1014. Wynn supplies a miscellany of material on a variety of individuals from Gwynedd, principally younger sons of gentry, who had entered the church, fought in the army and practised law. He begins by referring to John Williams of Conwy, Bishop of Lincoln and Lord Keeper of the Great Seal at the time—himself a younger son and Wynn's kinsman—and his namesake of Dolwyddelan, a royal goldsmith and son of William Coetmor, an illegitimate descendant of Maredudd ab Ieuan ap Robert. He was considered to be 'an antiquary of considerable eminence' who assisted Michael Drayton with information for his *Poly-Olbion* (1612), a long poetic topography of England. *DWB*, pp. 1044-7; *PACF*, pp. 186, 280-1, 393; *HGF* (1878), p. 87; D. E. Jenkins, *Bedd*

Gelert: its Facts, Fairies and Folklore (1899), pp. 119-20; 269-70; 281-3. Both were blood-relatives and it is, therefore, not surprising that Wynn, whose objective was closely in accord with his antiquarian pursuits, should have taken them as typical representatives of public figures on the upgrade. The section runs as follows:

Now haveing taken View and Survey of the soile and scituation of the County of Carnarvon, It would be considered and remembered what Witts and Worthy Members to the Common Wealth from time to time this poor County brought forth, and purposely omitting the Gentry and Ancient Houses of worth (whereof there are many) which I leave to some other Man's worke. I will only remember such as by there own Industry have Advanced their fortunes, and became Eminent, and because in these latter times hath bred the greater number thereof (and of more note) I will begin with this Time, makeing the History (like a Pyramides) Great in the bottome and Small at the topp.

The Children of Israel were commanded 26 Deut: ver. 3. That when they came to offer theire first Fruits to make a confession to God acknowledging that he had brought them to that Good land which he had promised their Fathers; soe I, bending the knees of my Hart to Almighty God, Doe acknowledge his goodness towards me in hearing my Prayer and performing my petition; For God's glory is to be published as the Angell said to Tobit, Chap: 12, verse 2 and thus it was: (some 45 years since or thereabouts) that Grindall was Arch-Bishop of Canterbury, and Ramsley L[ord] Maior of London. Two of the greatest subjects of this land (both as was then reported) born in Northumberland and poor men's children. The men I know but not the state of there parents, and therefore I speak but by heresay. This being voiced throughout the Cytty of London where I then was as rare accident, and coming to my Eares, Considering that Northumberland stood as far from the sun as Northwales did: I said, oh! that I might live to see the like out of Northwales in my time, Confessing ingeniously that I had little hope thereof, but it was spoken in the fer[v]our of my spiritt and Hart which it pleased Allmighty God to heare me granting my request in a greater measure then I could hope for. For at this time by God's especiale great goodness the R[igh]t Hon[ou]rable John Williams, Doctor in Divinity, and my Cousen in bloud, my Godson and One whome his Father had com[m]itted is Lord Keeper of the Great Seal of England, And Bishop of Lincoln. Born in the Town of Conway in this County of Carnarvon within Eight Miles of my Mansion House, and John Williams alsoe, the King's Goldsmith, who is well knowne, might be L[or]d Mayor of London. Both for his wealth and sufficient wherein (in my conceipt) few of the Cittizens can equall him, and none goe beyond him: was born in Dolethelyn within 5 Miles of my House on my̌ Land, and is alsoe my near kinsman by the Paternall Line of my House and Bloud. Now Judge you that read this whither God hath not amplie performed my petition.

HISTORY OF THE GWYDIR FAMILY

1.1 Gruffudd ap Cynan, prince of Wales: His dates are c. 1055-1137. King of Gwynedd (c. 1100-37). His grandfather, Iago, was assassinated by his followers c. 1039 and Gwynedd was ruled by usurpers until 1075 when Gruffudd, on his return from Ireland, regained the inheritance. His mother was Ragnhildr (Rhagnell), daughter of Olaf Arnaid (d. 1012) of the Danish royal line of Dublin, her grandfather being Sitric, 'King of the Silken Beard', who abdicated in 1035. Gruffudd was born in Dublin and reared at Swords monastery. Very little is known of Cynan, his father, and Gruffudd claimed the throne of Gwynedd through his grandfather Iago. Although he returned to Gwynedd in 1075 it was not until c. 1100 that he established himself firmly on the throne. He is regarded as the ruler who, because of his persistent opposition to the invading Normans, laid the foundations of the medieval Kingdom of Gwynedd. *HW*, ii, 462-9; *DWB*, pp. 310-11. On his death he was described as 'prince of Gwynedd and head, King, defender and pacifier of all Wales.' *BT*, p. 88a. He was not officially recognised as 'prince of Wales', a title first used by Dafydd ap Llywelyn in January 1245. M. Richter, 'David ap Llywelyn, the first Prince of Wales', *WHR*, v (no. 3), 1971, 205-7. The rulers of Gwynedd, in view of their leadership in the struggle for independence, were acknowledged as being of higher status than other lords in Wales. By c. 1160, Owain Gwynedd had been recognised as 'prince' of his own region or province. After c. 1156, two years after Henry II's accession, the title of 'prince' was substituted for 'King' only by the ruler of Gwynedd, and it is believed that this designation had a consti-tutional significance. The first officially recognised Prince of Wales was Llywelyn ap Gruffudd. Although he had assumed the title as early as 1258, as a vassal of Henry III he was, consti-tutionally recognised as Prince in the Treaty of Montgomery in September 1267. *HW*, ii, p. 723 et. seq; *MWS*, pp. 28-9; D. Jenkins, 'Kings, Lords and Princes: the nomenclature of authority in Thirteenth-century Wales', *BBCS*, xxv (Pt. iv), 1976, 451-62.

1.2 Angharad, the daughter of Owain ab Edwin, lord of Engle-field. He, through his father, traced his ancestry to Hywel ap Cadell. *HW*, ii, pp. 407-8. He and his brother, Uchtryd, assisted Hugh of Avranches in his attacks on Gwynedd in 1098. Tegeingl was one of the four *cantrefi* of 'Y Berfeddwlad'.

HW, i, pp. 241-2, Owain, as 'lord', was ruler over a minor *gwlad* (political Kingdom), a term which became more common in the first half of the twelfth century.

1.3-4 Cadwaladr and Cadwallon: Cadwaladr was the eldest and Cadwallon the youngest. All three were involved during their father's last years in extending the frontiers of Gwynedd southwards into Meirionnydd and Ceredigion, and eastwards beyond the Conwy river. Cadwallon was slain by his cousin, Cadwgan, son of his uncle Goronwy ab Owain, in Nanheudwy in 1132. *HW*, ii, pp. 467.

1.5 He reigned over Wales fifty years: Gruffudd strengthened his hold over Gwynedd c. 1100. Good relations between him and Henry I were established before Hervé, Bishop of Bangor, was translated to Ely in 1109. According to the author Gruffudd's reign would have begun c. 1087, the year of William I's death. David Powel, in his *Historie of Cambria* (1584), states that he had 'ruled worthilie 50 yeares'. *HC*, p. 191. Although Trahaearn ap Caradog, the last usurper to rule Gwynedd, had been killed by him at the battle of Mynydd Carn (1081), Gruffudd's position was still insecure until c. 1100. He returned from Ireland in 1099, with Cadwgan ap Bleddyn, and finally appeased the province. *HGK*, xxv-xxvi.

1.6 famous acts: Gruffudd's life was full of adventure and perils. Powel states that he died 'after he had escaped great dangers by sea and land ... and after manie worthie victories'. *HC*, loc. cit.

1.10-23 in a most ancient book written: See here Ca. MS. 83 (MS. 4.101). 165r; the Cartulary of Haughmond Abbey (late fifteenth century), Shrewsbury Public Library MS. 1, ff. 148v-149v where a number of charters relating to Gwynedd are recorded. U. Rees (ed.), *The Cartulary of Haughmond Abbey* (1985), no. 788, p. 160. A Welsh MS. version of the *Historia Gruffud vab Kenan* was discovered at Gwydir in the time of John Wynn ap Maredudd (d. 1559), the author's grandfather. The monk, Thomas ab Ieuan ap Dafydd ap Cynwrig ab Iorwerth, was a priest; he was 'a great traviler, and had some time studied at Rome ... and wrote with all integrity imaginable about the year 1500'. *TYP*, xlii. Ca. MS. 83 (MS. 4.101), 81r-88r. This version of the *Historia* was contained in 'The Booke of Sir Richard Wynn', the author's heir and the second baronet of Gwydir. The version, described as having been 'in a most ancient book written', was in the possession of Morus

Wynn (d. 1580), the author's father, who persuaded Nicholas
Robinson, Bishop of Bangor, in the years 1566-85, to translate
it into Latin. See 60.29-35n. *DWB*, p. 887. Professor D. Simon
Evans argues that 'The Booke of Sir Richard Wynn' and the
'most ancient book' were the same and is no longer extant. It
may have been destroyed in a fire at Wynnstay in 1858
because it had been acquired by Sir John Wynn, fifth baronet
(d. 1719). *HGK*, cclxviii-cclxxiii. The document recorded (in
part) by the author at this point refers to certain grants made
by Gruffudd ap Cynan ab Owain Gwynedd (c. 1194-1200)—
supporter of Llywelyn in 1194—to the Augustinian canons at
Haughmond near Shrewsbury for the church of St. Mary at
Nefyn in Llŷn. Other grants were made to the abbey by
Cadwaladr ap Gruffudd ap Cynan, Dafydd, his nephew, and
Dafydd's nephews, Gruffudd and Maredudd. Shrewsbury MS.
1, ff. 148v—149v, 214v. Nefyn was visited by Gerald, Archdeacon of Brecon, and Baldwin, Archbishop of Canterbury,
during their journey in Wales (1188). It had its own Prior in
1252. *AC*, 1860, 330-3; G. Williams, *The Welsh Church from
Conquest to Reformation* (1962), pp. 18, 21. Haughmond
Abbey was one of the oldest houses of the Augustinian order in
England. Gruffudd ap Cynan had been on close personal terms
with Henry I, and the abbey's founder, William fitz Alan, was
the King's tutor. Friendly relations were maintained between
the canons at Haughmond and other Welsh rulers such as
Cadwaladr ap Gruffudd ap Cynan, Dafydd ab Owain
Gwynedd (Henry II's son-in-law) and Llywelyn ab Iorwerth.
See also 2.23-4, 4.16-32, 8.6-28n. The author's intention in
including transcripts of this kind is merely to establish the
connections between Welsh rulers considered to be among his
earliest forbears. C. N. Johns, 'The Celtic Monasteries of
North Wales', *TCHS*, xxi, 1960, 28-9. The author's shortened
version of the Latin text of the grant made by Gruffudd ap
Cynan ab Owain Gwynedd to the Augustinian canons at
Haughmond Abbey, near Shrewsbury, reads as follows:

> Sciant tam presentes quam futuri quod ego Gruffinus
> filius Conani concessi dedi et confirmavi Deo et
> ecclesiae Sancti Johannis Evangelisti de Haughmond et
> canonicis ibidem Deo servientibus ad ecclesiam eorum
> de Nefyn tres acras in Nefyn et Abraham filium Aldredi
> sutoris et duos filios Serenne scilicet Wasdewi et
> Johannes in perpetuam Eleemosynam libere et quiete ad
> ecclesiam Sancte Marie de Nefyn et predictis canonicis
> de Haughmond iure perpetuo pertineat.

1.24 Owain Gwynedd: He was Prince of Gwynedd between 1137 and 1170 and was also known as Owain Fawr. He established for himself a reputation for strengthening the power and prestige of Gwynedd. *DWB*, pp. 692-3; J. B. Smith, 'Owain Gwynedd', *TCHS*, xxxii, 1971, 8-17.

1.26 Llywarch ap Trahaearn: He was in fact Lord of Arwystli, a *cantref* which was part of Powys Wenwynwyn but which ecclesiastically formed part of the diocese of Bangor. *HW*, ii, pp. 549-50; *WATU*, pp. 7-8, 239. For his father's military exploits see *HW*, ii, pp. 419, 435, 467. He assisted the sons of Gruffudd ap Cynan against the lords of Powys and died c. 1123. *BT*, pp. 82b-3a.

1.27 Iorwerth: He was the eldest legitimate son of Owain Gwynedd by his first marriage to Gwladys, daughter of Llywarch ap Trahaearn. 'Trwyndwn' = 'flat-nosed'. He married Mared, daughter of Madog ap Maredudd of Powys, and probably became lord of Nanconwy and Arfon before being disinherited by Dafydd, his half-brother. Owing to his facial deformity he was deemed unsuitable to succeed his father. His residence was Dolwyddelan castle, the caput of Nanconwy, where it is reputed that his son Llywelyn (the Great) was reared. He died c. 1174 at the time when Dafydd usurped northern Gwynedd. A tradition persists that his son, Llywelyn ab Iorwerth (the Great), was born at his father's residence at Dolwyddelan castle. *RCAM*, i, *Caerns. East*, p. 80.

1.28 Christina: She was the daughter of Gronw ab Owain ab Edwin of Tegeingl, Owain Gwynedd's first cousin and his second wife. *HW*, ii, pp. 488, 522. [See 1.24.] Owain was advised by Thomas Becket, Archbishop of Canterbury, and Pope Alexander III to put her away because the marriage was within the prohibited degrees, but he refused and was excommunicated. *HStA*, i, pp. 311-4. 'Owen, on account of his public incest with his cousin-german, had died excommunicated by the blessed martyr St. Thomas, the bishop of that see, having been enjoined to seize a proper opportunity of removing his body from the church'. *GC*, vi, pp. 133-4. Owain's refusal formed part of the much broader issue of resistance by the see of Bangor to the authority of Canterbury. Smith, op. cit., 13-17; *HW*, ii, pp. 480-6; 521-2. J. C. Robertson & J. B. Sheppard (ed.), *Materials for the History of Thomas Becket* (1875-85), v, pp. 225-40.

1.30 Dafydd: He was the illegitimate and ablest son of Owain Gwynedd and Christina. He came to power in Gwynedd in 1174 and his praises were sung by poets such as Gwilym Ryfel and Gwalchmai, O. Jones, E. Williams & W. Pugh (Pugh) (ed.), *The Myvyrian Archaiology of Wales* (1870), pp. 196, 199-200. He was expelled from Gwynedd by Llywelyn ab Iorwerth in 1203. *BT*, p. 125a.

1.31 Rhodri: He opposed his brother Dafydd who, in 1173, gained Anglesey and the other regions of Gwynedd. *BT*, loc. cit. In 1175, he was cruelly incarcerated by Dafydd. *HW*, ii, pp. 549, 551-2, 588-9. He refused to obey the ecclesiastical ban on his incestuous marriage to a daughter of the Lord Rhys ap Gruffudd and was expelled by Llywelyn ab Iorwerth. *GC*, pp. 445, 453,

1.31 Cadwallon: *HC*, p. 226; Dwnn, ii, p. 10. He was abbot c. 1169. *AC*, 1847, 63, 65-6; W. Dugdale (ed.), *Monasticon Anglicanum* (1665-73), iv, pp. 659-60.

1.33 Welsh chronicle: This is a reference to *Brut y Tywysogion*. The 'many victorious voyages' refers specifically to the successful attacks of Owain and Cadwaladr on Ceredigion in 1136. The Norman and Flemish armies lost about 3000 men during these attacks. Powel adds: 'that besides 3000 that were slain, a great number were drowned and taken and caried awaie captives'. *BT*, p. 87b; *HW*, ii, pp. 474-6; *HC*, p. 189.

2.2 The earl of Chester: Ranulph II de Gernon, earl of Chester, in alliance with Madog ap Maredudd of Powys, was defeated in 1149. *HW*, ii, p. 494; *BT*, pp. 98a, 99a.

2.4 *Itinerarium Kambriae:* It was one of the author's prime sources for the earlier part of the chronicle. He used Dr. David Powel's edition of both the *Itinerarium* and *Descriptio* published with two other works in one volume in 1585. The *Itinerarium* was a vivid travel-book, compiled in 1188, following the preaching mission of Gerald of Wales and Baldwin, Archbishop of Canterbury, around Wales with a view to seeking military support for the Third Crusade. He also wrote a sequel entitled *Descriptio Kambriae* (1194) which describes the peculiar features of the Welsh and their relations with the Normans. A. G. Prys-Jones, *Gerald the Welshman* (1955); T. Jones, *Gerald of Wales* (1947); M.

Richter, *Giraldus Cambrensis: the Growth of the Welsh Nation* (1972); L. Thorpe (ed.), *Gerald of Wales: the Journey through Wales, I, The Description of Wales* (1978), intro. p. 24 et seq.

2.5-6 three voyages royal: The author follows the *Brut* closely at this point when referring to Henry II's second expedition into Wales in 1165. *BT*, pp. 110b-111a; *HC*, p. 221.

2.7 the succours: 'to succour'. To give aid or assistance; in this case military aid and supplies such as auxiliary forces or reinforcements.

2.9 Coleshill Wood: It is near Flint, the assumed site of the battle between Owain Gwynedd and the forces of Henry II in 1157. *HW*, ii, p. 497; *HC*, p. 207; *GC*, vi, p. 130. See also D. J. Cathcart King, 'Henry II and the Fight at Coleshill', *WHR*, ii (no. 4), 1965, 367-73.

2.8-21 The author follows Powel's *Historie* (which quotes William Parvus) closely at this point. 'In this first viage of King Henrie against the Welshmen, he was put in great danger of his life in a strait at Counsylth not far from Flynt, where Henrie of Essex, whose office by inheritance was to beare the standard of England, cast down the same and fled: which thing incouraged, the Welshmen in such sort, that the King being sore distressed, had much adoo to save himself and (as the French Chronicle saith) was faine to flee'. *HC*, p. 207. Robert Montfort fought a duel with Henry, earl of Essex, on an island in the Thames six years after the battle and left him dying. He recovered, however, and became a monk in the abbey of Reading. This reference is adapted freely by Powel from the *Historia Rerum Anglicarum* by William Petit (or Parvus) of Newburgh. R. Howlett (ed.), *Chronicles of the Reigns of Stephen, Henry II and Richard I* (1884-8), i, pp. 106-9; J. Leland, *De Rebus Britannicis Collectanea* (1774), iv, p. 37.

2.18-19 After this prince had reigned . . . he died: He died on 23 November 1170. *HW*, ii, p. 522 (n. 136); *HC*, pp. 225-6.

2.22-4 Cadwaladr . . . was lord of Ceredigion: For further information on the conquest of Ceredigion in 1136 see *BT*, p. 86a/b; for his expulsion in 1144, ibid., p. 90a/b; and his recovery in 1157, ibid., pp. 103a-104a. The author, as in his first reference to Gruffudd ap Cynan, mistakenly assumes that the princely power of Gwynedd extended over *Pura Wallia*, or native Wales west of the March. Cadwaladr had married Alice, daughter of Richard de Clare, before 1153. *DNB* x, pp. 389-90; *HW*, ii, p. 491; Shrewsbury MS. 1, ff. 148-149v; Rees, *Cartulary*, no. 784, p. 159. See further Ca.MS. 83 (MS.4.101) 165r for a transcript of the document which follows. It is dated c. 1141-3 and records the grant of St. Mary's church at Nefyn by Cadwaladr ap Gruffudd ap Cynan to the Augustinian abbey at Haughmond. Johns, loc. cit. The first charter establishing canons regular at Haughmond was confirmed by Henry I who was on friendly terms with Gruffudd ap Cynan. It is not surprising, therefore, that the grant of Nefyn to Haughmond should have been made by his son Cadwaladr. It appears also that the Augustinian canons were known and respected in Gwynedd before the Cistercians made their appearance and settled in the province (c. 1200). The grant—which Wynn provides only in part—of St. Mary's church at Nefyn by Cadwaladr ap Gruffudd ap Cynan to the canons at Haughmond Abbey, c. 1141-3, reads as follows in Latin in the *History:*

> Cadwalladrus frater Owini magni salutem in domino. Notum sit universitati vestrae quod ego Cadwalladrus pro salute animae meae et omnium antecessorum et heredum meorum dedi et concessi Deo et ecclesiae Sancti Johannis Evangelisti de Haughmond et canonicis ibidem Deo servientibus in puram et perpetuam Eleemosynam ecclesiam de Nefyn. Teste. Alice de Clara, uxore mea etc.

> Ranulpho, comite Cestriae etc. praecipio quod Abbas Salopiae et conventus habeant totam tenuram suam inter Ryblam et Mersam. Teste. Ricardo, comite de Clara et Cadwalladro ap Gruffudd ap Cynan, Rege Walliarum, et Roberto Basset et Gauffrido Despenser apud Cestriam.

2.40 Kingly authority: i.e. regal rights in the kingdom of Ceredigion. J. G. Edwards, 'The Normans and the Welsh March', *Proceedings of the British Academy*, xlii, 1956, 155-77; *HW*, i, pp. 309-14, ii, pp. 549-50. The nature of 'regal rights' and 'regality' was not easily definable in Wales in the early Middle Ages. In this context it means that Cadwaladr had extended his supremacy over Ceredigion in the sense that he had superimposed a vague impression of overlordship over the region or *gwlad*. It is known that, by the mid-twelfth century, the minor rulers of *Pura Wallia* had abjured their regal title and had assumed the feudal designation of 'lord'. Owain Gwynedd acquired for himself the more grandiose title of Prince of Gwynedd, thus establishing the basis of the supremacy claimed by his successors in the thirteenth century. Cadwaladr, in this context, endeavoured to emulate his brother but attained no lasting success. *MWS*, pp. 26-30, 35-7. It was highly unlikely that an unstable ruler (as he was) claiming 'sovereign' power would maintain a permanent hold over Ceredigion. D. Jenkins, loc. cit. The practice of fosterage and the ensuing acrimony between the descendants of royal houses was also very much the order of the day since royal lands, like the institution of kingship, were divisible as were free kindred properties, and became the cause of disputes between blood brothers. *HW*, i, pp. 309-10.

3.3 The Welsh chronicle: Neither the *Brut* nor the *Historie* refer to him as such but Gerald praises his generosity. *GC*, v, p. 145.

3.4-5 the castle of Aberystwyth: His military exploits with Owain in 1136-7 are recorded in the *Brut*. *BT*, p. 86a/b. Aberystwyth castle was burnt on three successive occasions by Owain and Cadwaladr (1136), Hywel ab Owain (1142) and Maelgwn and Rhys Fychan (1211). *BT*, pp. 86b, 90a, 157a/b.

3.5 he was murdered by the English soldiers: There is no evidence to prove that this event took place. He died in February 1172 and was buried in Bangor cathedral alongside his brother Owain. *BT*, p. 121a/b; *GC*, vi, p. 133.

3.8-9 unfit to govern by reason of the deformity of his face: Iorwerth's deformity, it appeared, hindered him from aspiring to political domination in Gwynedd. He was described in an elegy by Seisyll Bryffwrch as 'ruler of Arfon' and tradition has it that he was buried at Llandudclud or Penmachno. *HW*, p. 550.

3.9-10 became prince: 'David gathered all the power he could and came against Hywel, and fighting with him slew him, and afterward enioied quietly the whole land of North Wales.' *HC*, p. 227; *HW*, ii. pp. 497-8, 549-51.

3.14 Nanconwy and Ardudwy: The hundred or commote of Nanconwy lay in the south-eastern region of Caernarfonshire adjacent to the march lordship of Denbigh, and formed part of the *cantref* of Arllechwedd. Ardudwy, in western Meirion-nydd, was divided into two commotes, Uwch and Is Artro, in the *cantref* of Dunoding. For more information on the supposed effigy erected in his honour in Pennant Melangell churchyard see 'Pennant Melangell, Montgomeryshire', *AC*, 1848, 138, 327-8; 1860, 379; 1956, 54-6. Thomas Pennant states that he fled there to avoid the persecutions of Dafydd ab Owain Gwynedd. A tradition exists that he was slain at Bwlch-y-groes in that area.

3.16-17 Prince Llywelyn: Llywelyn ab Iorwerth (1173-1240), one of the most renowned Welsh princes of north Wales who ruled Gwynedd Uwch and Is Conwy c. 1197-1240. It was he who laid the foundation of the principality established in the Kingdom of Gwynedd in the thirteenth century. Powel refers to him as 'Leolinus Magnus'. *HC*, p. 246; *DWB*, pp. 599-600; *HW*, ii, p. 693.

3.18 Madog ap Maredudd: Ruler of Powys between 1132 and 1160. He succeeded his father, Maredudd ap Bleddyn, and married Susanna, daughter of Gruffudd ap Cynan. He was the last King to rule over the whole of Powys. *HPF*, i, p. 111 et seq.; *HW*, ii, pp. 492-4, 587.

3.19 Cynan ab Owain Gwynedd: He was Owain's son by an unknown woman. His own son, Maredudd, was driven out of Meirionnydd in 1202. Cynan died in 1174. *Dwnn*, ii, p. 10; *HW*, ii, p. 549 (n. 65).

3.21 Emma: She was the King's half-sister, a natural daughter of Geoffrey of Anjou. The *Brut* offers an explanation for the marriage: 'That same Dafydd then married the King's sister—Emma was her name—because he thought that he could hold his territory in peace thereby'. *BT*, p. 126a. He died in England in 1203, ibid., p. 149a.

3.22 Owain: He and his parents lived in the manors of Ellesmere and Halesowen which they had received from Henry II after Dafydd's capture and banishment by Llywelyn ab Iorwerth. *HW*, ii, pp. 590, 616 (n.26), 640.

3.24 Rhodri: A blood-brother of Dafydd by Christina. This section compares closely with Powel's record of the same events. 'Rodericke brake his brothers prison, and escaping came to Anglesey, where all the countrie received him for their lord ... Thus Rodericke also was received as lord and prince in all the countrie above the river of Conway.' *HC*, p. 237. See also *BT*, pp. 126a, 128a, 135b.

3.29-30 Giraldus Cambrensis: Archdeacon of Brecon between 1175 and 1223. He was the youngest son of William de Barri and Angharad, daughter of Gerald de Windsor and Nest, daughter of Rhys ap Tewdwr, prince of Deheubarth. *HW*, ii, pp. 555-64; Richter, *Giraldus Cambrensis*, p. 66 et seq.; *DWB*, p. 279. See 2.4n.

3.29-30 Archbishop of Canterbury: He was Baldwin of Ford, primate of Canterbury from 1184 to 1190, described by Gerald as 'a venerable man, distinguished for his learning and sanctity'. *GC*, vi, p. 13. See 2.4. The journey in Wales occurred during Lent 1188. He and Gerald set out from Hereford on Ash Wednesday. *DNB*, iii, pp. 32-4.

3.32-4 Rhuddlan castle ... where the Archbishop lodged: In 1188, Dafydd entertained Baldwin and Gerald; 'a noble castle on the river Clwyd, belonging to David, the eldest son to Owain, where, at the earnest invitation of David himself, we were handsomely entertained that night'. *GC*, vi, p. 136.

4.1 Llywelyn, his nephew: He was Iorwerth's son by Mared, daughter of Madog ap Maredudd of Powys. By 1188, the year of Gerald's perambulation, he had asserted himself against his uncle Dafydd: 'This young man, being only twelve years of age, began, during the period of our journey, to molest his uncles, David and Roderic, the sons of Owain by Christina, his cousin-german'. *GC*, vi, p. 134.

4.6 the Lord Rhys: Rhys ap Gruffudd (1132-97), lord of Deheubarth, younger son of Gruffudd ap Rhys ap Tewdwr. His mother was Gwenllïan, daughter of Gruffudd ap Cynan. He is regarded as one of the greatest of Welsh leaders in Deheubarth, his chief aim being to maintain control and consolidate his authority over his territories which were threatened by the Normans. *HW*, ii, pp. 536-72: 'no prince did more for the independence of South Wales from the time of Rhys ap Tewdwr to the extinction of the southern dynasty'. J. E. Lloyd (ed.), *A History of Carmarthenshire* (1935), i, p. 158.

4.16-32 Shrewsbury MS. 1, ff. 148v-149v. See also Ca.MS.83 (MS. 4.101), 165r. This document (dated c. 1177-87) has little

relevance to the immediate context but, like others included
by the author in the earlier part of the text, it does establish
power and connections, in this case those of Dafydd ab Owain
Gwynedd. It records a grant of land in the town of Nefyn in
Llŷn to the abbot and canons of Haughmond abbey. Cf. the
grants made by his uncle Cadwaladr ap Gruffudd ap Cynan
See 2.23-4n. C. N. Johns, loc. cit. The author's version of the
document recording a grant of land in Nefyn to Haughmond
Abbey by Dafydd ab Owain Gwynedd (n.d.) reads as following
in the original:

> Omnibus sancte Dei ecclesiae filiis tam presentibus
> quam futuris, David Rex filius Owini salutem. Notum
> sit vobis me concessisse abbati et canonicis de
> Haughmond illam terram quam David habuit in villa de
> Nefyn ab omnibus terrenis consuetudinibus immunem
> concedoque similiter praedictis canonicis decimacion-
> em molendini mei de Nefyn ad perpetuam
> Eleemosynam.

> Testibus. Johanne de Burchelton, Radulfo de Lega,
> Einion Sais etc.

> David filius Owini Princeps Northwalliae universis
> Christi fidelibus Francis et Anglis salutem in domino
> sempiternam. Sciatis me assensu Emmae uxoris meae
> et Owini heredis mei etc. Hiis Testibus. Remo
> Episcopo, Radulfo de Lega.

> Domina Emma soror Henrici Regis uxor David filii
> Owini Principis Northwalliae etc. Sciatis me assensu
> David mariti mei et Owini heredis mei etc. Testibus:
> Einion Sais, Radulfo de Lega.

4.35 german: Now an obsolete form for 'first cousin'.

4.36-7 to Owain . . . and . . . Gruffudd: Cousins and rivals of
Llywelyn ab Iorwerth who contested supremacy in Gwynedd.
King John gave them the three *cantrefi*, excepting Deganwy
castle, and the commote of Creuddyn. The *cantrefi* of Arfon,
Arllechwedd and Llŷn were to be in their possession as well if
they could be conquered. *Rot. Chart.*, i, p. 188; *HW*, ii, p. 640.
The areas referred to at this point comprised three of the four
cantrefi of Gwynedd Is Conwy, hence the designation 'The
Four Cantrefs' also known as 'Y Berfeddwlad' ('the Middle
Country') between Gwynedd Uwch Conwy and Powys Fadog.

HW, i, pp. 239-42. The three *cantrefi* mentioned above formed part of Gwynedd Uwch Conwy, the Conwy river being considered throughout the Middle Ages as the natural boundary between the two regions. After the Act of Union (1536) as well it continued to be, for the most part, the dividing line between Caernarfonshire and Denbighshire. *HW*, i, pp. 233-5; but since the reorganisation of local government boundaries in 1974 it has lost its historical significance. Sir John Wynn referred to the ancient division in a letter to his eldest son and heir in 1624 when he prided himself on having raised the estate of Gwydir to a status above all others in Gwynedd above the Conwy. NLW. MS 9059E. 1188.

4.39 Deganwy: 'Gannow' or Deganwy in the commote of Creuddyn, alias Castell y Faerdref. *RC*, p. 2. It was the royal manor of Creuddyn and the seat of Maelgwn Gwynedd in the sixth century. *HW*, i, pp. 129-30, 240; *ELISG*, p. 4. It originally formed part of cantref Rhos.

5.1-33 *Rot. Chart.*, i, pp. 44, 188b. See also Ca.MS. 83 (MS.4.101) 168r. The author's version of the original grant of three *cantrefi* in Gwynedd Is Conwy by King John to Owain ap Dafydd and Gruffudd ap Rhodri (3 October 1214) reads as follows:

> Johannes Dei gratia etc. Sciatis nos concessisse et hac Charta nostra confirmasse Audoeno filio Davidi et Gruffino filio Rodheri tria contreda scilicet Rhos salvo nobis castro de Degannwy cum Creuddyn ubi castrum illud sedet Rhufoniog et Dyffryn Clwyd cum pertinentiis suis integre tenenda ipsis Audoeno et Gruffino et heredibus suis de nobis et heredibus nostris faciendis inde nobis et heredibus nostris servitutibus subscriptis singulis annis xii dextrarios de pretio suo de uno quoque cantredo quatuor dextrarios. Et preterea de illis tribus cantredis unam natam canum per annum et decem leporarum et omnes accipitres et falcones gentiles et spernarios dictorum trium cantredorum reddendo inde nobis et heredibus nostris singulis annis apud Salop ad festum Sancte Petri ad vincula. Preterea ipsi ambo ibunt in servicium nostrum cum gentibus de dictis cantredis et alius remanebit si volumus predicti vero Audoenus et Gruffinus obsides nobis dabit de fideli servicio suo si Audoenus filius David dabit filium suum de uxore sua desponsata etc.

Et si pro posse illorum et per licentiam nostram possunt conquirere Arfon, Arllechwedd et Llŷn ibidem servicium nobis facient de illis tribus predictis cantredis quod de aliis tribus predictis cantredis nobis futuris. Hiis Testibus: Domino Petro Wintoniae, episcopo, Willelmo, comite Sarum, fratre nostro, Galfrido filio Petri, comite Essex, Willelmo, comite Arundel, Willelmo, comite Warrenne, Stephano, comite Wintoniae, Willelmo, comite Ferrars, Willelmo Briwer, Petro filio Herberti, Thomaso de Ardminter, Philipo de Orby, Justicius Cestriae. Datum per manum magistri Ricardo de Marisco, Archdeaconus Northumberland apud Suwericae 3 die Octobris anno regni nostri xiiii.

5.34 the Welsh history: i.e. *Historie of Cambria*. 'About this time 1204 David sonne to Owen Gwyneth, after that prince Lhewelyn (his nephewe) had let him at libertie, fled to England, and got an armie to resolve him to his ancient estate in Northwales.' *HC*, p. 259.

5.39 Gruffudd: *Rot. Claus.*, i, p. 210; *HW*, ii, p. 640. Gruffudd ap Rhodri was a captain of Welsh troops in King John's service and was prominent in Llywelyn's service as well in the 1220s and 30s. D. Stephenson, *The Governance of Gwynedd* (1984), pp. 116-7.

5.40-6.1 'Llywelyn bravely expelled from North Wales those who were born in public incest, though supported by their own wealth and by that of others, leaving them nothing.' *GC*, vi, p. 134. Rhodri had, of course, married within the prohibited degree of consanguinity.

6.10 Sir Thomas Wiliems: Physician and cleric of Trefriw in the Conwy valley. He was born in 'Ardda'r Myneich' in the commote of Arllechwedd Isaf and was a descendant of Ednywain Bendew. He became curate of Trefriw in 1573 and later a 'physycwr gwledig' (country physician). He is most famous as a copyist of manuscripts and lexicographer, and was the author's kinsman and close friend, his mother, Catherine, being an illegitimate daughter of Maredudd ab Ieuan ab Robert (Sir John Wynn's great-grandfather) by Gwenllïan ferch Gwilym ab Ieuan Llwyd. *DWB*, pp. 1018-9; *HGF* (1827), p. 94. The author's information at this point was not obtained from Wiliems's copy of *Brut y Tywysogion* (NLW. MS. 5281) which was compiled from a parchment manuscript in the possession of Morus Wynn of Gwydir, the author's father. J. E. Caerwyn Williams, 'Thomas Wiliems, Y Geiriadurwr', *Studia Celtica*, xvi-xvii, 1981-2, 281-9, 302-3. The 'chronicle' referred to here was not one of the known versions of the *Brut* because the information differs from the texts, Stephenson, op. cit., p. 116.

6.10-11 Llywelyn killed his uncle Dafydd: This statement (from Wiliems's 'chronicle') is incorrect although the author seems to accept it. Dafydd, Llywelyn's uncle, was defeated by him at Aberconwy and imprisoned. He was released in 1198, expelled by Llywelyn in 1203, and died in England in that year. *BT*, p. 149a; *HW*, ii, pp. 588-90; *DWB*, p. 98; *HC*, p. 259. The author may have confused him with Owain, Dafydd's son. J. Williams, *Ancient and Modern Denbigh* (1856), p. 33. Even so, it appears that this Owain lived with his mother, Emma, and also obtained lands in Warwickshire and near Grimsby. *HW*, ii, p. 616 (n.26). No heirs of his are known.

6.15 Rhos and Rhufoniog: Two of the four *cantrefi* of Gwynedd Is Conwy or 'Y Berfeddwlad'. *HW*, i, pp. 184, 239-40. The lordship of Denbigh, created in 1282 and granted by Edward I to Henry Lacy, earl of Lincoln, comprised these two administrative divisions, and formed the largest of the four lordships created in 1282, its western boundary being the Conwy river. D. H. Owen, 'The Lordship of Denbigh, 1282-1415' (Unpublished Ph.D. dissertation, University of Wales, 1967), pp. 1-6; G. A. Holmes, *The Estates of the Higher Nobility in Fourteenth-century England* (1957), pp. 93-101. The grant was made in 1212. *Rot. Chart.*, i, p. 188; *HW*, ii, p. 640. They were also promised the *cantrefi* of Arfon, Arllechwedd and Llŷn in Gwynedd Uwch Conwy.

6.19 not wholly frustrate: i.e. their interests and influence were not limited to these areas since it is held by tradition that they were granted land by Llywelyn the Great in Eifionydd. NLW MS. 5281.

6.29 the daughter of Lord Rhys: She was Gwenllïan, youngest legitimate child of the Lord Rhys ap Gruffudd of Dinefwr. In the early thirteenth century, in a witness list to a charter of Llywelyn ab Iorwerth, a Einion ap Rhodri is recorded as an attestor. K. Williams-Jones, 'Llywelyn's Charter to Cymer Abbey in 1209', *JMHRS*, iii, 1957, 57. Her second husband was Ednyfed (Fychan) ap Cynwrig, seneschal of Llywelyn ab Iorwerth, and ancestor of the Tudors, *WG*, iii, p. 454; iv, p. 779.

6.33 invaded Anglesey: i.e. c. 1190. Rhodri, during his quarrels with Gruffudd and Maredudd, the sons of Cynan, his brother, obtained military aid from Reginald, King of Man (1188-1219), the illegitimate son of Godred II, and married his daughter. With his assistance Rhodri repossessed Anglesey. *HW*, ii, p. 588. Godred had died in 1187 but the author is following Powel who refers, mistakenly, to 'the help of Gothrike, King of Man'. *HC*, p. 243; *BT*, p. 134a. See T. Jones (ed.), *Brut y Tywysogion: Peniarth MS. 20 Version* (1952), p. 189.

6.37 Pennant: A free township which lies between the rivers Dwyfor and Henwy. *RC*, p. 39; *Eifionydd*, pp. 3-5.

6.37 Gwely: Literally a 'bed' or 'resting place', the original clan settlement established in the early Middle Ages sub-divided between the grandsons (wyrion) of the *priodor* or proprietor. *Gwely Wyrion Cynan* enjoyed free tenure and its owners were reputed to be the descendants of Cynan ab Owain Gwynedd. Eifionydd was probably in the possession of Maredudd ap Cynan who was forced to leave the region early in the thirteenth century. It is possible that his sons remained in Pennant where they established a *gwely*. *RC*, loc. cit., *Eifionydd*, pp. 6-7.

7.1 the cruel and unnatural wars: *HW*, ii, pp. 573-90; *GC*, p. 134; *HC*, pp. 227-56.

7.4 The collegiate church of Caergybi was served originally by twelve canons or prebendaries. *AC*, 1886, 176-209; *Monasticon*, viii, p. 1475; G. Williams, *The Welsh Church*, p. 63, 281-2; E. M. Fussell, 'Some Aspects of Monasticism in Anglesey', *TAAS*, 1921, 36-40; M. L. Williams, 'The Portionary Church of Caergybi and Jesus College', ibid., 1947, 38-42. Rhodri died in 1195. *HW*, ii, p. 589.

7.7 Thomas: i.e. Thomas, son of Rhodri ab Owain Gwynedd. *PACF*, pp. 280, 393; *Eifionydd*, pp. 343-4. Little is known about him but there is genealogical evidence for his existence, *Dwnn*, ii, p. 69.

7.7-8 Einion ap Seisyllt: Of Llanwrin and known as 'Lord of Mathafarn'. *WG*, iv, p. 831; *HPF*, v, p. 64. He was also called

'Lord of Meirionydd' and his father ruled that *cantref*. He held 'all the lands between the Dyfi and the Dulas and the lordship of Meirionydd *in capite* from the sons of Cynan ab Owain Gwynedd'. *HPF*, vi, pp. 36, 166. His wife was Nest, daughter of Madog ap Cadwgan of Nannau. He placed himself in the allegiance of the rulers of Powys and became a strong ally of Owain Cyfeiliog (1130-97). 'The Pryces of Gunley', *AC*, 1882, 131-2, 176.

7.9 Gwyn ap Gruffudd: *WG*, i, p. 48; iii, p. 455. He was a descendant of Brochwel ab Aeddan of Powys and had settled at Cegidfa (Guilsfield) in Montgomery. Nothing is known about Caradog ap Thomas.

7.10 Einion ap Caradog: c. 1261-74. An official of the Prince of Wales's curia in Gwynedd. *WG* (300-1400), iii, p. 455; *Eifionydd*, pp. 344-5; *AC*, 1851, 72; Dwnn, ii, p. 158; *HW*, ii, p. 743. He served Llywelyn ap Gruffudd (the Last) and Richard, Bishop of Bangor. T. Rymer (ed.), *Foedera, Conventiones, Litterae* (1819-69), i, pp. 370, 474; Stephenson, op. cit., pp. 23-4, 116-7.

7.11 Penychen: A bondvill in Eifionydd. *RCAM, Caerns. West*, cxli-cxliii; *Eifionydd*, pp. 343-4. It was held by Tudur ab Einion ap Caradog until 1284 when it was granted to Queen Eleanor, wife of Edward I.

7.12 Baladeulyn: 'The manor of Baladeulyn', claimed by the descendants of Owain Gwynedd in 1305. *RC*, p. 220; *RCAM, Caerns. West*, cxliii, cxlvi.

7.12 Pen-y-berth: A bondvill or township in the commote of Afloegion, Llŷn. *RC*, p. 220.

7.15 Ffriwlwyd: A bondvill between Afonwen and Afon Dwyfach. It was granted by Llywelyn ab Iorwerth as a grange to Aberconwy abbey c. 1201 when he drove Maredudd ap Cynan from Eifionydd, a fact which the author had not noticed. By 1352 the land (described as a manor and vill) was in the Crown's possession on an exchange basis. It was the author's invention to describe Gruffudd ap Caradog as Lord of Ffriwlwyd and the motte of the ancient *maerdref* as his manor house. *RC*, p. 43; C. A. Gresham, 'The Aberconwy Charter', *AC*, 1939, 132-4, 159; *Eifionydd*, pp. 338-41. Also by the same author 'The Aberconwy Charter: further consideration', *BBCS*, xxx (Pts. iii and iv), 1983, 339.

7.15 his manor house: Gruffudd ap Caradog's house may have been Tomen Fawr at Glan-llynnau, a fortified house sited in a central position. It is doubtful, however, that it was built c. 1200.

7.16 Ystrad Ysgeibion: 'Villata de Skeybeon'. Ysgeibion, a township in the commote of Cinmeirch. *SHD*, xx-xxi; G. M. Richards, 'Sgeibion, Llanynys', *TDHS*, ix, 1960, 187-8.

7.17-21 The author's narrative at this point is confusing. Thomas (ap Rhodri) married Mared, daughter of Einion ap Seisyll; their son was Caradog ap Thomas who married Efa, daughter of Gwyn ap Gruffudd, lord of Cegidfa. By her Caradog begat Einion, lord of Penychen ... Gruffudd, lord of Ffriwlwyd ... and Syna (or Senena or Senenam) who was married to the illegitimate Gruffudd ap Llywelyn ab Iorwerth. His son was Llywelyn ap Gruffudd (the Last) who was slain at Cilmeri in December 1282. This line, as Wynn was anxious to show, had descended from Gruffudd ap Cynan. *WG* (300-1400), iii, pp. 443-7, 454-5, J. B. Smith, *Llywelyn ap Gruffudd: Tywysog Cymru* (1985), p. 43. See also *RC*, p. 220.

7.20 Llywelyn ap Gruffudd: Second son of Gruffudd ap Llywelyn, who became Prince of Wales following the Treaty of Montgomery in 1267. *DWB*, pp. 597-8; *HW*, ii, p. 716 et seq.; J. G. Edwards (ed.), *Littere Wallie* (1940), xxv-lxix.

7.20 last prince of Wales: He was recognised constitutionally as Prince of Wales by Henry III on 29 September 1267. Ibid., xlix-l. He was killed in an ambush near Irfon Bridge on 11 December 1282. *HW*, ii, p. 763. 'This was the end of Lhewelyn, betraied by the men of Buelht who was the last Prince of Brytaines blood, who bare dominion and rule in Wales. So that the rule and gouernment of the Brytaines euer continued in some place of Brytaine, from the first comming of Brutus.' *HC*, p. 374; *BT*, p. 228b.

7.24 deposed his uncles: *HC*, p. 245; *HW*, ii, p. 588; *GC*, p. 134.

7.26-7 Llywelyn the Great: 'Llywelyn the Great, Prince of North Wales', *Chron. M.*, v, p. 718; 'Leolinus Magnus', *HC*, p. 246; 'the second great Achilles', *Ann. C.*, pp. 59-83.

7.27-8 His works and worthy deeds: *BT*, p. 135b et seq.; *HC*, pp. 246-98; *HW*, ii, chap. xvii, pp. 612-93; *Ann. C.*, pp. 59-83.

7.39 Richard Broughton: Second Justice of North Wales
(1594-1602), Vice-Justice of Chester (1599) and a native of
Lower Broughton, Bishop's Castle and Owlbury, Salop. P.
Williams, *The Council in the Marches under Elizabeth I*
(1958), pp. 344-5; W. R. Williams, *The History of the Great
Sessions in Wales 1542-1830 together with the Lives of the
Welsh Judges* (1899), p. 90.

8.6-28 The date is 1233 (17 Henry III). In fact, it is a letter
from Llywelyn to Henry III. Rymer, op. cit., i (Pt. i), p. 210.
The author ascribed this letter to Henry III probably because
of the phrases 'majestas vestra' and 'rogamus serenitatem'
which he applied to Llywelyn not Henry III, *HGF* (1878), p. 20
(n.3). Then follows a confirmation of the charter granted to
Haughmond abbey by Dafydd ab Owain Gwynedd, Llywelyn
ab Iorwerth's uncle (See 4.16-32n). The author's version of
the letter of Llywelyn ab Iorwerth to Henry III in 1233 reads as
follows in the original:

> Henricus Rex Anglie etc. Leolino, Principi Aberffraw
> domino de Snowdon salutem et se totum. Cum propter
> inundaciones aquarum et viarum discrimina nuncii
> nostri ad vos accedere non possunt per cursorem
> quendam litteras presentes duximus destinandas per
> quas majestati vestre significamus quod nos pro nobis et
> nostris vobiscum et cum omnibus vestris pacem
> tenuimus et tenebimus in futurum et hoc dedimus
> ballivis nostris et imprisiis in mandatis ut pacem cum
> suis comarchionibus firmiter teneant et observent
> quare vestram rogamus serenitatem quatenus ballivis
> vestris in marchia commorantibus detis si placet in
> mandatis quod cum nostris pacem teneant inviolatam
> beneplacitum vestrum si placet nobis significetis valeat
> excellentia vestra.

> Leolinus Princeps Northwalliae omnibus fidelibus tam
> presentibus quam futuris presens scriptum inspecta-
> turis salutem in vero salutari. Noverit universitas vestra
> nos concessisse Deo et ecclesiae Sancti Johannis
> Evangelisti de Haughmond et canonicis ibidem Deo
> servientibus pro salute animae nostre et patris nostri et
> David filii Owini avunculi nostri etc. sicut carta predicti
> David filii Owini testatur. Testibus: Remo episcopo
> Asaph etc. Radulfo de Lega etc.

8.29 Anno Domini 1253: The date is wrong. He died in 1200. *BT*, p. 145b. He ruled over Arfon, Arllechwedd and Llŷn. *HW*, ii, p. 589. He granted a charter to the community of Aberconwy abbey c. 1189-99. R. W. Hays, *The History of the Abbey of Aberconway, 1186-1537* (1963), p. 69, app. ii, p. 185.

8.30 a monk's cowl: A garment worn over the head and shoulders, the point being that Gruffudd died having 'donned the habit of a monk' at Aberconwy. *HW*, ii, p. 612.

8.32 Maredudd: Ibid., p. 613. Maredudd was Lord of Eifionydd and part of Ardudwy between 1173 and 1194. He also obtained a portion of Meirionnydd from his brother Gruffudd in 1194 when he divided his conquests in Gwynedd with Llywelyn ab Iorwerth. Llywelyn, in fact, was largely dependent on the aid given to him by Cynan's sons. On Gruffudd's death in 1200 Maredudd acquired Llŷn but lost it in the following year because of alleged treason, and he lost all his other lands in 1202. He was co-founder of the Cistercian abbey of Cymer in 1199 and he died in 1212. Ibid., pp. 497-8, 550-1.

8.34 Llŷn and Eifionydd: *GC*, p. 123. 'We continued our journey over the Traeth Mawr and Traeth Bychan . . . where two stone castles have newly been erected; one called Deudraeth, belonging to the sons of Cynan, situated in Eifionydd, towards the northern mountains; the other named Carn Fadryn, the property of the sons of Owen built on the other side of the river towards the sea, on the headland of Lleyn.' *HW*, ii, p. 613. In 1188 Llŷn was in the possession of Rhodri but in 1194-5 it passed to his nephew Gruffudd ap Cynan and subsequently to Maredudd, Gruffudd's brother, before it was acquired by Llywelyn ab Iorwerth.

8.39 Carnfadryn: Hillfort. *RCAM*, iii, *Caerns. West*, xxvii, pp. 69-70.

8.40 Deudraeth: The author has 'deudraeth juxta montana borealia de Erryri'. *GC*, pp. 123, 243. Deudraeth was in Ardudwy and not, as Gerald mentions, in Eifionydd. T. E. Morris, 'The Castle of Deudraeth', *AC*, 1927, 355-64; *RCAM*, *Merioneth*, p. 161.

9-7 the posterity of Rhodri: Rhodri died in 1195. *Ann. C.*, p. 59; *Eifionydd*, pp. 81, 339. If Llŷn and Eifionydd were granted, as the author states, to Rhodri's descendants, it must have been after 1202 when Llywelyn ab Iorwerth expelled Maredudd ap Cynan from Eifionydd. *HW*, ii. p. 613.

9.11 Joan: Natural daughter by Agatha, daughter of Robert Ferrers, earl of Derby. The marriage was arranged in the summer of 1204. *HW*, ii, p. 616; *Rot. Claus*, i, p. 12; the ceremony took place at Ascension-tide 1206. Joan died in 1237 at Aber, the royal seat of Arllechwedd Uchaf. *HW*, ii, p. 686.

9.14 lordship of Ellesmere: The castle and manor had been granted to Dafydd ab Owain Gwynedd as a gift, but fell to the Crown once again on his death in 1203. They were regranted to Llywelyn ab Iorwerth on his marriage in the spring of 1206. *Rot. Claus*, i, p. 23; *Rot. Chart*, i, p. 147; *HW*, ii, pp. 616-7.

9.21 Tangwystl ferch Llywarch Goch: Tangwystl Goch. Dwnn, ii, p. 107. A descendant of Llywarch Howlbwrch, 'chamberlain and treasurer to Gruffudd ap Llywelyn ap Seisyll'. *WG* (300-1400), iii, p. 604. See J. E. Lloyd, 'The Mother of Gruffudd ap Llywelyn', *BBCS*, i (Pt. iv), 1923, 335.

9.23 Gruffudd ap Llywelyn: *DWB*, pp. 317-8; Dwnn, ii, p. 107. He was the illegitimate son of Llywelyn ab Iorwerth (born before his father's marriage to Joan). *HW*, ii, p. 686 et. seq.; *Lit. Wal.*, xli; *BT*, p. 182b; *HC*, pp. 280, 282, 292, 307; *Chron. M.*, iii, p. 385, iv, pp. 8, 47-8, 296. For a discussion of the struggle between Gruffudd and his half-brother, Dafydd, for supremacy in Gwynedd, see G. A. Williams, 'The Succession to Gwynedd, 1238-47', *BBCS*, xx (Pt. iv) 1964, 393-413.

9.23 heir apparent: i.e. the eldest illegitimate son.

9.24 many wars: The bone of contention was Gruffudd's hold over Meirionnydd in 1222. *HW*, ii, p. 687; *HC*, pp. 280, 297; *Chron. M.*, iii, p. 385. Llywelyn ab Iorwerth was confirmed in his possession of these *cantrefi* in 1212 and in the Treaty of Worcester (1218). *BT*, p. 182b et. seq.

9.25 Englefield: The easternmost commote of 'Y Berfeddwlad' in Gwynedd Is Conwy. B. G. Charles suggests that the meaning is 'open land of the Angels' (OE. Engla-feld). See B. G. Charles, *Non-Celtic Placenames in Wales* (1938), pp. 231-3; *HW*, i, pp. 241-2; *WATU*, p. 202.

9.25 Rhos: The *cantref* was defined by the rivers Clwyd, Elwy and Conwy, its ancestral site being Deganwy. See 4.36-7n. *HW*, i, pp. 239-40.

9.25 Rhufoniog: Comprising the heartland of Hiraethog delineated by the rivers Elwy, Clwyd and Clywedog. *HW*, i, p. 240; *WATU*, p. 190.

9.26 Dyffryn Clwyd: The fertile *cantref* comprising the vale of Clwyd. *HW*, i, p. 241; *WATU*, p. 62.

9.27 countries next adjoining unto England: 'Y Berfeddwlad' had, since Saxon times, been a continual battleground between the English (and later Normans) and the Welsh.

9.30-36 *Chron. M.*, iv, pp. 295, 316, 318-9. See 7.17-21n.

9.33 daughter of the King of Man: See Dwnn, ii, p. 108 where it is stated (after 1586, when the visitation took place) that she was Ranult, daughter of Reginald, King of Man.

9.39-40 held the Principality against him: The author is inaccurate at this point. Llywelyn seems not to have joined with his father, Gruffudd ap Llywelyn, against his uncle Dafydd. *DWB*, p. 597; *DNB*, xii, p. 200-2; xxxiv, pp. 13-14. The narrative is confusing in this section.

10.2 Hywel ap Gruffudd ap Cynan: Lord of Meirionnydd. *HW*, ii, p. 613; *WG* (300-1400), iii, p. 445.

10.5 the honourable voyage: Llywelyn ab Iorwerth's first major show of strength in Deheubarth. Carmarthen was attacked on 8 December 1215. *HW*, ii, pp. 647-8; *BT*, p. 168a.

10.9 is buried at Conwy: He died in 1216. *BT*, p. 173a. He was a generous benefactor of Cymer Abbey.

10.18 Anno 1240: The year of Llywelyn ab Iorwerth's death. He died on 11 April. *BT*, pp. 197b-198a; *Chron. M.*, iv, p. 8; *Ann. C.*, p. 82; *HW*, ii, p. 693.

10.18 Einion: He was a prominent adviser and supporter of Llywelyn ap Gruffudd. *WG* (300-1400), iii, p. 455; *Lit Wal*, pp. 4, 23, 77-8; Stephenson, op. cit., p. 133. His wife was the daughter of Gruffudd ab Ednyfed Fychan.

10.20-21 after slain at Buellt: *Ann.C.*, p. 107; J. E. Lloyd, 'The Death of Llywelyn ap Gruffudd', *BBCS*, v (Pt. iv), 1931, 349-53. Gruffudd and Einion ap Caradog were not among the prominent servants of Llywelyn who remained loyal to Dafydd. In a charter of Llywelyn to Ralph Mortimer in the early 1240s Einion is a witness which suggests his support for Llywelyn. Stephenson, op. cit., pp. 117-8, 209-10.

10.22 We receive it by tradition: There is no evidence to substantiate this tradition. *Eifionydd*, pp. 343-4. Since these two clan leaders in Penychen were the author's ancestors he probably had it in mind to add some realism to their military power. Dafydd was not a strong ruler. *HW*, ii, p. 706; M. Richter, 'David ap Llywelyn', 218-9. There may well be some truth in Wynn's statement that he held his lands 'by the aid' of Henry III because he was in a weak position early in his reign and conceded to the King at Gloucester. *Lit. Wal.*, pp. 5-6.

10.34 Maesmynan: A township in the commote of Dogfeiling. *WATU*, p. 151. There is a tradition that Llywelyn ap Gruffudd held court at Maesmynan. The evidence supplied by a charter granted by Llywelyn to Einion ap Maredudd confirming land to him in Llannerch, Dyffryn Clwyd (27 September 1243) indicates that he had established a lordship in a part of that *cantref*. According to the settlement of Gwern Eigron in 1241 the King was to hold Rhos, Rhufoniog and Dyffryn Clwyd, but his charter shows that Llywelyn held part of Y Berfeddwlad probably against the wishes of his uncle Dafydd and the King. *Llywelyn ap Gruffudd*, pp. 40-41.

10.38 great possessions: Dafydd's territory, on his death in 1246, was divided between his two nephews, Owain Goch and his brother Llywelyn ap Gruffudd. *BT*, pp. 201b-202a; *HW*, ii, p. 707. The presence of Einion and Gruffudd ap Caradog on the side of Llywelyn ap Gruffudd helps to corroborate Wynn's account of the hostility of the brothers to Dafydd ap Llywelyn, and their flight from him. Stephenson, op. cit., pp. 230-1.

13.8 Tudur: *WG* (300-1400), iii, p. 455; *RC*, p. 220. According to a petition presented to Prince Edward at Kennington in 1305 he had held his lands for one year after the Conquest and, on his death, the lands were granted to Queen Eleanor. *Eifionydd*, p. 345.

13.11 Gruffudd ap Caradog married Lleucu: *WG* (300-1400), iii, p. 455. Little is known of him except that he was given hereditary tenurial privileges at Bryncelyn, Llŷn, by Llywelyn ap Gruffudd. He may also have granted him lands near Denbigh (recorded in 1334) which were held by his descendants. Stephenson, op. cit., p. 118. The second section of the chronicle begins at this point with the marriage of Dafydd ap Gruffudd (known also as Dafydd of Penyfed) and Efa, heiress of Gruffudd Fychan ap Gruffudd of Penyfed.

13.11-12 Llywarch Fychan ap Llywarch Goch: *WG*, loc. cit; *PACF*, p. 281; Dwnn, ii, p. 158; *Eifionydd*, p. 181. This Gruffudd (above-mentioned) was a descendant of Rhodri ab Owain Gwynedd. His family possessions in Eifionydd had been usurped by Rhodri's nephews (his brother Cynan's sons), and his ancestors subsequently settled on lands granted to them by Llywelyn ap Gruffudd in the vicinity of Denbigh. Following the policy of land exchange, adopted by the lord of Denbigh, Gruffudd's son Dafydd and his kindred were re-settled in less favourable lands in the commote of Uwchdulas. *SHD*, pp. 27-8, 32, 193, 205, 274; D. H. Owen, 'Lordship of Denbigh', p. 147. On his marriage and settlement in Eifionydd Dafydd became known as Dafydd of Penyfed. *RC*, p. 39; *MWS*, p. 234.

13.14 Efa: The heiress of Gruffudd Fychan ap Gruffudd ap Moreiddig Warwyn of Penyfed. *WG* (300-1400), iii, p. 455; *RC*, p. 39; *MWS*, p. 233; *Eifionydd*, p. 81.

13.17-18 record of the extent: *WG*, loc. cit.; *SHD*, p. 285. The author is confusing at this point. The Extent was compiled in 1334, in the eighth year of Edward III, and not, as stated, 'in the time of Edward the first'.

13.23-4 to exchange their possessions: To consolidate his position in Denbigh and the surrounding areas Henry Lacy, earl of Denbigh, exchanged the landed possessions which Dafydd ap Gruffudd's immediate ancestors held in the township of Ysgeibion for other lands in the westernmost part of the lordship in the commote of Uwchdulas. This movement probably occurred between 1284 and 1311, the year of Lacy's death. Resettlement or exchange of lands and kindred group proceeded apace during this period and native tenants were resettled in other vills, usually escheat lands, in exchange for their original holdings. *SHD*, xx-xxi; Owen, 'Lordship of Denbigh', pp. 147-57.

13.26-7 the words of the record do follow: The author at this point either forgot to include a transcript of the record or intended to add it on a later occasion. This indicates that the original manuscript copy of the *History* was not intended by the author to be the final version.

13.28 How they lost the lordship of Ffriwlwyd: *Eifionydd*, pp. 338-41. See 7.15n.

13.30-31 it was taken from them by the King's officers: Llywelyn ab Iorwerth had granted the township to the abbey of Aberconwy in 1201 after he had driven Maredudd ap Cynan from Eifionydd. It remained a monastic grange until 1 October 1350 when Edward III exchanged it for the advowson of the church of Eglwys Rhos. *RC*, p. 107; *Eifionydd*, p. 340. The reasons for the exchange are not clear. Its distance from Aberconwy may have been one but sea encroachment had also taken its toll. *History of Aberconway*, pp. 107-8; 'Aberconwy Charter', 159.

13.33-4 considering what befell the other cousins: i.e. which is not unlikely considering what had befallen the other cousins.

13.38 Tudur ab Einion: *WG* (300-1400), iii, p. 455; *RC*, pp. 220, 262. Petitions submitted by the heirs of Tudur ab Einion in the post-conquest period show that Einion had many lands in Penychen (where he held a *llys*) and Pen-y-berth and parts of Llŷn. *Eifionydd*, pp. 345-6; Stephenson, op. cit., p. 118; *Cal. Anc. Pet.*, pp. 389, 454.

14.2-3 found themselves aggrieved for the wrongs: For a further discussion of this theme see W. H. Waters, *The Edwardian Settlement of North Wales in its Administrative and Legal Aspects, 1284-1343* (1935), pp. 29-32; G. Roberts, *Aspects of Welsh History* (1969), pp. 303-4; J. B. Smith, 'Crown and Community in the Principality of North Wales in the Reign of Henry Tudor', *WHR*, iii (no. ii), 1966, 121-44; F. M. Powicke, *The Thirteenth Century* (1953), pp. 429-38.

14.4-5 their general and private griefs: *RC*, pp. 212-4, 220, 437-44. A reference to one in a series of petitions submitted to Edward, Prince of Wales, in 1305. The author's reference to 29 Edward I (i.e. 1301) is incorrect; it should be 33 Edward I. Smith, op. cit., 146-7; C. R. Cheney (ed.), *Handbook of Dates*

(1978), p. 20. The author's version of the original petition from the men of north Wales to Edward, Prince of Wales, at Kennington in Lent 1305 reads as follows:

> Petitiones de Kennington facte apud Kennington pro hominibus Northwalliae tam pro comitatibus quam pro singularibus personis exhibite domini principi filio Regis Edwardi, conquestoris Walliae et consilio suo apud Kennington extra London tempore parliamenti predicti Regis habiti apud Westminesterium prima dominica quadragessie anno regni regis predicti Edwardi xxxiii; et responsiones ad easdem petitiones facte et liberate Justiciis Northwalliae sub privato sigillo dicti domini principis ad executionem responsionum predictorum faciendam et eos firmiter observandos in partibus Northwalliae.

> Ad petitionem Leolini et Gruffini filiorum Owini ap Llywelyn de eo quod Tudur ab Einion avunculus erat dominus de Baladeulyn, Penychen et Penyberth in comitate Caernarfon et seisitus post pacem proclamatam fere per unum annum post cuius descessum tenementa predicta ad Gwerfilam sororem dicti Tudur tanquam ad propinquiorem heredem eiusdem Tudur descendisse debuerunt sed domina Regina mater principis affectavit tenementa illa et ea a domino obtinuit que quidem tenementa nunc sunt in manu principis et ad eos iure hereditatis spectant, unde petunt remedium. Responsum est quod Justicius informet se supra contenta in petitione predicta et quo tempore dictus Tudur obiit et si forisfecit necne et de omnibus aliis circumstantiis et certificet inde dominum.

> Ad petitionem eorum dictorum Llywelyn et Gruffudd quod dominus velit concedere eis aliquas ballivas in comite Caernarfon pro debita firma inde reddenda quosque discusserimus quid de eorum hereditate fuerit faciendum responsum est quod pertinet ad Justicium ordinare de ballivis prout utilitati domini melius viderit expedire.

15.4 proclamation of peace: i.e. Statute of Wales (1284). In the preamble the Crown proclaimed that 'the people or inhabitants of those lands who have submitted themselves absolutely unto our will, and whom we have thereunto so accepted, should be protected in security within our peace under Laws and Customs'. *SW*, p. 2.

15.12 Gwerfyl: i.e. the daughter of Einion ap Caradog. *WG* (300-1400), iii, p. 455.

15.15 the Queen: Eleanor of Castile (d. 1290). A petition presented to Edward, Prince of Wales, at Kennington in 1305 confirms that Tudur, lord of Penychen, Pen-y-berth and Bala-deulyn, died a year after the conquest of Wales and that his lands were granted to the Queen. *RC*, p. 220; *Cal. Anc. Pet.*, p. 454.

15.24 William Sutton: Justice of North Wales (1301-6). *Edwardian Settlement*, pp. 124-5, 168. The role of estreats of fines and amerciaments, which he imposed during his period of office, displayed the harshness of his administration, ibid, pp. 144-5, 165.

15.34 Hywel: He was the eldest of the three sons and it was in the author's interests to trace the fortunes of his descendants since it was from this time onwards that the ancestors of the Wynn family recognisably emerge. *WG* (300-1400), iii, pp. 13-14.

15.37 gavelkind: Originally, the name of a land-tenure existing chiefly in Kent but in the sixteenth century used to denote a system of dividing a deceased man's patrimony equally among his sons. 'Cyfran, cyfrannu'; it is also known as partible inheritance. *MWS*, pp. 223-4, 236-7, 338; *GC*, vii, p. 211; J. Thirsk (ed.), *The Agrarian History of England and Wales*, iv, 1500-1640, (1966), pp. 357-81.

15.38 brought to the estate of mean freeholders: 'humbled in birth and rank'.

16.4 the book of Moses: 'And he said, 'I will make all my goodness pass before you and will proclaim before you my name 'The Lord'; and I will be gracious to whom I will be gracious, and will show mercy on whom I will show mercy'.' (*Exodus*, xxxvi, 19).

16.6 Commonwealth: The whole body of people; body politic.

16.8 Sodom or . . . Gomorra: The 'Cities of the Plain', south of the Dead Sea, which were destroyed by fire from heaven because of their wickedness. (*Genesis*, xix, 24-5).

16.9-10 continue in the reputation of gentlemen: i.e. we are by reputation gentlemen. 'In these days he is a gentleman who is commonly taken and reputed'. T. Smith, *De Republica Anglorum* (1586), repr. 1970, pp. 39-40.

16.14 township of Esgair Ebrill: 'villata de Escorebrithl' in the commote of Uwchdulas. *SHD*, pp. 284-5.

16.14 Eglwysbach: A parish in Uwchdulas comprising originally the five townships of Esgair Ebrill, Pennant, Cefn-y-coed, Bodnod and Maenan. D. R. Thomas, *A History of the Diocese of St. Asaph* (1908-13), ii, p. 308.

16.15 Mathebrwd: 'villata de Mathebrut' in the commote of Uwchdulas extending into the uplands to the east of the town of Llanrwst. *SHD*, pp. 275-9; see also Ca. MS. 51. *Estreats and Memoranda, 1491-95.*

16.22 the Extent of North Wales: *The Record of Caernarfon: Registrum vulgariter nuncupatum* (1352), compiled by John de Delves, deputy justice of North Wales, on behalf of the Black Prince. It contained an official record of the value of kindred lands in the Principality of North Wales among other administrative details, and is a source used regularly by the author. 'Wele Werion Griffri'; *RC*, p. 39.

16.24 quit rent: A small rent paid by a freeholder or copy-holder in lieu of the services required of him.

16.27-8 is descended of Sandde Hardd: Presumably Moreiddig ap Sandde Hardd ap Caradog Hardd. This Sandde was the Lord of Fortyn and Burton in the parish of Gresford and eldest son of Caradog or Cadrod Hardd, lord of Tref Bodafon, Anglesey. *WG* (300-1400), i, p. 44; iv, p. 821.

16.29-30 another in South Wales: Of Cantref Selyf, a son of Drymbenog ap Maenyrch. The Vaughans of Tretŵr and their cadets sprang from him. *WG* (300-1400), ii, pp. 242-3.

16.38 Ieuan ap Hywel: Of Cefn-y-fan in the township of Pennant, a descendant of Collwyn ap Tangno, Lord of

Eifionydd, Llŷn and Ardudwy, head of the fifth royal tribe of Gwynedd. *PACF*, p. 280; *Eifionydd*, xvii, pp. 17, 154, 185.

17.1-2 yet mangled with division and subdivision of gavel-kind: Economic dislocation had caused a crisis in the social structure of Wales, the continual morcellation of land making kindred patrimonies less economically viable. *CCQSR*, lxi-ii; W. O. Williams, 'The Social Order in Tudor Wales', *TCS*, 1967 (Pt. ii), 175-6.

17.3 Ieuan ap Hywel: Of 'Y Llys yng Nghefn-y-Fan' in Pennant, seventh in line from Collwyn ap Tangno. He had three daughters and Efa, the youngest, married Hywel ap Dafydd, inheriting Cefn-y-fan and other properties in Pennant, Trefan and Abercain. *Eifionydd*, p. 17; *PACF*, p. 281.

17.5 Rhirid Flaidd: *WG* (300-1400), ii, p. 431, iv, p. 754 [See n. 154]. 'He took his surname of Blaidd . . . from his maternal ancestor Blaidd Rhirid . . . of Gest, near Penmorfa'. P. Yorke, *The Royal Tribes of Wales* (1887), pp. 14, 116-7.

17.6 Ieuan ap Gruffudd: Fifth in descent from Rhirid Flaidd whose effigy lies in Llanuwchllyn church (d. 1370). He was appointed a Justice's escort in North Wales. *PACF*, p. 394; *WG* (300-1400), iv, p. 754.

17.9-10 Hywel ap Goronwy: A descendant of Tudur Trefor of Maelor. *WG*, ibid, p. 916. 'Lord of Gloucestershire, Hereford, Maelor, Oswestry and other areas in the borders of Wales'.

17.12 Hobydili: *WG*, ibid, pp. 699, 916. Gwerfyl married Tudur ap Robert (or 'Hobydili'), a descendant of Marchweithian of Is-Aled. 'Hob' (Robert) 'dil' (possibly ME. 'dull, foolish').

17.8-13 Alicine, married to Puleston: The author is confusing at this point. Ieuan ap Hywel ap Maredudd of Cefn-y-fan's third daughter married Hywel ap Goronwy ab Ieuan of Maelor. Their daughter Alicia married Hywel ab Ieuan ap Gruffudd of Bersham, another descendant of Tudur Trefor. *WG*, ibid, pp. 908, 916. Her daughter, Alicine, inherited her mother's estate of Hafod-y-wern and married John Puleston of Bersham, second son of Robert Puleston of Emral.

17.16 The author makes a serious error at this point. The original text reads 'father to Einion ap Gruffudd ap [*sic*] Hywel ap Gruffudd'. The reference is clearly to two blood-brothers and not to one person.

17.16 Hywel ap Gruffudd: i.e. Sir Hywel y Fwyall, or Hywel ap Gruffudd ap Hywel ap Maredudd, a descendant of Collwyn ap Tangno, lord of Eifionydd and Ardudwy. He distinguished himself at the battle of Poitiers, 19 September 1356. He was appointed Constable of Cricieth castle in 1376, a post which he held to c. 1381. Dwnn, ii, p. 101; *DWB*, p. 404; *IGE*, pp. 25-7, 344; B. H. St. J. O'Neil, 'Criccieth Castle, Caernarvon-shire', *AC*, xcviii, (Pt. i), 1944, 9-10. See also D. R. Johnston (ed.), *Gwaith Iolo Goch* (1988), pp. 6-8, 185-91. His home was Bron-y-foel, Eifionydd. According to the Journal of Payments made in the Ports of Gascony in the time of John Henxeworth, Controller of the Prince of Wales, he was Knighted before Poitiers. D. L. Evans, 'Some Notes on the History of the Principality of Wales in the time of the Black Prince, 1343-1376', *TCS*, 1925-26, 63.

17.18-19 reported to have taken the French King: *IGE*, pp. 26, 344; Yorke, *Royal Tribes*, pp. 184-5. Iolo Goch praises him for his accomplishment ('Y Ffrwyn ym mlaen brenin Ffrainc'): 'there is a tradition among the Welsh that it was Sir Hywel who captured John II (1350-64) by enbridling him and obtained an allowance for himself and his axe from the King, and subsequently obtained the rents of Chester mills and latterly the castle of Cricieth' (preface to the 1587 copy of Iolo Goch's *cywydd* in his honour (in translation). NLW. Add. MS. 14866.118). The author may have used this copy but seems not to be convinced that there is any truth in this tradition. Jean Froissart, the contemporary chronicler, stated that, although a number of knights had claimed to have captured him, it was Denis de Morbeke of Artois, who fought for the English, who actually forced him to surrender. B. Emerson, *The Black Prince* (1976), pp. 129-30; M. McKisack, *The Four-teenth Century*, 1307-99 (1959), pp. 139-40. Hywel was Constable of Cricieth between November 1359 and 21 June 1377.

17.25-6 Einion, his brother: Sheriff of Caernarfonshire 1351-5 and 1358 and brother of Sir Hywel ap Gruffudd (y Fwyall). He was followed in this office between 1385 and 1390 by his son Ieuan ab Einion of Chwilog. *LS*, p. 248. He was a substantial landowner in the townships of Gest, Trefan and Treflys. *Eifionydd*, passim; *HPF*, i, p. 290; *PACF*, p. 262; *IGE*, no. x, lxxxii, pp. 28-30, 249-50, 379; D. R. Johnston, op. cit., pp. 13-18, 191-7.

17.28 Maredudd ap Hywel: i.e. Maredudd ap Hywel ap Dafydd of 'Y Llys yng Nghefn-y-Fan' which lies in the detached portion of Pennant township. The remains of this stone-built house are still visible, being on the site of an earlier house owned by Efa, daughter of Ieuan ap Hywel ap Maredudd. See 17.37-18.20. Y Gesail Gyfarch became the ancestral home of the Wynn of Gwydir forbears and lies on good arable land south-east of Y Clenennau between Cwm Ystradllyn and Alltwen.

17.31 Yr Henblas: A farmstead which still stands in the township of Mathebrwd in the commote of Uwchdulas. It lies adjacent to the borough of Llanrwst.

17.32 Morfudd: Her grandfather, Dafydd Goch of Penllyn, was Abbot of Bardsey. Dwnn, ii, pp. 119, 158; *WG* (300-1400), iii, p. 457, iv, pp. 876-8.

17.37 heirs of Gwely Gruffudd: *RC*, p. 39.

17.37-18.2 The author is totally confused and misleading at this point and seems not to have researched his material or revised his text sufficiently. However, he does appear to be aware of the main lineal succession. See 17.6n. Angharad Llwyd states that this section should probably read as follows: 'Dafydd ap Hywel married the grand-daughter of Ieuan ap Hywel ap Maredudd, the daughter of Gwenllïan and Ieuan ap Gruffudd ap Madog, 'who was presumably the widow of Rheinallt ap Bleddyn. It is Dafydd's father, Hywel, who married Efa, daughter of Ieuan ap Hywel ap Maredudd of Henllys, Cefn-y-fan, a descendant of Collwyn. Efa was Gwenllïan's sister (not her daughter) and it was this sister who married Ieuan ap Gruffudd ap Madog, a descendant of Rhirid Flaidd of Penllyn. It was presumably her daughter (unnamed) who married Rheinallt and later Dafydd ap Hywel but this is not borne out in the pedigrees. It may well be that Gwenllïan had another daughter who married Dafydd. *WG* (300-1400), ii, p. 431, iv, p. 754; *HGF* (1878), pp. 30-1. All this is not easily acceptable because by this arrangement Dafydd would have married his first cousin. The lineal descent would appear to be as follows:

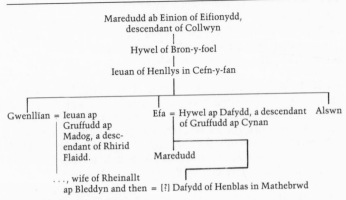

Of Ieuan's three daughters and co-heiresses Efa obtained the principal lands in Pennant, Trefan and Abercain. Her lands in Pennant formed the basis of three large estates established by her descendants in the late fifteenth century. Gwenllïan, her sister, also inherited lands in Pennant, Penyfed and Trefan among others. *Eifionydd*, p. 15.

This vague and confusing section seems to have been an unnecessary interpolation; the main point is that Dafydd ap Hywel's son, Robin Fychan, had an only daughter, Catherine. *WG* (300-1400), iii, p. 456, ii, p. 428; *PACF*, p. 221; *HGF* (1878), p. 30. Neither Angharad Llwyd nor Askew Roberts are clear on the exact line of descent here but it appears from the text that the naming of Rheinallt ap Bleddyn had caused the most serious ambiguity.

This section in the original manuscript is imprecise and confusing and serves only to reveal the author's passion for genealogical details even to the point of irrelevance and error. It also indicates that Wynn had allowed himself insufficient time to correct and revise when he decided to bring his chronicle history to an abrupt end c. 1616. It is hardly conceivable that he would have left this section, which established some vital clues about his Mathebrwd descendants, if he had adopted a systematic method of checking the whole manuscript. Other uncertainties with regard to distant lineal descents are found in the text and some of them are queried.

18.5 Rhys ab Einion Fychan: Of Plas Ucha, Llanrwst, a descendant of Iorwerth Penwyn of Gwely Wyrion Iddon, Betws-y-coed and of the stock of Marchudd, Melai (Llannerch) and Uwchdulas. *PACF*, pp. 221, 361, 377; *WG*

(300-1400), iv, p. 693; (1400-1500), viii, p. 1319. Robin Fychan married the daughter of Madog ap Rhys ap Gruffudd, a descendant of Ednyfed, and not as the author states at this point. *WG* (300-1400), iv, pp. 676.

18.10-11 Robert Salusbury: Son of Thomas Salusbury Hen (d. 1471). He settled at Plas Isa, Llanrwst and was the grand-father of William Salesbury, the Protestant humanist scholar. He was sinecure rector of Llanrwst (1515) and Llansannan (1535). It was probably the case that the lands held by English tenure fell to Salusbury and that those held by Welsh tenure were inherited by Ieuan ap Robert. *WG* (1400-1500), ix, p. 1573. Gwenhwyfar inherited Brynsyllty and Plas Isa. In 1543-44 she was assessed at £22, in land, the highest in Llanrwst parish. See G. A. Williams, 'Edmwnd Prys (1543/4-1623): Dyneiddiwr Protestannaidd', *JMHRS*, viii, 1980, 350, 364 (citing PRO, Exchequer, Subsidy Rolls. E179/220/166). See also by the same author 'Edmwnd Prys, un arall o enwogion Llanrwst', *TDHS*, xxiii, 1974, 294-7. Rhys ab Einion Fychan's great-great grandson was Edmwnd Prys, Archdeacon of Merioneth and the versifier of the Psalms in Welsh.

18.25 Morfudd: She was the daughter of Ieuan ap Dafydd ap Trahaearn Goch of Llŷn.

18.28 official of the archdeacon: Saethon(?) a farm in the parish of Buan, Llŷn. The Archdeacon of Merioneth installed 8 April 1416 was John Estcourt. Browne Willis, *A Survey of the Cathedral Church of Bangor* (1721), p. 141.

18.31-2 Conway of Rhuddlan: The Conways were of English stock who settled at Botryddan, Flintshire, in the late thir-teenth century. Jenkyn Conway (d. 1432) was the father of John, Aer Hen y Conwy (d. 1486). *PACF*, p. 260: Dwnn, ii, pp. 296-7; *DWB*, p. 1115-6; E. Roberts, 'Seven John Conways', *Flints. Hist. Soc. Jnl.*, xviii, 1960, 61-3. The John Conway mentioned in this context as the author's cousin was probably he who died in 1606—a translator of two treatises into Welsh, namely *Apologia Musices* by John Case (1588) [*Klod Kerdd dafod ai dechreuad*] and *A Summons for Sleepers* by Leonard Wright (1589) [*Definiad i Hennadirion*].

18.37 Siôn Tudur: One of the most renowned late-sixteenth-century Welsh poets; a native of Wigfair, St. Asaph. He was raised to the rank of apprentice chief-poet in the Caerwys eisteddfod in 1568 and was a domestic poet to John Conway of Botryddan. *DWB*, p. 915; E. Roberts (ed.), *Gwaith Siôn Tudur* (1978), ii, xi-xxxiii; idem, 'Siôn Tudur,' *Llên Cymru*, ii, 1952, 82-96.

18.39 Ithel Fychan: A descendant of Ednywain Bendew of Ysgeifiog, Flintshire, who married Angharad, daughter and heiress of Robin ap Dafydd. The Bithels were the descendants of this Ithel. Dwnn, ii, pp. 303, 305; *WG* (300-1400), ii, p. 264.

19.9-10 to part certain tenements: Robert ap Maredudd had not claimed a share of the inheritance of Y Gesail Gyfarch. His late marriage and the birth of his son, Ieuan, changed matters. This Ieuan was probably reared by John ap Maredudd at Y Clenennau. When John's father died c.1460 the situation again changed. Political faction may also have played its part. Owen Tudor had been executed in 1461 after the battle of Mortimer's Cross. John ap Maredudd may have decided not to campaign further but to accept Edward IV as King, settle on his divided inheritance and leave Ieuan to continue fighting in the Lancastrian cause. *Eifionydd*, pp. 21-2. Ieuan's property in Eifionydd was inherited, for the most part, by his eldest son Maredudd who owned 56 properties, according to a rental compiled in 1528. NLW MS. 9051E.210. In 1463 Ieuan, aged about 25 years, claimed half the inheritance. John ab Maredudd had to obey the law with regard to partible inheritance and he obtained Ystumcegid and other lands in Pennant and Penyfed (including Y Clenennau). Ieuan settled at Y Gesail Gyfarch in Penyfed and possessed other lands in the area.

19.11 Hywel ab Einion: *PACF*, p. 394. He is known as Hywel Gwynedd. His grandfather, Hywel Coetmor of Castell Cefel Ynghoedmor, Betws-y-coed and Gwydir, and grand-uncle, Rhys Gethin, of Hendre Rhys Gethin (the present Hendre Farm in Pentre Du), Betws Wyrion Iddon, fought for Owain Glyndŵr, and the family descended from Llywelyn ab Iorwerth through an illegitimate line. *HPF*, iii, 33; *WG* (1400-1500), v, p. 832; Dwnn, ii, pp. 133, 255; *PACF*, p. 394. The family had been well-established in Nanconwy and Hywel Coetmor's sepulchral effigy lies in Gwydir chapel in Llanrwst. Also, his ancestor, Gruffudd ap Dafydd Goch of Y Fedw Deg, Nanconwy, is commemorated in an effigy on the north wall of the chancel of St. Michael's church, Betws-y-coed. He was the foreman of the Nanconwy jury in 1352 and the tenant of Cwmllannerch. *RC*, pp. 9, 11; *PACF*, pp. 328, 394; *HPF*, i, pp. 192-3, iii, 33, 44; *SHD*, pp. 142, 144, 283; *AC*, 1874, 128; *RCAM*, *Denbs.* p. 148; Yorke, *Royal Tribes*, p. 22; Dineley, op. cit., p. 144; *WG* (300-1400), iii, pp. 447-9. Gruffudd ap Dafydd was one of the heirs of Gwely Cynwrig ab Iddon and held lands in Penmachno, Cwmllannerch, Llanrwst and Talybolion in Anglesey. *HPF*, iv, pp. 275-6. See also C. A. Gresham, *Medieval Stone Carving in North Wales* (1968), pp. 194-6, 205-7. Dafydd Goch, his father, was the reputed illegitimate son of Dafydd ap Gruffudd, youngest brother of Llywelyn, Prince of Wales.

19.12 umpire: 'meditator, daysman' (dyddiwr, cyflafar-eddwr): an arbitrator in property matters.

19.18 Ieuan, then Constable of Cricieth: It is known that a 'Ieuan ap Willie Boy' was under-constable c. 1398-9. *CPR*, 1396-9, p. 520; 'Cricieth Castle', op. cit., 10.

19.27 Thomas ap Robin: Of Cochwillan near Llandegái who was executed in 1468. He was the son of Robin ap Gruffudd, brother of Gwilym ap Gruffudd who established the Gruffudd family of Penrhyn by a second marriage. He, like his father (who abandoned Glyndŵr in 1408), supported the Lancastrians. *PACF*, p. 186; *DWB*, pp. 1123-5. Ballinger transcribes the last clause incorrectly as 'Gwenhwyfar *and* Ieuan ap Maredudd'. *HGF* (1927), p. 19. Wynn, in fact, does not go on to record the names of those who arranged the partition. This Thomas married Gwenhwyfar ferch Ieuan ap Maredudd ap Hywel of Cefn-y-fan (Ystumcegid). He probably was one of the arbitrators but Wynn is confusing two ïssues here. He is recording that he had married 'Gwenhwyfar ferch Ieuan ap Maredudd'. *PACF*, pp. 86, 232; Ca. MS.83 (MS.4.101). 94r.

19.31 the Lord Herbert: William Herbert, earl of Pembroke, son of Sir William ap Thomas of Raglan. He rose in Yorkist favour and was raised to the peerage on Edward IV's coronation on 4 November 1461. *DWB*, p. 354; *WWR*, p. 74 et seq.

19.38 Maredudd: Very little is known about Maredudd, his son John being a far more prominent and forceful character. *WG* (1400-1500), v, p. 845. He was, however, active in maintaining law and order in Eifionydd as the following writ shows, and the poets Ieuan Llawdden and Llywelyn ab y Moel each sang a *cywydd* to him. NLW Cwrtmawr MS. 11.52; *IGE*, lxvii, pp. 200-2. He was created an Esquire by Henry V and

Cochwillan

(Crown Copyright, Royal Commission on Ancient and Historical Monuments in Wales)

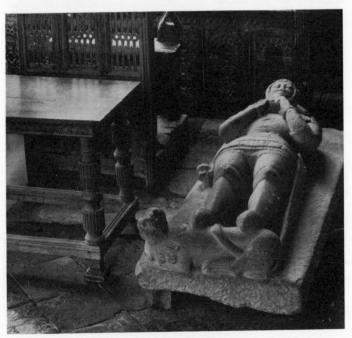

Hywel Coetmor's effigy in the Gwydir Chapel,
St. Grwst's church, Llanrwst

Brynsyllty, Mathebrwd
(Crown Copyright Royal Commission on Ancient and Historical Monuments in Wales)

Henblas, Mathebrwd
(Crown Copyright Royal Commission on Ancient and Historical Monuments in Wales)

inherited the Rhiwedog estate through his wife. He died c. 1460 and John, his son, inherited a substantial estate in Penyfed, Pennant, Llanfrothen and Nanmor. He did not rebuild Cefn-y-fan or Y Gesail Gyfarch on their original sites. Instead, he probably built Ystumcegid on a more favourable site. *Eifionydd*, pp. 19-20.

20.4 Ieuan is come of the elder: The author's main contention that Robert ap Maredudd, his ancestor, was the elder of two brothers is based on the content of this paragraph. Regardless of other subsidiary arguments which he introduces later it is the fact that Robin Fychan ap Dafydd's inheritance in Uwchdulas fell to Robert's son, Ieuan, and not to his kinsman John ap Maredudd which makes him convinced that Ieuan was a son of the elder brother. The reasoning at this point is completely false. Ieuan ap Robert inherited Robin Fychan's lands because of his affinity within the third degree, Robert and Robin being cousins. John ap Maredudd was of a different generation and was not within the kindred grouping which could have claimed Robin Fychan's inheritance. The line of descent, as described in this paragraph, is as follows:

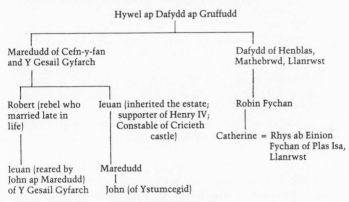

Ieuan ap Robert was Maredudd ab Ieuan's cousin german and a first cousin once removed of John ap Maredudd.

20.14-21.3 The author's version of the original Latin version of this writ (dated 28 August 1441), issued by Henry VI to Robert ap Maredudd and others for the capture and arrest of Ieuan ap Robin and other outlaws, reads as follows:

Henricus Dei gratia Rex Anglie et Francie et dominus Hibernie dilectis sibi Roberto ap Maredudd, Maredudd ab Ieuan ap Maredudd, Rhys ap Tudur, Hywel ap Madog ab Ieuan, John ap Goronwy et Hywel ab Ieuan Fychan salutem. Quia pro certo sumus informati quod Ieuan ap Robin et alii diversi notorii utlegati et incogniti de die in diem vi et armis cum diversis felonis in comitiva sua ut dicitur faciunt ambulaciones supra diversos fidelium nostrorum infra comitatem nostram de Caernarfon, et diversos de eisdem fidelibus nostris spoliaverunt et male tractaverunt in destructionem et de paupertacionem ligeorum nostrorum manifestam ac contra formam statutorum progenitorum nostrorum in hac parte provisorum. Assignavimus vos et unumquemque vestrum conjunctim et divisim ad arrestandum et capiendum predictas Ieuan ap Robin et alios in comitiva sua existenses pro corpora ubicumque inventi fuerint infra commotum de Eifionydd et eos salvos et securos usque castrum nostram de Caernarfon indilate duci faciendum constabulario nostro ibidem liberandum et in eodem castro morantur quosque de eorum deliberatione aliter duximus ordinandum. Et ideo vobis mandamus quod circa permissa diligenter intendatis et ea faciatis cum effectu sicut inde coram nobis respondere volueritis. Damus autem universis et singulis fidelibus nostris tenore presentium firmiter in mandatis quod vobis et quilibet vestrum in omnibus quae ad arrestionem et captacionem predictorum Ieuan ap Robin et aliorum pertinent intendentes sint auxiliantes fortificantes et per omnia respondentes. In cuius rei testimonium has litteras nostras fiere fecimus patentes. Teste mei ipso apud Caernarfon 28 die Augusti anno regni nostri vicesimo.

21.6-7 it is not a matter to be stood upon: The younger son, in fact, could benefit because he was usually given a choice and was in a position to retain the family home.

21.9 Hywel Sele ap Meurig: Hywel ap Meurig, a descendant of Bleddyn ap Cynfyn, and Glyndŵr's cousin. *PACF*, p. 200. He opposed Glyndŵr during the revolt. E. D. Jones, 'The Family of Nannau (Nanney)', *JMHRS*, ii, 1953, 8-9; B. Parry, 'Hugh Nanney Hen (c. 1546-1623), Squire of Nannau', ibid., v, 1957, 189.

21.12 Einion ab Ithel: He came from the stock of Rhirid Flaidd and was Esquire of the Body to John of Gaunt, Duke of

Lancaster. He was appointed sheriff of Merioneth in 1400. The pension which he received was awarded for military service in Guienne. *LS*, p. 260; Yorke, *Royal Tribes of Wales*, p. 13; W. W. E. Wynne, 'Sheriffs for the County of Merioneth', *AC*, 1847, 126-7. Rhiwedog lies in the parish of Llanfor and in the commote of Penllyn. Maredudd's praises were sung in a *cywydd* composed by Ieuan Llawdden. NLW. Cwrtmawr MS. 11.52. He is described as having resided at Ystumcegid. He was very young when he inherited the estate of Cefn-y-fan and Y Gesail Gyfarch but the two houses had been destroyed. He also inherited the Rhiwedog estate through his wife. Maredudd chose not to rebuild the houses on their original sites and Ystumcegid was erected to the south-west of Cefn-y-fan. There is no doubt that this Maredudd, in spite of his apparent obscurity, had inherited and consolidated a strong patrimony for his son John ap Maredudd. *Eifionydd*, pp. 18-9.

21.14-15 Hywel ab Ieuan ap Maredudd: Practically nothing is known of Hywel ab Ieuan ap Maredudd other than that he married Mallt ferch Rhys of the line of Collwyn. *WG* (300-1400), iii, p. 457. He was known as Hywel Fychan of Y Gesail Gyfarch.

21.17 Owen Holland of Berw: Owen Holland of Berw (Llanfihangel Ysgeifiog), the author's contemporary, married Elizabeth, daughter of Sir Richard Bulkeley, thus strengthening his landed status in Anglesey. *DWB*, p. 361; *PACF*, p. 110. Rhydderch ap Rhisiart of Myfyrian, Llanidan was a poet (fl. 1580-1620). Only a few of his poems have survived. *Board of Celtic Studies: Mynegai i Farddoniaeth Gaeth y Llawysgrifau* (1978), p. 3246. Rhisiart Gruffudd ap Huw o Fôn was also an Anglesey poet (fl. 1569) and well-versed in local genealogy. Some of his work appears in manuscript. Ibid, p. 2934. *DWB*, p. 316. Wynn's reference to the descent of the families of Berw and Myfyrian from Hywel's line by females can be established. His daughter, Gwenhwyfar married Ithel ap Hywel ap Llywelyn, a descendant of Llywarch ap Brân of Menai from which the Berw families emerged. Ithel's daughter, Mallt, married Dafydd ab Ieuan of Myfyrian. *WG* (300-1400), iii, p. 595; (1400-1500), vi, p. 1042, vii, p. 1158; *PACF*, pp. 110, 115; Dwnn, ii, p. 210.

21.22 John of Gaunt: Of Ghent, third surviving son of Edward III and Duke of Lancaster (1362). S. B. Chrimes, *Lancastrians, Yorkists and Henry VII* (1966), p. 6 et. seq.

21.24 his manor of Halton: an honour in Runcorn, Cheshire, within the Duchy of Lancaster. R. Somerville, *History of the Duchy of Lancaster* (1953), i, 1265-1603, pp. 510-13.

21.26 The Charter I have seen: Owain ap John ap Maredudd's settlement (1486) has survived. *Eifionydd*, pp. 23-4; C. A. Gresham, 'The Origin of the Clenennau Estate', *NLWJ*, xv, 1967-8, 336-7. John Owen (i.e. John ab Owain), was the blood-thirsty enemy of Hywel ap Madog Fychan of Abercain. See 52.36n. The document referred to by the author was probably in the possession of his contemporary, John Wyn Owen (he died *c.* 1605-10). *Eifionydd*, p. 26. He, like his great-grand-father, Owain ap John ap Maredudd, inherited Ystumcegid. Dwnn, ii, pp. 169-70.

21.34 Abbot of Bardsey: Confusion has arisen as to the identity of this Robert ap Maredudd, abbot of Bardsey. The narrative is ambiguous at this point. He was a brother of John ap Maredudd (Ieuan ap Robert's protector) and *not* Ieuan's father (as historians have made him out to be). This Robert has erroneously been identified as the brother of Ieuan ap Maredudd who supported Henry IV and defended Caernarfon castle against Glyndŵr. *Eifionydd*, pp. 19, 154; 'Bardsey Abbey: Grant of Prayers 1464', *AC*, 1860, 188-9.

21.35 Robert: i.e. Ieuan ap Robert's father, not the abbot.

21.35-6 The third section of the chronicle begins at this point with the marriage of the author's direct ancestor, Robert Maredudd, in his old age. Since it is known that his son Ieuan died in 1468-9 aged 31 years, the marriage may be dated c.1436-7. See 25. 13-14n. His wife, Angharad, was the daughter of Dafydd ap Llywelyn ap Dafydd of Cefnmelgoed (a farm which still exists in the parish of Llanychaearn), a descendant of Llawdden. Angharad's mother, Margaret, was a descendant of Cydifor ap Gwaethfoed and the daughter of Rhydderch ab Ieuan Llwyd of Parc Rhydderch, a prominent office-holder and lawyer in the commote of Mabwnion as well as in Cardiganshire. He was also a keen supporter of Glyndŵr. *WG* (300-1400), i, p. 179; iii, p. 588; R. A. Griffiths, 'Gentle-men and Rebels in Later Medieval Cardiganshire', *Ceredigion*, v, 1965, 152-5.

22.1-2 and [several?] daughters: In the original MS. the number of Robert ap Maredudd's daughter is omitted. The author also forgets to name them as he had intended. He had three; Morfudd, Margaret (Maud?) and Angharad. *PACF*, p. 280.

22.2 Of this Robert, abbot, are descended: The author, keen to establish his family's reputation, offers this information about remote kinsmen (whom he calls 'pencenedl', i.e. senior members of their respective families) who were his contemporaries. Gruffudd ap Richard of Madryn Isa, Llŷn, and Robert ap Richard of Llecheiddior Ganol in Eifionydd were the abbot's great-grandsons. The third kinsman mentioned, Owen ap John (b. 1532), was of Cefn Cyfannedd (in the free township of Treflys) and not, as the author states, of Bron-y-foel. *Eifionydd*, pp. 154-5, 205. The line of descent is as follows:

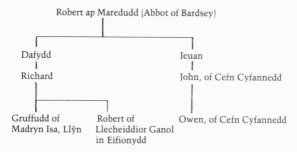

22.12 Einion ab Ithel's daughter: See 21.12n.

22.14 Owain Glyndŵr: Owain ap Gruffudd (c. 1354-1416), lord of Glyndyfrdwy and Cynllaith Owain in Powys Fadog. Sycharth, his seat, was situated in Cynllaith. He quarrelled with Reginald de Grey, lord of Ruthin, over land and inspired a national revolt against Henry IV (of Lancaster) who had usurped the throne on the deposition of Richard II in 1399. *DWB*, pp. 691-2; J. E. Lloyd, *Owen Glendower* (1931); G. Williams, *Owen Glendower* (1966); R. R. Davies, *Conquest, Coexistence and Change: Wales 1063-1415* (1987), pp. 431-59.

22.15 Maredudd ap Hwlcyn Llwyd: It was Hwlcyn Llwyd, not his son, Maredudd (as the author states), who defended Caernarfon castle. He was the son of Tudur Goch, a freeholder in Dinlle in 1352, and the ancestor of the Glynn family of Glynllifon. Dwnn, ii, p. 147; *DWB*, p. 280; Roberts, *Aspects of Welsh History*, pp. 160-2; Lloyd, *Glendower*, p. 77.

22.18 his two houses: They were burnt at the time when Glyndŵr's forces were moving from Caernarfon to Cricieth castle. Cefn-y-fan was built of stone by Maredudd ap Hywel. Neither house was erected again on the original sites and Ieuan's son Maredudd probably built Ystumcegid within a short distance away south of Cefn-y-fan. The timber structure of Y Gesail Gyfarch was probably not replaced but rebuilt. *Eifionydd*, pp. 1-2, 86; C. A. Gresham, 'Platform Houses in North-West Wales', *AC*, 1954, 36-7.

22.20-1 died Ieuan at Caernarfon: Ieuan and his comrade Hwlcyn died on 4 November 1403 (when Caernarfon was besieged by French ships) and 18 January 1404 respectively. Lloyd, op. cit., pp. 76-8. Penmorfa church is dedicated to St. Beuno and the window in the chancel once contained stained glass to commemorate Maredudd ab Ieuan ap Robert and his wife Margaret, daughter of Morus ap John ap Maredudd of Y Clenennau. The stained glass in the east window of Dolwyddelan church also commemorated him, See 55.25n. C. E. Breese, 'Old Stained Glass in St. Beuno's Church, Penmorva'. *AC*, 1905, 147-52; *Eifionydd*, p. 79.

22.25 a pardon granted: The pardon was granted on 20 September 1409. See NLW MS. 9061E.1504 (i) for a copy of the pardon preserved among the muniments at Gwydir. When fighting with Glyndŵr he had joined with Ieuan ab Einion ap Gruffudd of Bron-y-foel, a nephew of Sir Hywel y Fwyall. See 17-16n. *PACF*, p. 264; Lloyd, op. cit., p. 78; *Eifionydd*, p. 187. This Ieuan was sheriff of Caernarfonshire in 1385-90. *LS*, p. 248. The author's version of the pardon originally granted to Robert ap Maredudd by Henry, Prince of Wales (20 September 1409) reads as follows:

Henricus illustris Regis Anglie et Francie primogenitus, Princeps Walliae, Dux Aquitaniae, Lancastriae, et Cornubiae, et comes Cestriae locum tenens metuendissimi domini nostri Regis et patris in partibus Southwalliae et Northwalliae. Omnibus et singulis presentes litteras nostras inspectaturis salutem. Sciatis quod nos authoritate et potestate nobis per ipsum metuendissimum dominum nostrum regem et patrem commissis ac etiam per quadam fine nobis per Robertum ap Maredudd ap Hywel nuper rebellem dicti domini nostri regis et patris in partibus Walliae ad opus eiusdem domini nostri regis et patris soluta. Recipimus et admisimus dictum Robertum ad gratiam predicti domini nostri Regis et

patris et ei perdonamus nomine eiusdem domini nostri
Regis et patris sectam pacis sue que ad ipsum dominum
nostrum regem et patrem pertinet pro omnimodis
predictis omnibus insurrectionibus rebellionibus
incendiis feloniis adhesionibus transgressionibus
misprisionibus et maleficiis quibuscumque per
predictum Robertum in partibus et marchiis Walliae
ante hec tempora factis sive perpetratus unde indictatus
rectatus vel appellatus existit. Ac etiam utlegariis si
quae in ipsum hiis occasionibus fuerint promulgate et
firmam pacem predicti domini nostri regis et patris inde
concedimus ac ei bona et catalla sua quecumque dicto
domino nostro regi et patri occasionibus premissis
forisfacta nomine et authoritate predicta concedimus
per presentes. Ita tamen quod stet recto in curia predicti
domini nostri regis et patris ac nostra si qui versus eum
loqui voluerint de premissis vel aliquo premissorum. In
cuius rei testimonium has litteras nostras fieri fecimus
patentes. Datum London vicesimo die Septembris anno
regni dicti metuendissimi domini nostri regis et patris
Henrici quarti post conquestum nono.

Irrotulatur ad Sessionem tentam apud Caernarfon die
Lune proxima post festum assumptionis beatae Mariae
virginis anno principatus domini Henrici Principis
Walliae undecimo.

23.28 Rhys Goch Eryri: An early fifteenth-century poet, a
descendant of Collwyn and a native of Hafod Garegog in
Nanmor, Beddgelert. *WG* (300-1400), ii, p. 430; *DWB*, p. 842.
The *cywydd*—of which only the first sixteen and last twenty
four lines are quoted—was probably composed in honour of
Robert ap Maredudd although he is not mentioned by name.
The poem is dated c.1416-36, the period after Robert had been
pardoned, because it does not portray a hunted outlaw but
rather an ageing nobleman descended from Gruffudd ap
Cynan enjoying the comforts of his home. Sir Ifor Williams
suggests that his name was kept anonymous in the poem
because of the jealousies which had wrecked relations
between the immediate descendants of this Robert and his
brother Ieuan, the poet not wishing to displease either
kindred. *IGE*, xlii-liii, c, pp. 301-3. In the lines quoted the
person eulogised is compared favourably with Alexander the
Great (1.23) and Trystan, the lover of Esyllt (1.25). This
extract from the *cywydd* composed by Rhys Goch Eryri in
praise of Robert ap Maredudd reads as follows in modern
Welsh:

Hir y bu Ruffudd ruddbar
Waywdan fab Cynan ein câr
Ar groesgeirch hir grae ysgwyd
Yn gorwedd, llew fflamgledd llwyd,
A'i dalaith llwybr goddaith llaw,
Ffynnodd gynt, yn celffeiniaw.

Taw, oerfab, bid tau arfoll,
Na chrŷn, ddyn, ni chrinodd oll.
Mae arno gainc, llathrfainc llu,
Etifedd propr yn tyfu,
Yn dwyn ystod, fragod frig,
Garw ben hydd, gŵr bonheddig,
O bryd a llafn hyfryd hedd,
Ac ysgithr brwydr a gosgedd,
A champau anwydau naid
Frutyniawl hen Frytaniaid . . .

O'm gofyn, emyn ymwal,
Dyn annosbarthus ei dâl,
Pwy ei henw, ni'm difenwir,
Bedydd, ar du gwerydd dir;
Y gŵr a elwir yn gainc
Dylwythfawr ar daleithfainc;
Alexander niferoedd,
Mur a phen, mawr oroff oedd;
Trystan ddoethran oddeithryw,
Tulath aur ein talaith yw;
Bonedd ond odid beunoeth
Y cwsg ein hen farwn coeth,
Rhwng Hafren hoyw ddwfr gloyw glân,
Llu gwrth a Lli ac Arthan.
Ni ad gwawd, pechawd heb bwyll,
Ogandaith genfigendwyll,
Sôn am y Cymro, os iach,
Pwyllog doeth, a fo pellach.
Pei megid, eurid araith,
Cenau o neb Cynan iaith,
Hir ddewr lân hardd eryr lid,
Henw mygr, o hwn y'i megid.
Ymgroesed gwawd tafawd hen,
Ymgais, ni wn i amgen.

Rhys Goch Eryri ai cant

24.17-18 the utter destruction of that sort of man: Welsh poetic tradition had certainly suffered a setback during the fourteenth century but this tale, seemingly invented by the author, has since been disproved by Thomas Stephens. It is conceivable, nonetheless, that the poets themselves were originally responsible for creating such a myth to explain the decline in their output during this century. Whatever the truth the author is keen to extract as much information as possible from the poets to enhance his family's reputation. It is the dearth of poetic material in honour of his antecedents that probably caused him to invent such a story. It was used by Thomas Carte in his *History of England* (1747-55) and became an important theme in a poem by Thomas Gray (1757), and the nineteenth century Hungarian poet, János Arány who based his poem 'A Welski Bárdok' on this theme. T. Stephens, *The Literature of the Kymry* (1876), pp. 327-9; N. Masterman, 'The Massacre of the Bards', *The Welsh Review*, vii, 1948, 58-66; *HGF* (1927), xvii-xviii; M. H. Jones, 'Wales and Hungary', *TCS*, 1968 (pt. i), 25-6. For the literary background to this period see C. W. Lewis, 'The Content of Poetry and the Crisis in the Bardic Tradition', in A. O. H. Jarman and G. R. Hughes (ed.), *A Guide to Welsh Literature*, ii, chap. iv, pp. 97-110. Wynn was constantly aware of the need to offer as much source evidence as possible to strengthen his claim to lineal descent from Owain Gwynedd. Where it was not available he was obliged to invent it or try to explain its non-existence (as in this case) in the most imaginative way possible—yet another indication of his antiquarian leanings and over-reliance on hearsay and unfounded traditions. Gray's 'The Bard' inspired paintings by artists like Paul Sandby and Thomas Jones of Pencerrig. See P. Morgan, *The Eighteenth-Century Renaissance* (1981), pp. 120-1; idem, 'From a Death to a View: the hunt for the Welsh past in the Romantic period' in E. Hobsbawm and T. Ranger (ed.), *The Invention of Tradition* (1983), pp. 82-3.

24.25 the Prince's records: For more information on the changes and disorder among muniments in the Tower see L. Fox (ed.) *English Historical Scholarship in the Sixteenth and Seventeenth Centuries* (1956), pp. 14-19. Although there had been a strong tradition of record-keeping at Caernarfon records were not kept there with the care and safety that they deserved in the sixteenth century. Documents were often taken away to be perused privately. *CCQSR*, xxi; *CWP*, no. 1390; R. I. Jack, *The Sources of History: Studies in the Uses of Historical Evidence: Medieval Wales* (1972), p. 19.

24.35-6 farmer of Dolbenmaen: Dolbenmaen was a bond township between the rivers Dwyfach and Dwyfor. *Eifionydd*, p. 370. It was farmed out by the Crown in the late fourteenth century, Robert ap Maredudd being Crown farmer. Aberglaslyn lands lay within the eastern boundary of the free township of Pennant. The mill of Aberdwyfor was in the free township of Rhwng Dwyfor a Dwyfach. Ministers Accounts show that, in 1469-70, the mill and fishery of Aberdwyfor had recently been granted to Robert ap Maredudd. C. A. Gresham, 'Townships in the Parish of Llanystumdwy', *TCHS*, xix, 1958, 36. Robert ap Maredudd became a prominent public figure in Eifionydd in 1430; together with others he negotiated with the Crown on behalf of the free communities of the Principality of North Wales. J. B. Smith, op. cit., 154-5.

24.39 Ieuan: He assumes a central role in the chronicle, being the author's direct ancestor and a man of military strength for whom Wynn shows considerable respect. He was born c.1437. *PACF*, pp. 280-1; *WG* (1400-1500), v, p. 850. See 20.4n.

24.41 John ap Maredudd: He was the son of Ieuan's cousin Maredudd and his own first cousin once removed. Since Ieuan's father was very old at his birth John ap Maredudd was many years his senior and became his foster parent, a role quite common in the Middle Ages and recognised by Welsh Law. T. P. Ellis, *Welsh Tribal Law and Custom in the Middle Ages* (1926), i, pp. 385-6; *WG* (1400-1500), v, p. 846. He was born probably in the first decade of the fifteenth century, lived to a ripe old age and died c.1486. *Eifionydd*, pp. 19-20. He has been described as 'one of the most interesting of all historical persons known in medieval Eifionydd'. Robin Ddu, the Anglesey poet, sang to him c.1430-70. *Mynegai*, p. 4477; *HGF* (1878), pp. 44-5(n2); *DWB*, p. 886. In a grant of lands to his son Owen ap John in Pennant and other townships in Eifionydd in 1485 he is described as an 'esquire' and a free tenant of the King's township of Pennant, *HGF* (1878), p. 47(n.2); Dwnn, ii, p. 169.

25.3 Bron-y-foel: It is situated in the free township of Treflys. Hywel ap Rhys's mother was the daughter of Rhys Gethin, the soldier and rebel, of Hendre Rhys Gethin, Betws-y-coed, in the commote of Nanconwy, See 19.11n., *PACF*, p. 264. His father had been busily occupied bulding up a small estate. It was not, as the author declares, a family with extensive possessions but it was in his interest to describe, in the most elaborate manner, how the powerful Hywel, who was Ieuan ap Robert's bitterest enemy, was finally overcome. According to the matrimonial arrangements Hywel married Ieuan's sister Margaret, and Ieuan married Hywel's sister Catherine, *PACF*, p. 232; *Eifionydd*, pp. 150-3; C. A. Gresham, 'The Townships of Gest, Treflys and Ystumllyn', *TCHS*, xviii, 1957, 12-13.

25.7 widow of Robert ap Maredudd: She was Angharad, daughter of Dafydd ap Llywelyn ap Dafydd of Cefnmelgoed in Cardiganshire. See 21.37n. Her second husband, Maredudd ap Rhys ab Ieuan Llwyd of Gorddinog, Aber (near Bangor), was a descendant of Iarddur of Arllechwedd Uchaf. *WG* (300-1400), iii, p. 530.

25.13-14 fell a dislike and variance: Ieuan ap Robert died in 1468-9 at the age of 31 years. He was born, therefore, in 1437. See 20,4n. His father was reputed to have been 80 years of age on his birth. He could have survived much longer because he also had three daughters. His death can possibly be dated c.1440-50. It was at that time that the disagreement referred to in this section occurred. The author refers to Gwilym (Fychan) ap Gwilym of Penrhyn (c.1420-83), known as 'Siambrlen Hen'. He appears not to have held the office of Chamberlain of North Wales but did function as deputy to a number of them. He was the son of Gwilym ap Gruffudd (who came to terms with Henry IV in 1407) by his second wife Joan Stanley of Hooton, Cheshire, and his career illustrates the rise of the individual Welsh landowner in spite of many legal disadvantages. He inherited the Penrhyn lands on his father's death in 1431, and in 1440 was made an English citizen by Denization. He married Alice, heiress of Sir Richard Dalton of Apthorp, Northamptonshire. The feud reveals the animosity which could occur, in unsettled times, between powerful heads of kindreds who did not hold office and the new office-holders who would stop at nothing to upgrade themselves and their families. *DWB*, p. 1124; *PACF*, pp. 184-5; E. I. Rowlands, 'Tri Wiliam Gruffudd', *Llên Cymru*, ii, 1952-3, 256-7; *IGE*, p. 390.

25.22-3 *Nec Caesar . . .*: A Latin tag. *'Nec quemquam iam ferre potest Caesarve priorem Pompeiusve parem'*. ('Caesar could no longer endure a superior, nor Pompey an equal'), Lucan, *The Civil War: Pharsalia*, ed. J. D. Duff (1977), pp. 12-13.

25.25 burrs: Any rough or prickly seed-vessel or flower-head of a plant; in this context a person or persons who clings to another; the loyalty of members of a clan to their chieftain.

25.26 sect: A section of a tribe; a clan; it is a variant of 'sept' and was used with reference to Irish kin structures.

25.26 *Tylwyth:* 'Kinsmen, Kinsfolk'. Blood relatives.

25.32 Owen Tudor: Owain ap Maredudd ap Tudur of Penmynydd, Anglesey, a descendant of Ednyfed Fychan and kinsman of John ap Maredudd. He was Henry Tudor's grandfather who served in the household of Henry V and married his widow, Katherine de Valois, secretly in 1429 apparently without official consent. He favoured the Lancastrians in the dynastic wars and was executed at Hereford after the battle of Mortimer's Cross (1461). *DWB*, p. 693-4; T. A. Jones, *Without My Wig* (1945), pp. 11-32.

25.35 Usk castle: Yorke states that he had been imprisoned at Usk (Brynbuga) castle and that John ap Maredudd and his retinue were beset by enemies in the vicinity of Caerllïon-ar-Wysg. *Royal Tribes*, pp. 14-16.

26.6-7 Hywel Llywelyn ap Hywel: Unidentified but probably a descendant (possibly grandson) of Hywel Fychan ap Maredudd who was John ap Maredudd's uncle. *WG*, iii, p. 457.

26.9 vanward: voweward, 'vaward', 'vanguard': the foremost division of an army or warring party. It could also be interpreted in this context as 'for-ward', 'being in the fore', or near or towards the front.

26.14 Queen Katherine: The youngest daughter of Charles VI of France.

26.29 five sons: Morus settled at Y Clenennau, Ieuan at Bryncir, Gruffudd at Isallt, Llanfihangel-y-Pennant, and Owain at Ystumcegid. *WG* (1400-1500), v, p. 847.

26.34 Thelwalls: The Thelwalls settled in Ruthin c.1380 with Reginald de Grey and, through marriage, settled at Plas-y-ward. The lordship of Ruthin was created in 1282 out of the *cantref* of Dyffryn Clwyd. *DWB*, p. 933. It was granted in fee to Reginald de Grey of Wilton on 23 October 1282 who also obtained the castle of Ruthin. *Complete Peerage*, vi, p. 173. 'The Lord Grey', referred to by the author, was Edmund, created Earl of Kent on 30 May 1465 and appointed Lord High Treasurer on 24 June in the same year. Ibid, p. 160; vii, p. 164; *CPR*, 1461-7, p. 286. See also R. Newcome, *An Account of the Castle and Town of Ruthin* (1836), pp. 47-50.

27.13 Thomas ap Gruffudd ap Nicholas: He was the son of the most powerful administrator and strongest Lancastrian supporter in south-west Wales in the mid-fifteenth century. *DWB*, pp. 313, 840. He was the father of Rhys ap Thomas, supporter of Henry Tudor, and was slain in an encounter at Pennal, Merioneth, during the Yorkist attacks in north Wales in 1468.

27.21-28.8 this letter ... to John ap Maredudd: *WWR*, pp. 221-2. A copy, with slight variations, is included among the Clenennau papers. T. Jones Pierce (ed.), *Calendar of the Clenennau Letters and Paper in the Brogyntyn Collection. NLW Jnl. Supp.*, Ser. iv, pt. 1, 1947, 139(i). The present rendering is a copy since Henry, earl of Richmond, would hardly have designated himself 'H.7' or have added 'By the King' before Bosworth'. Letters seeking support, however, were sent to England in semi-regal style. S. B. Chrimes, *Henry VII* (1977), p. 39. Humphrey Humphreys, Bishop of Bangor, notes in his version of the *History*: 'I have seen ye original of this letter and perused it at Gwedir 1690'. *HGF* (1878); NLW, Wynnstay MS.130.

28.12 Catherine: i.e. Catherine, sister of Hywel ap Rhys of Bron-y-foel. Maredudd ab Ieuan was the founder of the Gwydir estate. *PACF*, p. 280.

28.14 the house of Llwyndyrus: Ibid., pp. 231, 280. Llwyn-dyrus, Abererch. Sir Gruffudd Llwyd was the chief Welsh supporter of the Crown in north Wales in the early fourteenth century and a great-grandson of Ednyfed Fychan. *DWB*, p. 319; J. G. Edwards, 'Sir Gruffydd Llwyd'. *EHR*, xxx, 1915, 577-601. Gruffudd Fychan received ancestral lands in Uwch-dulas in the Conwy valley. Nothing is known of the other two children of this second marriage. *WG* (1400-1500), v, p. 850. *PACF*, p. 28 is wrong in stating that this Gwenhwyfar married Thomas ap Robin of Cochwillan. His wife was Gwenhwyfar, daughter of Ieuan ap Maredudd ap Hywel of Ystumcegid (See

19.27n). It was Maredudd, Ieuan ap Robert's eldest son by his first wife who received most of the lands in Eifionydd. It was he who began the task of consolidating the *rhandir* or hamlet of Penyfed into the demesne of Y Gesail Gyfarch. NLW MS.9051E.210, and later extended into Nanconwy. He followed the same pattern as did Morus ap John ap Maredudd in Y Clenennau. *Eifionydd*, pp. 87-8.

28.17 Ieuan: i.e. Ieuan ap Robert. He died late 1468 or early 1469. A safe-conduct was issued on 4 October 1468.

28.21 burned the duke of York's lands of Denbighland: See *WWR*, pp. 164-70 for the background to Jasper Tudor's inroads in Denbigh in 1468 and Herbert's attacks on north Wales. See 19.31n.

28.24-5 to recover the castle: The castle had to be captured by the Yorkists if Lancastrian connections with Ireland and Scotland were to be severed. It surrendered to Herbert on 14 August 1468, *WWR*, p. 169. Dafydd ab Ieuan ab Einion was the son of Ieuan ab Einion of Cryniarth (Llandrillo) in Edeirnion in the cantref of Penllyn. His mother, Angharad, was the heiress of Dafydd ap Giwn Llwyd, baron of Hendwr, again in Edeirnion. Dwnn, ii, p. 215; *PACF*, p. 223. Ieuan was influential in Merioneth in the years after the Glyndŵr revolt. Dafydd ab Ieuan was appointed constable and defender of Harlech castle (1461-8). W. W. E. Wynne 'Lists of Constables of Harlech Castle', *AC*, 1846, 264-5. Dafydd fought in France and, on his return (probably in 1450), he became a staunch Lancastrian supporter. He was in many ways a turbulent fellow and patron of bards. G. Davies, *Noddwyr Beirdd ym Meirion* (1974), pp. 45-9.

28.33-29.9 in these words: NLW MS. 9061E. 1504(ii). The document issued on 4 November 1468 offered protection during negotiations. The regnal style is confused in the original copied by the author. It should read: 'in the eighth year of the reign of King Edward, the fourth after the conquest'. The author's version of the original document which records the safe-conduct issued by William Herbert, Earl of Pembroke, to Ieuan ap Robert (4 November 1468) reads:

> Omnibus Christi fidelibus ad quos presens scriptum pervenerit Williamus Comes Pembroke, Justicius

domini regis in partibus suis Northwalliae salutem.
Sciatis nos dedisse et per presentes concessisse Ieuan ap
Robert de commoto Eifionydd in comitati Caernarfon
salvum et securum conductum intrandi veniendi
ambulandi expectandi comorandi ac salvo eundi et
redeundi per et infra comitates de Caernarfon et
Merioneth pro se bonis et catallis suis sine arrestacione
molestacione impeachimento dampno violencia manu
capcione perturbacione seu gravamine aliquali tam ad
sectam domini regis quam ad sectam partis alterius
persone cuiuscumque a die confectionis presentium
quosque per nos habuerit premonitionem sex dierum.
Datum sub sigillo nostro quarto die mensis Novembris
anno regni regis Edwardi quarto post conquestum
octavo.

29.12 most valiant withal: Contemporary poets referred
continually to his physical stature. They were Inco Brydydd,
Hywel Rheinallt and Ieuan ap Tudur Penllyn. The latter poet
called him 'Gŵr mawr lluniaidd' ('a great figure of a man'). T.
Roberts (ed.) *Gwaith Tudur Penllyn ac Ieuan ap Tudur
Penllyn* (1958), nos. 37-8, 45, pp. 69-71, 80-1. These poets
sang to him at Y Gesail Gyfarch and drew attention to his
martial prowess and generous hospitality. Ca.MS.83
(MS.4.101) 21r-21v, 23r-25r, 26v-27r.

29.13 deadly feud: It is the persistent feuding in Eifionydd
which preoccupies the author over a large section of his
narrative history from this point onwards and emphasis is
placed on internecine jealousies which exacerbated kin
relations and created prolonged and bitter quarrels.

29.16 Hywel ap Rhys: See 25.3n.

29.18-19 Tudur Gruffudd ab Einion's daughter: She was
Mared, heiress of Tudur Fôn ap Gruffudd ab Einion, a descend-
ant of Osbwrn Wyddel of Llanaber. *WG* (300-1400), iv, p. 727;
Dwnn, ii, p. 94.

29.26 Dafydd ap Siencyn: A famous mid-fifteenth-century
outlaw and a descendant (paternally) of Maredudd and
(maternally) of Llywelyn ab Iorwerth. He sided with the Lancastrians and, until 1468, defended Nanconwy against the
Yorkists, his outpost being Carreg-y-gwalch above Gwydir
near Llanrwst. Dwnn, ii, pp. 102, 132; *HPF*, iv, p. 274, v, p.

235, vi, p. 221. He was also a poet of some repute. Together with Ieuan ap Robert he defended Nanconwy against Yorkist incursions and also raided parts of the lordship of Denbigh on behalf of the Lancastrians. Tudur Penllyn sang his eulogy, combining in his verse a description of Dafydd as a man of gentle birth who, as an outlaw, was excluded from the benefits of English law. He also drew attention to his military expertise and to his power over loyal followers of his own type. *Gwaith Tudur Penllyn*, no. i, p. 1.

> Dy gastell ydyw'r gelli,
> Derw dôl yw dy dyrau di . . .
> Glanaf y medrit, Dafydd,
> Gerddoriaeth, helwriaeth hydd . . .
> Caredig i'r ceirw ydwyd,
> Câr yr iarll, concweriwr wyd.
> Tithau, gleddau arglwyddi,
> Teyrn wyd yn ein tir ni . . .
> Gwylia'r trefydd celfydd call,
> A'r tiroedd o'r tu arall . . .
> Da yw ffin a thref ddinas,
> Gorau yw'r glyn a'r graig las . . .
> Cadw o'r dref, cadw'r coed a'r drws,
> Cadw batent coed y Betws.

(Thy castle is the woodland, thy towers are the oak trees. Thou art a poet, a hunter of stags, a conqueror and a king in our land. Beware of towns and their surroundings. Better is the glen and the grey rock. Keep away from them: remain in the woods of Betws and defend them.)

Outlaws such as he operated on the boundaries of the Principality of north Wales and the lordship of Denbigh and were able to slip with ease from one region to the other to avoid their respective legal jurisdictions. Poems composed in their honour condemned the settled life of the court and the town. Llywelyn ap y Moel, for example, complimented outlaws on their ability to undermine the law and offer popular leadership in frontier regions. *IGE*, no. lxiii, lxvi, pp. 191-2, 198-9. Criminals who were not apprehended and brought to justice were regarded as outlaws and risked being lawfully slain on sight. Outlawry was also the penalty for failure to make appearance at four successive shire courts when summoned to do so. Since outlaws were considered to be beyond the reach of the law they were looked upon as being no better than wild animals. In Richard I's reign, for example, five shillings was paid for every outlaw's head. It is hardly surprising, therefore, that Dafydd ap Siencyn was considered to be a man who was admired and feared; admired by those who despised English law and legal procedure and feared by those who had submitted to royal authority in the Principality and who endeavoured to maintain good order and governance. In times of political and economic stress such people were regarded often as popular leaders of discontent and local unrest. In the political climate described by Sir John Wynn renegades could easily become the tool of others in their efforts to seize the main chance in the acquisition of land or to pay back old scores. Dafydd ap Siencyn was described by the author of the *History* as a 'man of great valour' and as a contender for the 'sovereignty' of the commote of Nanconwy in spite of his alliance with Hywel ap Rhys against Ieuan ap Robert, Wynn's ancestor. In turbulent days courage and contempt of law was often admired. *PACF*, pp. 264, 396; *DWB*, p. 99. Dafydd ap Siencyn and Hywel ap Rhys were first cousins, their mothers being daughters of Rhys Gethin of Nanconwy.

29.36 This woman: i.e. Mared, daughter of Tudur Fôn ap Gruffudd ab Einion.

29.37 my ancestor: i.e. Ieuan ap Robert. For fosterage see *HW*, i, p. 310; *Welsh Tribal Law*, i, p. 385; G. D. Owen, *Elizabethan Wales: the Social Scene* (1962), p. 51. The rule seemed to be that sons of the *uchelwyr* were fostered by men of lower status and succeeded the foster-fathers as heirs obtaining a share of the property equally with his own sons. This is probably a reference to Maredudd (who was subsequently fostered at Crug in Is Gwyrfai). Ieuan had two other sons from his first marriage and two from his second.

30.8-9 nothing was punished by law whatsoever happened: It is on the basis of such broad generalisations that historians have drawn conclusions that Wales was remarkably violent in the fifteenth century. It is not now accepted that quarrels between kindreds linked through intermarriage were as devastating as historians considered them to be. See M. Gluckman, 'The Peace in the Feud,' *Past and Present*, viii, 1955, 1-14.

30.16 the sum of his rancour: The author suggests that it was the close ties between Ieuan ap Robert and his foster, John ap Maredudd, which led to Hywel ap Rhys's jealousy. That supposition cannot be accepted as the only reason. The unoccupied Crown lands in the township of Gest probably provided a more immediate reason. 'Townships of Gest, Treflys and Ystumllyn', 12-13.

30.26-7 to avoid the fury of the revengement of blood: The feud did not end until Gruffudd ap John ap Goronwy of Gwynfryn who sided, not with his kin descended from Collwyn, but with the sons of John ap Maredudd, was killed in an assault on Hywel ap Rhys's house of Bron-y-foel. His father, John ap Goronwy, was John ap Maredudd's brother-in-law. *Eifionydd*, p. 152; *PACF*, pp. 164, 232. Furthermore, this John ap Goronwy, was among those directed to apprehend the outlaw Ieuan ap Robin on 28 August 1442. The quarrel occurred over fishing rights in Ystumllyn. *Eifionydd*, pp. 24-5.

30.28 partition of the inheritance: i.e. according to partible inheritance. He had married twice, having three sons from the first marriage and two from the second.

30.30 Mathebrwd: A township in the commote of Uwch-dulas, adjacent to the town of Llanrwst, forming a portion of the ancestral lands originally granted in exchange to the author's forbears by the Earl of Lincoln. See 16.15n. Henblas still survives as a farmstead. The lands were granted to Gruffudd Fychan, his second son by his second marriage. Gruffudd married the daughter of Gruffudd ap Madog Fychan. *PACF*, p. 280.

31.2 a mortgage: The 'gage' (mortgage) or *prid* was an important feature of the land market in late medieval Wales. It was a device to facilitate the alienation of land regardless of the fact that Welsh property laws forbade it. Lands, however, could be mortgaged for a consideration over a period of four years but the vendor reserved the right to redeem that property. If it had not been redeemed within four successive quadrennial periods it was deemed to have been alienated to the mortgagee or his descendants. The purchaser in this case was Robin Fychan's son-in-law, Rhys ab Einion Fychan, who paid £12 for the lands. According to Welsh law relating to north Wales a woman could not inherit land and since Robin had no son to succeed him the property (in this particular region) would normally have escheated to the lord of Denbigh. In this instance, however, the inheritor was Ieuan ap Robert (according to the division in 1463) but it was Robin's wish that the land might eventually pass into Rhys's ownership before his own death. At this point he transfers the land to Gruffudd ab Ieuan, the next male heir, in 1496 because he was within three degrees of affinity. Ll. B. Smith, 'The Gage and the Land Market in late Medieval Wales', *Economic History Review*, xxix (iv), 1976, 537-50; D. Jenkins & M. E. Owen (ed.), *The Welsh Law of Women* (1980), pp. 100-101; A. Rh. Wiliam (ed.), *Llyfr Iorwerth* (1960), c. 86, 56. The author has made an error in recording that Gruffudd Fychan had married the daughter of Owain ap Gruffudd. In fact he had married Gruffudd ap Madog's daughter, Margaret. *WG* (1400-1500), vi, p. 1029. S. J. Williams and J. E. Powell (ed.), *Cyfreithiau Hywel Dda yn ôl Llyfr Blegywryd* (1942). p. 75.

31.7 the copy whereof follows: The copy of a release granted by Rhys ab Einion Fychan to Gruffudd ab Ieuan ap Robert (20 October 1495) reads as follows:

> Omnibus Christi fidelibus ad quos presens scriptum pervenerit Rhys ab Einion Fychan salutem in domino sempiternam. Sciatis me prefatum Rhys remisisse relaxasse duodecem libras de *prido* que habeo supra terram Robin Fychan ap Dafydd ap Hywel cum pertinensiis iacentibus et existentibus in commoto de Uwchdulas in dominio de Denbigh Gruffino ab Ieuan ap Robert heredibus et assignatibus suis imperpetuum. Ita videatis quod ego predictus Rhys nec heredes mei neque executores mei neque aliquis alius per nos pro nobis seu nomine nostris aliquid ius statutum titulum clameum interesse sive demandere de vel in predictis duodecim libris neque in predicta terra et tenementa cum pertinensiis ut predicitur iacentes et existenses in commoto predicto et in dominio predicto nec vel in aliqua inde parcella de cetero exigere clamare vel vindicare sive demandere poterimus neque poterit in futurum quovismodo sed ab omni accessione iure statuto titulo clameo interesse et demandere inde imposterum exinde sumus penitus exclusi imperpetuum per presentes.

> In cuius rei testimonium huic presenti scripto meo sigillum meum apposui coram hiis testibus: Maredudd

ap Dafydd ab Einion, Dafydd ap Maredudd ap Dafydd Lloyd, Sir Robert Cowsyth clericus, Thomas Cowsyth et Ieuan ap Dafydd ap Llywelyn cum multis aliis datum vicesimo die mensis Octobris anno regni regis Henrici Septimi undecimo.

32.5 Einion ap Caradog: Caradog was the son of Thomas ap Rhodri ab Owain Gwynedd. See 7.17-21n. Einion was lord of Penychen. The author has mistaken Sir William Caradog (alias Wilcock Cradock) for another. There seems not to have been a son of that name, the confusion being with Wilcock Cradock ap Caradog of Newton (Pembs.) ap Hywel ap Goronwy of the line of Rhydderch ab Iestyn. *WG* (300-1400), iv, pp. 758, 761; Dwnn, i, p. 143.

32.8 Tudur ab Einion: One of the petitions presented to Edward, Prince of Wales, at Kennington in 1305 states that Tudur, lord of Penychen, Pen-y-berth and Baladeulyn, died a year after the conquest of Wales, and that his lands were granted to Queen Eleanor of Castile, and remained in the Crown's possession. *RC*, p. 220; *Eifionydd*, pp. 345-6.

32.11 Gruffudd [was] lord of Ffriwlwyd: He owned lands in Rhos and Rhufoniog as well as Ffriwlwyd in Eifionydd. His grandchildren, Dafydd and Maredudd, were forced to exchange lands with the lord of Denbigh.

32.16 William alias Wilcocke Caradog: This Wilcock Cradock of Newton in Rhos near Milford married Joan, daughter of Mathew Morgan. His great-great grandson, Robert Cradock, married Margaret, daughter of Nicholas Sherborn. *WG* (300-1400), i, p. 147, iv, p. 761.

32.24-5 the posterity of Hywel: Hywel ap Dafydd ap Gruffudd ap Caradog. It is from his line that the author of the *History* traced his direct ancestry.

32.29-30 I presage God's mercy to the kindred: This is special pleading on the author's part. The lineal descent is as follows:

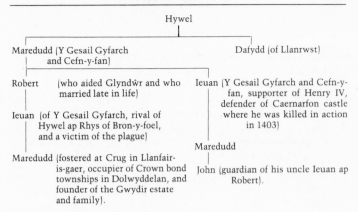

Hywel

Maredudd (Y Gesail Gyfarch
and Cefn-y-fan)

Dafydd (of Llanrwst)

Robert (who aided Glyndŵr and who
married late in life)

Ieuan (of Y Gesail Gyfarch, rival of
Hywel ap Rhys of Bron-y-foel,
and a victim of the plague)

Maredudd (fostered at Crug in Llanfair-
is-gaer, occupier of Crown bond
townships in Dolwyddelan, and
founder of the Gwydir estate
and family).

Ieuan (Y Gesail Gyfarch and Cefn-y-
fan, supporter of Henry IV,
defender of Caernarfon castle
where he was killed in action
in 1403)

Maredudd

John (guardian of his uncle Ieuan ap
Robert).

32.39 to build the house: i.e. in Mathebrwd, Uwchdulas. This section reveals how the author had depended, in part, on oral evidence. The meaning is that because they had insufficient corn to be used as straw to thatch the house, since the corn in the furrow was not ready to meet the circumstances, they reaped the corn exposed to the rain.

33.3 The wars of Lancaster and York: They began in 1460 when the Duke of York claimed the throne of England. J. R. Lander, *The Wars of the Roses* (1965), p. 107 et. seq.

33.10 wasted with fire and sword: A reference to the assistance given to Jasper Tudor during his attacks on Denbighland and the surrounding areas in 1468. *WWR*, pp. 164-70.

33.13 William, earl of Pembroke: The son of Sir William ap Thomas of Raglan and Gwladys, daughter of Sir Dafydd Gam. He was a soldier, statesman and powerful administrator. *DWB*, p. 354.

33.17-18 Edmund, earl of Richmond: Edmund Tudor, father of Henry Tudor, was created earl of Richmond by his half-brother Henry VI in 1452-3 and his brother Jasper created earl of Pembroke at the same time. *DWB*, pp. 985-6.

33.21-4 this Welsh rhyme: Ca. MS.83 (MS.4.101). 220v. 'Pann aeth y tir yn gaeth yn Nankonwy' (in the hand of Huw Machno). See also T. Roberts & I. Williams (ed.), *The Poetical Works of Dafydd Nanmor* (1923), no. lii, p. 117. It is an *englyn* composed anonymously. In his ode to Sir William Herbert, Guto'r Glyn describes his ravages in Gwynedd in 1468.

> Dyrnod anufudd-dod fu,
> Darnio Gwynedd a'i dyrnu

('Because of its disobedience, the province of Gwynedd was struck a heavy blow and devastated'). I. Williams & J. Ll. Williams (ed.), *Gwaith Guto'r Glyn* (1939), xlviii, p. 130. Ieuan ap Tudur Penllyn commented on his outstanding courage in defending Snowdonia. *Gwaith Tudur Penllyn*, p. 38. The *englyn* is translated as follows: 'At Harlech and Denbigh every house was in flames, and Nanconwy in ashes; the year of my Lord 1400; and sixty and eight more'.

33.29 the wrest: The instrument used to tune or tighten the strings of a harp; it was the hollow iron used for this purpose. The reference indicates that Ieuan was a proficient harpist as well as a soldier. Ability to play the harp was considered to be one of the twenty-four feats expected of an accomplished *uchelwr*. See 36.29n.

34.1 to cold coals: 'Kynau Nanconwy yn varwor' ('Burning Nanconwy to cold ashes').

34.8 his uncle: Wynn is completely confused at this point. What he is trying to say is that John ap Maredudd was the son of his cousin german. The section should read: 'John ap Maredudd, being son to Ieuan ap Robert ap Maredudd's cousin german, not withstanding ...'. Robert ap Maredudd's late marriage can cause much confusion. Ieuan ap Robert was Maredudd ab Ieuan's cousin and a first cousin once removed of John ap Maredudd.

34.23 Brynsyllty: *PACF*, p. 221. A farmstead which still exists in the township of Mathebrwd.

34.31 Rhys Llywelyn ap Dafydd: It was his father who received the nosegay (or bouquet of flowers) from Robin Achwr (the Genealogist) at Llanrwst in the presence of Maredudd ab Ieuan ap Robert, the founder of the Gwydir estate.

34.33 Lancellet: Probably Lanncelot, a weaver, who dwelt in Mathebrwd. 'Tyddyn Lancelet' was valued at £1.12s.0d. in 1685, UCNW. Mostyn MS. 5440. 'Tyddyn Lancellott' is referred to in a lease in 1734-5, UCNW, Mostyn MS. 1855. Gruffudd Wynn was the second son of John Wyn ap Maredudd of Gwydir and brother of Morus Wynn (Sir John Wynn's father) who inherited the estate on his father's death in 1559. Gruffudd obtained his father's lands in the vicinity of

Llanrwst and acquired Y Berthddu, south of the town, through his marriage to Gwen, co-heiress of Robert Salusbury of Y Berthddu and Cae'r Milwr. The land referred to here was situated in Mathebrwd and augmented a growing estate established by Gruffudd Wynn, mainly in Uwchdulas. *PACF*, 184.

34.35-6 into so little parts did the gavelkind ... chop our inheritance: In this section the author is particularly critical of the destructive effects of partible inheritance upon the economy and ancestral pride of his kindred in Uwchdulas.

34.40 what common ancestor they were descended: They were descendants of Ednyfed Fychan ap Cynwrig, seneschal to Llywelyn the Great through his grandson Rhys Fychan ap Rhys. Branches were eventually established in the townships of Tybrith and Garthgarmon, adjacent to Mathebrwd and Bryniog in that township. *WG* (300-1400), iv, p. 676; *Dwnn*, ii, p. 284. The author was not correct in assuming that all freeholders in Tybrith were descendants of Ednyfed. Many were descended from Marchweithian. *WG*, iv, p. 699; T. A. Glenn, *The Family of Griffith of Garn and Plasnewydd in the County of Denbigh* (1934), p. 238. The author at first claimed (but later scored out) that most of these inhabitants in Tybrith and Garthgarmon were related to him. Ca.MS. 83 [MS.4.101].98v. ['Where the most parte of the Towne, blessed be God, is in our blood and kindred are mine and my cozen Hugh Gwynns'].

35.5-6 they were foreigners: i.e. either that they came from the area where foreigners (Englishmen) had settled in and around Denbigh or that they sprang from clans 'foreign' or alien to those in Mathebrwd and surrounding townships. They were the descendants of Rhodri ab Owain Gwynedd in Rhos and Rhufoniog and, by means of exchange, they were moved to Uwchdulas. See 13.23-4n. Rhys Llywelyn ap Dafydd, a freeholder, was the son of Llywelyn to whom a nosegay was given in the presence of Maredudd ab Ieuan ap Robert. See 34.31n.

35.9-10 Mathebrwd is in our blood: The author adds later the sentence that most of the tenants in Mathebrwd were kinsmen of the Wynns. The lands were principally owned by Owen Wynn of Cae'r Milwr, the author's uncle, with whom he quarrelled concerning rights of transport from Trefriw to Cae'r Milwr. See 47.21n. The lands were purchased by Sir John Wynn from John Wyn ab Owen. NLW Add. MS.465E.375.

35.11 Robin Achwr: Robert ab Ieuan ap Hywel (Robin or Robert Iachwr) a genealogist of some repute and disciple of Gruffudd Hiraethog. He probably was acquainted with Sir Thomas Wiliems since both were in the fellowship of Gruffudd. He compiled pedigrees for north Wales families such as Myfyrian and Plas Newydd (Anglesey) and Mostyn (Flintshire). NLW Peniarth MSS. 134.364; 136.20; 139.3; 176.167; 177.97; 298. W. O. Williams, 'Social Order', 167.9; F. Jones, 'An Approach to Welsh Genealogy', 365, 367, 374. Wynn's great-grandfather was Maredudd ab Ieuan ap Robert who had settled at Gwydir c.1500.

35.13 chwaraefa gampau: A hurling match; athletic meeting. Gardd-y-felin was probably the land where Y Felin Isaf and Cae'r Felin are sited at present in Llanrwst. It was later acquired by Gruffudd Wynn of Y Berthddu. UCNW Mostyn MS.5972.

35.17-18 deliver this nosegay to the best gentleman: Maredudd most probably expected Robin to return the nosegay to him.

35.25-6 for it is an ancient received saying: i.e. the saying (explained here in the author's own words) contained in the doggerel which follows.

35.28-31 When Adam delved ...: A familiar doggerel first cited in a slightly different version by Richard Rolle of Hample in *Religious Pieces from R. Thornton* MS.75 c.1340. The priest, John Ball, executed in 1381 for his part in the Peasants' Revolt, is made to utter the first two lines quoted here in his 'sermon' on equality composed as part of the play *Life and Death of Jack Strawe* (1593), composed possibly by George Peele, a London actor and playwright. R. B. Dobson (ed.), *The Peasants' Revolt of 1381* (1970), p. 390. James Pilkington (c.1520-76), first Protestant Bishop of Durham, in his *Aggers* quotes the rhyme almost as it is recorded by Wynn. *Oxford Dictionary of English Proverbs* (1970), p. 3; G. G. Perry (ed.), *Religious Pieces* ... edited from *Robert Thornton's MS.*, Early English Text Society (1867), vii, p. 79.

35.32 a great temporal blessing: The oft-quoted statement which refers specifically at this point to Llewelyn ap Dafydd (and not the author himself) who received the nosegay. Gentlemen of the 'first head' were *nouveaux riches*, upstarts who possessed no gentlemanly pedigrees. *Dict. of Eng. Prov.*, p. 299. The term 'first head'' was used with reference to deer and was applied to a young buck of the second year called a 'buck of the first head'. The fluidity of the economic structure increased social mobility and led to the emergence of new families claiming gentility. W. O. Williams, 'Social Order', loc. cit.

36.1-5 The conditional promise: On his deathbed King David told his son and heir Solomon: 'Fulfil your duty to the Lord your God: conform to his ways, observe his statutes and his commandments ... so that you may prosper in whatever you do and wherever you turn, and that the Lord may fulfil this promise that he made about me: If your descendants take care to walk faithfully in my sight with all their heart and with all their soul, you shall never lack a successor on the throne of Israel' (1 *Kings* 2, 3-4).

36.6 The Rechabites: The religious order in Israel founded by Jonadab, son of Rechab, which preached against Canaanite luxury and advocated a return to asceticism. Its members abstained from drinking wine. 'We will not drink wine for our forefather Jonadab, son of Rechab, laid this command on us: 'You shall never drink wine, neither you nor your children ... these are the words of the Lords of Hosts the God of Israel: Because you have kept the command of Jonadab your ancestor and obeyed all his instructions and carried out all that he told you to do ... Jonadab son of Rechab shall not want a descendant to stand before me for all time'.' (*Jeremiah* 35, 7, 18-19).

36.12 Meillionen: The house of Meillionen on the Prior's Land in Beddgelert; the home of Humphrey Jones, a kinsman of the Wynns and receiver of the King's revenues in north Wales in the early seventeenth century. The rock where the cave (known as Ogof Filen or Ogof Elen) is situated in the upper reaches of Cwm Meillionen through which ran the river Colwyn. W. Jones, *Plwyf Beddgelert: ei Hynafiaethau a'i Gofiannau* (1862), p. 31. The reputed site of the forays of Ieuan ap Robert is Bwlch-y-fatel in Nanmor, ibid., p. 66.

36.15 Nanhwynan: Also called Nanhwynain, the original form of Nant Gwynant in Beddgelert, *ELISG*, p. 70; a township granted by Llywelyn ab Iorwerth to the Cistercian abbey of Aberconwy c. 1200. G. A. Gresham 'Aberconwy Charter', 150-7.

36.18 under his hand and seal: see 28.33-27.9n.

36.25 continual debate: The prime reason for the animosity most probably was the competition between them for the occupation of lands in the township of Gest.

36.29 to try masteries: The twenty-four feats which an *uchelwr* was expected to master. The ten physical feats were termed feats of valour, six of which were (a) strength (b) running (c) jumping (d) swimming (e) wrestling (f) horse-riding. The remaining four were (a) shooting (b) duelling with sword and buckler (c) fencing with a two-handed sword (d) duelling with a quarterstaff. See J. Davies, *Antiquae Linguae Britannicae . . . Dictionarium Duplex* (1632).

36.35 healthing: i.e. drinking of health; toasting. Not only was the keeping of the winehouse considered to be a source of profit; it was also a source of disorder. Flenley, op. cit., p. 15.

36.37 draft: A plot or artifice; applied to mean a plan or devising a scheme.

37.2 Llanfihangel-y-Pennant: The free township of Pennant was co-terminus with the ecclesiastical parish of Llan-fihangel-y-Pennant. The hurling or archery contest took place near John ap Maredudd's house at Ystumcegid. R. Kelso, *The Doctrine of the English Gentleman in the Sixteenth Century* (1964), chap. viii, pp. 149-56.

37.17 Robin ab Inco: Robert ab Inigo, said to be the son of the poet Inco Brydydd (c. 1480) who composed an eulogy to Ieuan ap Robert, *DWB*, 415 (where the details recorded are incorrect); J. Jones, *Enwogion Sir Gaernarfon* (1922), pp. 149-50; *Mynegai i Farddoniaeth Gaeth*, p. 1855.

37.24-5 in sort: i.e. a company of friends, kindred or allies.

37.27-8 Ieuan ap Robert's wife: i.e. Catherine, Hywel's younger sister, Ieuan's first wife. She died soon after (but not necessarily as a consequence of) her courageous act in this encounter.

38.4 *canllaw:* In this case probably a wooden hand-rail.

38.7 *Furor arma ministrat:* 'Unthinking rage furnishes its weapons'. Vergil, *Aeneid*, i, 1.150. H. R. Fairclough (ed.),

Virgil (1960), p. 250. It is used in a passage about a tumultuous mob using whatever weapons or missiles are at hand.

38.10 greatly over-matched: The impression given is that the companies were large, especially Hywel ap Rhys's, but the extent of such encounters should not be exaggerated. It has been argued that clan rivalries were not as extensive as supposed. In this particular incident, in spite of the violence and serious injuries caused, only one person, namely the butcher, was killed. P. Williams, 'The Welsh Borderland under Queen Elizabeth,' *WHR*, i, No. i, 1960, 20. 27.13, 30.8-9n.

38.26-7 the parson of Llanfrothen took a child: It is not possible to date these incidents but this child was probably Maredudd, Ieuan's son by his first wife (the sister of Hywel ap Rhys), and he was subsequently moved to Crug in Llanfair-is-gaer. See 49.7-8n.

38.40 damned crew: i.e. Hywel ap Rhys's faction.

39.4 Ogo'r Llychwin: i.e. in the parish of Llanfrothen. Ogof Llychwin was a Wynn tenement in that parish valued, in 1569, at £4 per annum. NLW. Llansteffan MS.179 (b) 59.

39.5 Chirkland: The march lordship of Chirk (Swydd y Waun), previously part of Powys Fadog. In October 1282 it was granted by Edward I to Roger Mortimer, third son of Roger de Mortimer, Baron Wigmore. It was the scene of disorder in the fifteenth century with the continual change of ownership. Sir Robert Trefor of Plas Teg in Ystrad Alun died in 1487 and his wife Catherine, daughter of Llywelyn ab Ithel of Plas Teg, married Rhys ap Hywel of Ystumllyn, Hywel ap Rhys's son. The author, therefore, is inaccurate. The Trefor connection appears through Hywel ap Rhys's daughter-in-law, not his wife. *PACF*, pp. 254, 264.

39.10 llawrudd: 'llawf' (hand) + 'rhudd' (red), red-handed i.e. a murderer with blood on his hand.

39.14 Oswestryland: A small march lordship owned by the Fitzalan family early in the twelfth century. They became Lords of Oswestry and Clun. *DWB*, p. 263.

39.14-15 two sects or kindreds: The frequent changing of lords under the Crown in Chirk during the fifteenth century led to social and political dislocation in a region where a strong sense of kindred allegiance prevailed. The contest for local offices resulted in the prominence of some families at the expense of others. Robert Trefor (d. 1492) was Steward of Denbigh and Justice of north Wales. G. P. Jones (ed.), *The Extent of Chirkland, 1391-93* (1933), intro., xiii-iv; *DWB*, p. 978. The author is referring to the contest between family factions for the special powers which offices in the March gave them. George Owen refers to the 'jura regalia' possessed by the lords: 'And diverse small meane lordships in Wales, in process of time, and at such tyme as their chiefe Lords went into England, and leave their tenantes and servantes holding Lordships of theim, to be their Stewards and Lieutenauntes ... did usurpe and encroche diverse authorities and Jurisdictions regall to themselves ... whereupon you shall finde great quarrels and suites of later tymes'. *A Treatise of Lordshipps Marchers in Wales* in H. Owen (ed.), *The Description of Penbrokeshire*, (1906), iii, pp. 174-5. For the importance of officeholding in this seemingly turbulent period in the northern March see *Aspects of Welsh History*, pp. 308-10.

39.17 the Kyffins: Of Glascoed, Llansilin, represented by Hywel ap Morus Gethin of Oswestry (d. 1481) and descended from Bleddyn ap Cynfyn. Morus obtained Glascoed through his marriage to the heiress. *HPF*, iv, pp. 263-4; Dwnn, i, p. 307.

39.21 kept as very precious jewels: The once laudable custom of 'arddel' was abused in the March whereby notorious criminals from neighbouring lordships and elsewhere could, by means of advowry payments, obtain the protection of a lord and immunity from other jurisdictions. Such a practice exacerbated the chronic disorder prevalent in the borderlands. W. Rees, *The Union of England and Wales* (1948), pp. 9-10. Such men were regarded as being particularly valuable in the service of unscrupulous lords in such disordered times which may account for the author substituting 'juells' for 'dwellers' in the text. Ca. MS.83.100r.

39.27 Maredudd ap Hywel: The son of Hywel ap Morus Gethin of Oswestry. His ancestor, Madog ap Madog Goch, adopted the name Kyffin (from Cyffin, near Llanerfyl, where he was fostered) to distinguish him from his father. *PACF*, pp. 196, 198; *WG* (300-1400), i, pp. 35, 38.

39.28 a Kin: The relationship was not close; Owen Kyffin (of the Maenan, Llanrwst branch of the family) had married the daughter of Rhys ab Einion Fychan of the house of Penwyn, Nanconwy. See 18.5n. Her mother was Catherine, only daughter of Robin Fychan ap Dafydd ap Hywel of Henblas in Mathebrwd township.

39.36 Tŷ-yn-Rhos: Or Tŷ'n-y-Rhos in Minffordd, Merioneth: an old inn now called 'Rhos'. Until recently 'Brewery y Rhos' had been carved on an adjoining cowshed. F. Edwards, 'Penrhyndeudraeth', *JMHRS*, i (no. 3), 1951, 197-8; *HGF* (1878), p. 62. According to *HGF* (1878), p. 62, it 'was a public house unto 40 years ago. It is just under the Castell Deudraeth drive and close to Plasnewydd. Before the embankment was made, the ford across the Glaslyn was near it'.

39.39-40.1 *Hwyr y dial fo i dadmaeth:* 'The wrong done to a foster father is not avenged in haste'. Such a saying may have arisen from the fact that, since no blood affinities or *galanas* payments were matters of consideration in such circumstances in early medieval Wales, the act of vengeance was not treated as urgently as would have been the case if clan relations were involved.

40.7-28 This passage displays the immunity which criminals enjoyed. In this case they were partisans of the Trefors who would defend them against any attempt on the part of law officers to seek their extradition so that they might stand trial at Caernarfon.

40.17 for a fine to the lord: A common practice in the March lordships whereby felons, or their partisans, would pay substantial fines for the remission of the proper penalty which, in cases of felony, was execution. Fines or exactions collected for the 'Redemption of any Murther, or any other Felony' were forbidden by law in 1534. *SW*, p. 57.

40.20 new ordinance of Wales: i.e. St. 27 Hen. VIII, c. 26, or the 'Act of Union' (1536). Mawddwy, then in the lordship of Powys, was notorious for its disorder in the fifteenth century. It was attached to the shire of Merioneth in that statute (cap. 19), *SW*, 87; J. B. Smith, 'The Regulation of the Frontier of Meirionnydd in the Fifteenth Century', *JMHRS*, v (no. ii) 1966, 106-10.

40.30 Dafydd Llwyd ap Gruffudd Fychan: Of Cwm Ystradllyn, son of Gruffudd Fychan (alias Wynn) and grandson of Ieuan ap Robert by his second wife Gwenhwyfar (or Mallt), daughter of Madog Fychan of Llwyndyrus. *PACF*, p. 281; *WG* (1400-1500), v, p. 850. He was an attendant to Hugh ap Robert of Plas Iolyn, Ysbyty Ifan who became abbot of Aberconwy (d. 1528). Both his grandfather and father served Henry VII and Wolsey respectively. *PACF*, p. 204. His brother was the notorious ecclesiastical commissioner, Dr Ellis Prys of Plas Iolyn. 'History of Aberconwy', pp. 139, 159-60.

40.32 Mr. Robert ap Rhys: Chaplain to Cardinal Wolsey and descendant of Marchweithian. He was granted lands by Henry VIII in Dolgynwal (Ysbyty Ifan) and Penllyn. His father, Rhys ap Maredudd (Rhys Fawr), was Standard Bearer to Henry Tudor at Bosworth. *DWB*, p. 805; *PACF*, p. 204; E. Roberts, 'Teulu Plas Iolyn', *TDHS*, xiii, 1964, 57-9.

41.3-4 Lowri ferch Hywel: i.e. Lowri heiress of Hywel ap Gruffudd Goch of Rhos, a descendant of Marchudd. *PACF*, pp. 204, 290; *HGF* (1878), p. 63. This passage is yet another comment on Ieuan's physical stature. The 'spur' is the hind part of a wooden settle.

41.8 'Gallt y Morfa Hir'. It cannot be identified but it was a hill probably south of Llanfrothen adjacent to 'Morfa Gwyllt' and 'Hir Ynys'.

41.21 Ieuan ap Robert's mother: She was Angharad, daughter of Dafydd ap Llywelyn ap Dafydd of Cefnmelgoed. Her mother, Margaret, was the daughter and not, as the author states, the sister of Rhydderch ab Ieuan Llwyd. Dwnn, ii, p. 225(n.1).

41.31 the assizes: Justices Sessions in the Northern Principality were set up in the Statute of Wales (1284) by Edward I. They were normally held at Caernarfon castle before the Chief Justice of North Wales who administered civil and criminal justice. Waters, *Edwardian Settlement*, p. 123ff.

41.39 Carreg-y-gwalch: The rocky ledge immediately above Gwydir mansion. Beneath it was built Gwydir Uchaf house in 1604 chiefly for entertaining guests. 'Gwell yw'r glyn a'r graig las' ('He preferred the safety and protection of the gorge and the rock'). *Gwaith Tudur Penllyn*, p. 4.

42.11 wort: Plants or herbs fermented to produce 'metheglin' ('meddyglyn'), a spiced or medicated mead which, when prepared, was very hot. 'Metheglyn, whiche is moste used in Wales, by reason of hotte herbes boyled with hony, is hotter than mead'. Sir Thomas Elyot, *Castle of Helthe* (1541), p. 36; See Ca. MS.83; 227v. for a reference to the recipe for 'the Making of right good Metheglin by Doctor Lobell, a nertherlander in anno 1610'.

42.19-20 the country did rise: It is difficult to believe that the 'great numbers' referred to implied that the gathering was extraordinarily large. Family feuds did not necessarily entail large numbers of combatants and hardly any widespread upheaval was caused. It does not seem that Y Gesail Gyfarch had been built anew after the Glyndŵr Revolt. The author's description of it suggests that it was the old timber structure repaired with small outhouses. C. A. Gresham, 'Platform Houses in North-West Wales', 37-8; *Eifionydd*, p. 86.

42.31 Ieuan Grach: Ifan Grach ap Siencyn of Y Gellilydan, parish of Maentwrog, a descendant of Iorwerth Goch, was related to the Rhiwgoch family of Trawsfynydd. Dwnn, ii, 89. Ieuan ap Robert was his kinsman through Ifan's mother, Elsbeth, daughter of Maredudd ap Hywel of Cefn-y-fan and Y Gesail Gyfarch. *WG*, iii, pp. 457, 572.

45.9 See 28.17n.

45.11 his three eldest sons: i.e. his three sons by his first marriage to Hywel ap Rhys's sister, a point which again emphasises the fact that feuds between clans were generally restrained in primitive societies. Nor were the numbers involved very large and the author does tend to exaggerate for effect. The sons were Hywel's nephews and were prepared to forego their differences.

45.13 Enmity did continue: The rivalry continued over landed interests between the houses of Bron-y-foel and Ystumcegid, and the author, at this point, graphically describes the final assault on Bron-y-foel.

45.16 Gruffudd ap John ap Goronwy: A descendant of Collwyn ap Tangno and grandson of the founder of Gwynfryn. Although his grandfather was a brother to Hywel's grandfather, his father's sister, Gwenhwyfar, had married John ap Maredudd, a family tie which probably accounted for the support. Men who had returned from service in the French wars were in a position to cause social disorder. Fighting was quite often their sole occupation and experienced soldiers contributed significantly to the armies in the dynastic wars. Gruffudd ap John ap Goronwy was in a position to lead unruly and disreputable men on such occasions as described at this point. C. L. Kingsford, *Prejudice and Promise in 15th Century England* (1962), pp. 75-6. For the background to Welsh military service in France see A. D. Carr, 'Welshmen and the Hundred Years War', *WHR*, iv (no. 1), 1968, 26-46.

45.16-22 The family had consolidated its hold over property along the right bank of the river Dwyfor, in parts of Treflys, in freehold land in the bond township of Gest and in lands at Abererch and Penrhos in Llŷn. As owner of freehold lands in Gest and Treflys he probably claimed fishing rights in Llyn Ystumllyn. Gruffudd ap John ap Goronwy was descended from Collwyn and Einion ap Gruffudd (the brother of Sir Hywel y Fwyall). He lived at Gwynfryn in the township of Rhwng Dwyfor a Dwyfach. His grandfather was a brother to Hywel ap Rhys's grandfather, but his father's sister had married John ap Maredudd of Cefn-y-fan (Ystumcegid), and it was this connection which probably accounts for John's assistance in the feud. Following the incident at Llyn Ystumllyn Gruffydd obtained the aid of his cousins, sons of John ap Maredudd, in an attack on Bron-y-foel. *Eifionydd*, pp. 151-2, 212; *PACF*, p. 164.

45.23-4 in such dugeon: i.e. resentment, ill-will or offended indignation.

45.32 beaver: The lower face-guard of a helmet.

45.23-34 The attack followed the practice of siege-warfare in France at the time. The out-houses were burnt and the doors gutted by burning straw. The house was thus filled with dense smoke with the intention of forcing Hywel ap Rhys to surrender. P. Earle, *The Life and Times of Henry V* (1972), pp. 153-8. A glaive (M.Eng. 'glaive', O.Fr. 'glaive'), is a broad sword. It can also mean a spear or lance (Cf. 'glaif' in Welsh). It is probably a sword in this context.

46.10 Morus ap John ap Maredudd: He married Angharad, daughter of Ellis (Eliza) ap Gruffudd ab Einion and probably inherited ancestral land in Y Clenennau, his father's principal holding in Penyfed. A tradition does exist, however, that it was a foster-father, a smallholder in Y Clenennau, and not his father who gave him his stake in land. C. A. Gresham, 'Origins of Clenennau', 336-7; *Eifionydd*, pp. 34-7, 102-7. In a period of tension and strife Morus seems to have been more circumspect and responsible than his other kinsmen and became the founder of the Clenennau estate in Eifionydd. *MWS*, pp. 238-40. Together with his son Ellis he purchased many lands in Pennant township. On his death in 1512 his properties in Eifionydd were inherited by Ellis. *PACF*, p. 218.

46.14 who was cousin german removed: Their fathers were first cousins, the grandfathers, Hywel ab Ieuan of Bron-y-foel and Gronw ab Ieuan of Gwynfryn being blood-brothers. Hywel ap Rhys and Gruffudd ap John ap Goronwy, therefore, were second cousins. *PACF*, p. 264.

46.18 kept and defended him: Such was the anger of Gruffudd ap John ap Goronwy's kindred following his death that Hywel ap Rhys, by then an aged man, had to be guarded very closely when escorted to Caernarfon castle by Morus ap John ap Maredudd.

46.19-20 Owain ap John ap Maredudd: The younger son of John ap Maredudd and a turbulent fellow. He received Ystum-cegid and lands in the townships of Abercain, Treferthyr and Treflys. He was doubtless determined to maintain his inherit-ance despite the attacks of Hywel. 'Origins of Clenennau', loc. cit.

46.21 like a camp: i.e. they moved gradually like an army on campaign.

46.28 for the fear of the kindred: Hywel's friends and followers discreetly kept at a safe distance since they feared an ambush which might cause his death.

46.30 constable of Caernarfon castle: In the Statute of Wales (1284), the Constable of Caernarfon castle was made respons-ible for the custody of prisoners and their appearance in court to stand trial. *CCQSR*, xlvii.

46.31 assizes: i.e. of the Justice's Sessions at Caernarfon.

47.2 his mother's kindred: His mother was Gwerfyl, daughter of Rhys Gethin of Hendre Rhys Gethin near Betws-y-coed. *PACF*, p. 264. The author had added (but had scored out) the following phrase to complete the sentence: 'a note worth the observation'.

47.6-7 being four descents besides himself: The author goes on to explain this statement in greater detail in the following paragraphs. It was the ties of marriage, however, and not loss of face, as Wynn seems to suggest, which accounted for this estrangement from Bron-y-foel itself, but the family still owned the lands in Treflys.

47.10 his first wife: His first wife was Catherine, daughter of Llywelyn ab Ithel of Plas Teg, Ystrad Alun, widow of Robert Trefor, a kin of the Trefors of Bryncunallt. *PACF*, p. 254; *HPF*, v, p. 259. His second wife was Margaret, daughter of Hugh Conwy Hen of Bryneuryn, Llandrillo, the widow of Rheinallt ap Meurig of Glynllugwy in the upper Llugwy valley adjacent to Trewydir township ('His next neighbour'), a great-grandson of Hywel Coetmor. Dwnn, ii, p. 102. Maredudd's daughter, Gwen, by his third wife, Margaret, daughter of Morus ap John ap Maredudd, married Owain ap Rheinallt ap Meurig of Glynllugwy, Dwnn, ii, pp. 132-3; Ca. MS.83 (MS.4.101), 134r. It was Rhys ap Hywel ap Rhys who helped Maredudd ab Ieuan ap Robert, the author's great-grandfather, to build the original house at Gwydir and he was buried in Llanrwst parish church. *PACF*, pp. 264, 290, 394.

47.16 William Dafydd ab Elis Eyton: Grandson of Elis Eyton of Rhiwabon. His father, Dafydd Elis Eyton, had married Marsli, daughter of Hywel ap Rhys of Bron-y-foel. This Rhys ap Hywel was, therefore, Wiliam ap Dafydd Elis Eyton's uncle. *HPF*, ii, p. 175; *PACF*. p. 264.

47.20 Cadwaladr ap Robert Wyn: Of Hafod-y-maidd, Cerrig-y-drudion in Hiraethog. He married Elen, daughter of Gruffudd Wynn of Berthddu, second son of John Wyn ap Maredudd, and the author's uncle. *HPF*, v, p. 392; *PACF*, p. 184.

47.21 Owen Wynn: Gruffudd Wynn's younger brother of Cae'r Milwr, who obtained the inheritance on his marriage to Elin, co-heiress of Robert Salusbury of Cae'r Milwr. *PACF*, p. 228. It was with him that the author quarrelled over right of way. See 48.2n.

47.23 Thomas ap Rhys ap Hywel: The grandson of the notorious Hywel ap Rhys of Bron-y-foel.

Interior of St. Gwyddelan's church, Dolwyddelan
(Crown Copyright Royal Commission on Ancient and Historical Monuments in Wales)

The Gwydir Memorial in St. Gwyddelan's church, Dolwyddelan
(Crown Copyright, Royal Commission on Ancient and Historical Monuments in Wales)

47.24 Hopesland: 'Estyn' or 'Queen's Hope' or 'Yr Hob' adjoining Ystrad Alun in Flintshire, a commote (originally in Powys Fadog) which became the Norman lordship of Hope or Hopedale. It formed part of the new shire in 1284. Since his mother's lands were situated in Ystrad Alun the author may be referring here to Moldesdale and not Hopesland.

47.25 Cadwaladr ap Thomas: His wife was Eleanor (or Elen), daughter of Rhydderch ap Dafydd of Myfyrian in Anglesey, of whom he had three children. *PACF*, p. 264.

47.28 my uncle Owen Wynn's daughter: He married Elin, daughter of Owen Wynn of Cae'r Milwr and the author's cousin. He was born in 1557 and died in 1597. He built for himself a new house called Ystumllyn in that township, a fine example of Elizabethan architecture. *Eifionydd*, p. 164; *PACF*, p. 228.

47.30-1 one Doctor Davies: John Davies or Siôn Dafydd Rhys, physician and grammarian, a native of Llanfaethlu, Anglesey. He went to the continent in 1555 and graduated Doctor of Medicine at the University of Sienna in 1562 or 1563. He eventually settled at Brecon in the early 1580s. In 1592 he produced a Welsh grammar in Latin entitled *Cambro-brytannicae Cymraecaeve Linguae Institutiones et Rudimenta*, dedicated to Sir Edward Stradling of St. Donat's. T. Jones, *History of Brecknockshire*, iv (1930), pp. 171-2; T. Parry, 'Siôn Dafydd Rhys,' *Y Llenor*, ix, 1930, 157-65, 234-41; x, 1931, 35-46; R. G. Gruffydd, 'The Life of Dr. John Davies of Brecon', *TCS*, 1971 (Pt. ii), 175-90; *DWB*, pp. 845-6..

47.32 This man's name: i.e. Ellis ap Cadwaladr, a person known for his integrity and good counsel.

48.2 grew to a great heat: It appears that Ellis's good counsel (he died in 1597) on this occasion had prevented the author and his uncle from going to law in this matter. They had tried to settle their differences earlier c.1595 in the Court of Exchequer with regard to Crown meadows and fisheries and right of way to Trefriw mill. E. G. Jones (ed.), *Exchequer Proceedings concerning Wales Henry VIII—Elizabeth* (1939), pp. 59-60.

48.9 with headiness and rashness: This is a reference to the impetuosity and indiscretions of his great-grandfather,

Hywel ap Rhys, which led to a decline in the fortunes of Bron-y-foel.

48.12 bridled my choler: The irascibility or bad temper for which the author was notorious. On another occasion, however, he considered himself to be 'a quiet orderly and civill gentleman'. NLW MS. 9051E.141.

48.14-49.5 The following two paragraphs are but a repetition of what the author has already explained. Ieuan ap Robert inherited Robin Fychan's lands because he was related to him within three degrees of affinity, their fathers being cousins. See 30.16n.

48.25-26 bad customs: i.e. partible inheritance and the custom, adhered to more strictly in Gwynedd, of allowing a male within three degrees of affinity to inherit instead of a female. Robin Fychan, in this case, could mortgage the land which would thereby not escheat on his death to the lord of Denbigh. On Robin Fychan's death, however, Ieuan ap Robert inherited the lands of Henblas in Mathebrwd and returned to Rhys ab Einion Fychan his £12. *HW*, i, pp. 229-30; *Welsh Law of Women*, pp. 100-2.

49.1-5 The author raises an old issue at this point, namely that since he believed Robert ap Maredudd to have been the elder of two brothers his son Ieuan ap Robert had inherited the lands. If Ieuan ap Maredudd had been the elder of the two then John ap Maredudd (Ieuan's protector), says Wynn, would have inherited. His reasoning, however, is doubtful. John ap Maredudd belonged to a different generation and was not within the degree of affinity to be able to claim Robin Fychan's patrimony according to the laws.

49.6 Maredudd, son to Ieuan: The fourth and last section of the chronicle begins at this point. It traces the early career of Maredudd ab Ieuan ap Robert, the founder of the Wynn family who established himself in the commote of Nanconwy. It was he who laid the foundations of the Gwydir estate in that commote.

49.7-8 an honest freeholder: The identity of this freeholder is not known but it appears that, following the murder of the parson of Llanfrothen, he was willing to foster Maredudd so that he might avoid the wrath of his mother's kindred at Bron-y-foel. Maredudd was born c.1460. Crug stands in the parish of Llanfair-is-gaer in the commote of Is Gwyrfai, north-east of Caernarfon. The author is vague about the place and its owner and about the extent of Maredudd's inheritance there. It is not impossible that the freeholder was a scion of the Cochwillan family which later established a prominent branch at Y Faenol nearby. G. Roberts, 'Biographical Notes', *BBCS*, xvii (Pt. 1), 1956, 48-49; *WG* (1400-1500), v, 851. Crug and other adjacent properties were inherited by John Wynn ap Maredudd; later references appear to lands held by the Wynns of Gwydir in Llanfair-is-gaer and at Crug. *CWP*, nos. 451, 1135; BM. Add.MS.8533. The author himself held five small tenements in and around Crug and had built a 'new house' there. *NLW*. MS.463(b).74; *RCAM, Caerns (Central)*, p. 200. Morus Wynn bequeathed all the glass of the windows at Gwydir and Crug to his son and heir.

49.13 **to have a patron:** It was this movement which initially laid the basis of Maredudd's fortunes and enabled him to acquire a taste of urban life and the social graces. The custom of fosterage was, in some ways, similar to the protection granted in the March lordships but without the military element. Elder sons fostered in this way became gradually more estranged from their blood-brothers. In a community where physical violence was a serious threat responsible men became more inclined to rely on the support of 'patrons' rather than on the existing legal framework even though, as in this case, the patron resided but a few miles from Caernarfon itself. *HW*, i, pp. 309-10.

49.14-15 **though they sought him never so far off:** Rural communities in those days were confined to the immediate locality, usually to the township or commote. It is hardly likely that a patron or protector in the vicinity of Caernarfon would be troubled by any retaliation from Eifionydd (except in more pressing circumstances) because Arllechwedd Uchaf would be virtually unknown to all apart from those who had occasion to attend the courts or conduct business at Caernarfon.

49.17-18 **In those days Caernarfon flourished:** The author describes Caernarfon, the legal and administrative centre of the Northern Principality since 1284, as a flourishing town. The Chamberlain was the head of the Exchequer (the accounting branch of the treasury) and was subordinate to the central exchequer at Westminster. The Chancery, headed by the Chancellor or Controller, recorded all moneys paid out by the Chamberlain. The Justice of North Wales kept his Sessions which usually met quarterly to deal with pleas of the Crown, English criminal law having been made official in the Principality by the Statute of Wales (1284). Caernarfon castle was the centre for all governmental activities but the Exchequer and Chancery were, at an early stage, occasions rather than specific places. In 1610, however, Speed's map of the town located the Exchequer at the junction of High Street and Pepper Lane, west of the town. *BMW*, p. 72; *CCQSR*, liv; Waters, op. cit., pp. 123-33, 134-48.

49.22 civility and learning: Two main features of the new lay society which was emerging during this period of new developments in social life and education. Civility implied conformity to the principle of social order through the acquisition of liberal education; a sense of urbanity was gradually emerging in the local towns. F. Caspari, *Humanism and the Social Order in Tudor England* (1954), pp. 132-56; J. Simon, *Education and Society in Tudor England* (1967), chap. xiv, pp. 333-68. Such qualities were exemplified in Castiglione's *Il Cortegiano* (1528) and Sir Thomas Elyot's *The Boke named the Governour* (1531); J. G. Jones, 'Educational Activity among the Wynns of Gwydir', *TCHS*, xlii, 1981, 8-11; W. P. Griffith, 'Beth oedd y Dyn Tuduraidd?', in D. G. Jones and J. E. Jones (ed.), *Bosworth a'r Tuduriaid* (1985), pp. 31-9.

49.23 they were called the lawyers . . .: The three most important boroughs in the northern Principality, created by Edward I around fortified castles. Lawyers, merchants and gentry represented the three main social orders which were thriving in that period. Caernarfon naturally, had acquired a reputation for its legal expertise, many of its burgesses having been associated with administrative or legal posts or having descended from families with a background of public service. *BMW*, p. 80. The re-grouping of tenants' rights by Bartholomew Bolde of Conwy in the mid-fifteenth century is indicative of the growing prosperity of urban inhabitants. Ibid., pp. 195-227; C. A. Gresham, 'The Bolde Rental' (Bangor MSS. 1939), *TCHS*, xxvi, 1965, 31-49. The Bulkeley family had entrenched itself at Beaumaris by mid-century, acquiring prestige locally, developing the port, holding offices and positions of influence and establishing matrimonial connections with other north Wales families. D. C. Jones, 'The Bulkeleys of Beaumaris, 1440-1547', *TAAS*, 1961, 1-9.

49.32-3 a matter of great moment in those days: an oft-quoted sentence to indicate how much emphasis was placed by progressive families and individuals on the value of literacy and a classical education. Such instruction was viewed as a prime need of gentle life and not merely as an avenue to social betterment. All young gentlemen were expected to have mastered Latin at a fairly early age since it was considered necessary for the cultivation of the social graces. A knowledge of the English language was also considered essential for the aspiring Welsh gentry intent on making their mark in the world in government and property matters. Bilingualism was becoming a prime feature of the social development and many of them became proficient in three and even four languages. According to Speed's map of Caernarfon in 1610 'the Free Schole' was sited at the bottom end of Ditch Street, but whether that school existed in the late fifteenth century is not known. *BMW*, p. 72; W. O. Williams, 'The Survival of the Welsh Language after the Union of England and Wales: the First Phase, 1536-1642', *WHR*, ii (no. 1), 1964, 68-71. It may have been the case that Maredudd had acquired some 'schooling' in the company of Caernarfon administrators, lawyers and merchants.

49.33-4 losing their father young: Ieuan ap Robert died c.1468-9 and Maredudd was born c.1460. Assuming that he was nine years of age on his father's death the other four sons, from two marriages, were very young and were fostered locally.

49.36 breeding: i.e. good up-bringing, enabling Maredudd to become accomplished in the social graces. The author is obliged to admit that God's providence was not the only factor which accounted for his great-grandfather's good fortune!

50.1-2 the age of twenty years or thereabouts: i.e. c.1480.

50.4 daughter-in-law: i.e. step-daughter. She was Alice (Ales), illegitimate daughter of William Gruffudd ap Robin of Cochwillan, appointed sheriff of Caernarfonshire for life in 1486, the year when he was granted denizenship. *LS*, p. 248; *CPR*, 1485-94, p. 55. Her parentage is borne out by Lewys Môn. *GLM*, xlviii, p. 172. His father, Gruffudd ap Robin, related to the Gruffudd family of Penrhyn, had functioned on royal commissions from 1459 to 1475. Her mother was Mallt, daughter of Cynfrig ap Llywelyn ap Madog ap Rhys Goch.

Dwnn, ii, p. 252; *DWB*, p. 252. She married Thomas Spicer, a prominent burgess and alderman of Caernarfon and member of a respected family, originally from Carmarthen, which had settled there in the mid-fourteenth century. *BMW*, p. 95; *PACF*, p. 225. Dwnn, ii, pp. 120-1; G. P. Jones & H. Owen (ed.) *Caernarvon Court Rolls, 1361-1402* (1951), p. 181 passim. The line is as follows:

This flaw in the Wynn lineage accounted in part for the action brought against the author by William Williams of Cochwillan in Star Chamber (1592) where he was accused of having descended from bastardy, his great-grandfather 'being mean by birth' and a servant of Cochwillan. I. ab O. Edwards (ed.), *A Catalogue of Star Chamber Proceedings relating to Wales* (1929), p. 37; Roberts, op. cit., 49. Wynn did not seem embarrassed however, when he referred to his ancestor's marriage. Lewys Môn, the poet who sang to Maredudd, openly acknowledged his first wife's birth:

> Uchel yw merch Wiliam Wyn,
> O Sir Gaer, siri gorwyn.

('William's daughter is uppermost; he is the prestigious sheriff of Caernarfonshire'). *GLM*, xlviii, p. 172.

50.9-10 John Spicer: He was the eldest son of Thomas Spicer who acquired property around Caernarfon as well as in Merioneth and Anglesey. He had also demised lands and tenements in Caernarfon to Welshmen. *BMW*, p. 90; *CCQSR*, lxxv, 13-19. He was in the Merioneth Commission of the peace in 1543. J. R. S. Phillips (ed.), *The Justices of the Peace in Wales and Monmouthshire 1541 to 1689* (1975), p. 37.

50.11-12 brother by the mother: i.e. step-brother of Alice ferch William Gruffudd ap Robin.

50.14 the Bangors: The Bangor family, i.e. descendants of Dafydd Daron, Dean of Bangor (1399). Dwnn, ii, p. 252; *PACF*, p. 386. The relationship between Mallt ferch Cynfrig and this family cannot be fully established. Roberts, op. cit., p. 49.

50.1-15 Ibid., loc. cit.; Professor Roberts believed that the chronicle can be dated at this point and suggested that the author would never have made such a blatant admission of illegitimacy after 1592, the year of the Star Chamber suit. See 50.4n. This suggestion is not easily acceptable because Wynn did not delete references from his narrative which might appear to be embarrassing, and the latter part of the *History* was not amended in any way. In fact, when writing his *Survey of Penmaenmawr* (c.1621-5), he traced the lineage of the house of Cochwillan without any hint of bad-feeling, and regarded it as the 'chieffest and pryme brannch which descendeth and houldeth most landes from Yerwerth ap Iarddyr'; J. O. Halliwell (ed.), *An Ancient Survey of Penmaenmawr* (1859), p. 17. It may well be that it was William Williams's action in Star Chamber in 1592 which prompted the author to write his chronicle and to set the record right regarding his reputable ancestry, but this cannot be proved.

50.18 Edmund Gruffudd: Of Porth-yr-aur, Caernarfon. The founder of Carreglwyd estate in Anglesey. He was the son of Gwilym Fychan ap Gwilym of Penrhyn, deputy Chamberlain of North Wales, by his second wife Gwenllïan, daughter of Iorwerth Ddu, a descendant of Cadrod Hardd. *PACF*, pp. 26, 185. See 25.13-14n.

50.18 Sir John Puleston: The Pulestons of Caernarfon were a branch of the Pulestons of Hafod-y-wern near Bersham, Wrexham. Janet was his second wife. Sir John Puleston (d. 1551), a descendant of Sir Roger de Puleston and son of John Puleston Hen of Hafod-y-wern and Bersham, was a public figure in his day: Sheriff of Caernarfonshire (1543-4), M.P. Caernarfon (1541-4), M.P. Caernarfonshire (1545-7, 1547-51), Chamberlain of Gwynedd (1547), Constable of Caernarfon castle (1523-51). *PACF*, p. 275; *DWB*, p. 817; *LS*, p. 248; *PH*, p. 58; *CCQSR*, p. 247.

50.19-20 Rowland Gruffudd: Grandson of Gwilym Fychan ap Gwilym of Penrhyn. Through his second marriage Gwilym granted his son, Robert Gruffudd, lands in Anglesey and he became the founder of the Gruffudd family of Plas Newydd, *PACF*, pp. 56, 185.

50.22-3 he was minded to have returned: Maredudd had not resided in Eifionydd long enough to really want to return there. If he had he would not have known his blood-brothers very well. Furthermore, since it appears that he had purchased some land in Eifionydd which enlarged the Gesail Gyfarch inheritance as Ieuan had received it in 1463, his presence there might easily have caused a great deal of embarrassment. Most important perhaps was the fact that he was the eldest son of a marriage between two members of rival families—Y Gesail Gyfarch and Bron-y-foel—which could have created much resentment if he had returned to his patrimony. He must have been sadly affected by conflicting loyalties to both paternal and maternal kinsfolk. *Eifionydd*, pp. 24, 88, 188.

50.24 killing and fighting: A reference to the deadly feud, probably over landed affairs, between John Owen ap John ap Maredudd of Ystumcegid and Hywel ap Madog Fychan of Abercain, a kinsman of the Bron-y-foel family.

50.24-6 he did purchase a lease of the castle and *ffriddoedd* of Dolwyddelan: This movement was remarkable in view of the fact that Maredudd, having broken away from his kin, was settling in an area entirely new to him and his wife. When his ancestor, Dafydd of Penyfed, moved to Eifionydd to marry Efa, heiress of Gruffudd Fychan ap Gruffudd ap Moreiddig Warwyn, he did at least have contacts there and did inherit lands through marriage. Maredudd, most probably, entered upon Dolwyddelan lands from Is Gwyrfai via Bwlch Ehediad forming an entry into Blaenau Dolwyddelan from Nanhwyn-an and Beddgelert. O. G. Jones, *Gweithiau Gethin* (1884), ed. T. Roberts and E. Humphreys, p. 291.

The exposed *ffriddoedd*, including the castle of Dolwyddelan, in the Lledr valley, commote of Nanconwy, had been leased in 1483 by Richard III to Sir Ralph Birkenhead, an official at Caer-narfon. The family came from Backford, Wirral, and he was the fourth and youngest son of Adam Birkenhead of Huxley, Protonotary and Clerk of the Crown at Chester and Flint. Sir Ralph was sheriff of Cheshire (1481) and was described as 'late clerk of the Crown in north Wales' (1508). He functioned as commissioner enquiring into royal lands in the northern Principality. There is no evidence to show that he held the office of Chamberlain of North Wales. G. Ormerod, *History of Cheshire* (1819), i, p. 187; ii, p. 199. *CPR*, 1494-1509, pp. 438, 583; *CSPFD*, 1509 (Pt. i), p. 8; 1513, i (Pt. ii), p. 1157.

50.28 an act of resumption: *Rot. Parl.* vi, pp. 403-4; *SW*, p. 49 (St. 11 Hen. VII c. 33); Chrimes, *Henry VII*, pp. 123-5. According to the Act of Resumption (1487) the Crown did resume all lands granted by Richard III and those lands were to be regranted to tenants on favourable financial terms to Henry VII.

50.34 the castle of Dolwyddelan: A native fortification overlooking the Lledr valley, consisting of one keep, a tower and a courtyard. It is the reputed birthplace of Llywelyn ab Iorwerth. The keep may have been built by his father Iorwerth Drwyndwn, lord of Nanconwy. It appears that Maredudd lived in the south-east tower or keep and that he added a second floor and three windows to it. *RCAM*, ii, *Caerns. East*, pp. 80-1. See 1.27n.

50.35 Hywel ab Ieuan ap Rhys Gethin: A grandson of Rhys Gethin ap Gruffudd Fychan, Hendre Rhys Gethin of Pentre Du near Betws-y-coed. His family lived at Y Cwm, Penmachno. *WG* (300-1400). iii, p. 448, iv, p. 676. It is believed that Dolwyddelan castle was in the custody of the Gethin family after the Conquest (1282-4). *Gweithiau Gethin*, pp. 236, 280. See 25.3n.

50.39 See 29.26n.

50.40 the Sovereignty of the country: i.e. for domination in a disordered countryside.

51.3 Penamnen: A sheltered valley south-east of Dolwyddelan and adjacent to the modern village. It is a corrupt form of Pennant Beinw (the river of that name running through it). *ELISG*, p. 105; *Gweithiau Gethin*, pp. 307-8. It may be that it was Hywel ab Ieuan's house at Penamnen that was later rebuilt and extended by Maredudd ab Ieuan. *RCAM*, p. 83.

51.5 brought him to Conwy castle: i.e. to be imprisoned until he could be moved to Caernarfon for trial before the Justice's Sessions of North Wales. The Sessions, however, were occasionally held at Conwy castle. *CCQSR*, xlvii (n.2).

51.16 the whole country then was but a forest: The upper reaches of Nanconwy were sparsely populated, heavily wooded and hemmed in by the eastern ridges of Snowdonia and the uplands bordering on the Hiraethog moorlands. Rainfall is heavy and the damp climate ideal for a stock-rearing economy. The Lledr valley consisted mainly of alder—oak—birchwood and scrub. E. G. Owen (ed.), *Wales: an Historical, Regional and Physical Geography* (1957), p. 270.

51.18-19 Owain Glyndŵr's wars: The revolt of Owain Glyndŵr, 16 September 1400—c.1415.

51.21 green grass grew: The oft-quoted phrase which vividly describes the effects of revolt. The borough of Llanrwst, consisting originally of five free *gwelyau*, had probably been established by the princes. By 1334, however, it was in decline and a policy was adopted whereby English burgesses were attracted to settle there. The Glyndŵr revolt did seriously affect its economy since no income was recorded for the years 1410-11. Owen, 'Lordship of Denbigh', pp. 234-5, 243-4. Serious losses of revenue were incurred, according to the accounts, up to 1424. Bryn-y-boten was the site occupied later by the old Town Hall (demolished in 1965).

51.22 the deer fed in the churchyard: Ballinger wrongly transcribes 'fed' as 'fled'. The present west tower of the parish church dates from the late fifteenth century—early sixteenth century, and its principal feature is the rood loft and screen work. An earlier church was probably destroyed during the ravages of the earl of Pembroke in 1468 and it is said that it was rebuilt c. 1470. *HStA*, ii, p. 336.

51.24-5 that the English should find not strength ...: Cf. George Owen of Henllys's remark, writing in the same period: 'theare grewe about ye tyme deadly hatred betweene them and the English nation insomuch that the name of a Welshman was odyous to ye Englishmen, and the name of Englishman woefull to the Welshman'. *Penbrokshire*, iii, p. 37.

51.33-4 Carreg-y-gwalch: See 29.26n.

51.34 the earl Herbert: See 33, 21-4n.

51.38-9 having few inhabitants: Of the ten commotes in Caernarfonshire it is estimated that Nanconwy, in the period 1545-63, was the least populated with about 152 households and 760 inhabitants. L. Owen, 'The Population of Wales in the Sixteenth and Seventeenth Centuries', *TCS*, 1959, 109.

52.2-3 from . . . Conwy to Bala: i.e. the regions to the east of Nanconwy, namely the western fringes of the lordship of Denbigh and lands adjacent to Merioneth which had contributed to the devastation; a reference doubtless to the contents of the following paragraph.

52.4 Hiraethog: The reference here is to the region of Hiraethog not the mountains. In south-east Nanconwy at Ysbyty Ifan (Dolgynwal) lay the old sanctuary of the Knights Hospitallers of St. John of Jerusalem established c.1190 on land called Tir Ifan granted to them by Ieuan ap Rhys of Trebrys. A hospice and church, dedicated to St. John the Baptist, were built there. In 1221-24 Llywelyn ab Iorwerth did confer upon the hospice the church of Ellesmere, acquired by him from Henry III. Before 1338 the estates were combined with those of Halston and, in the fourteenth century, were entrusted to lay stewards. The steward of the Hiraethog lands in 1450, about the time when the brigands became operative, was Maredudd ap Tudur of Plas Iolyn. E. Roberts, 'Teulu Plas Iolyn', *TDHS*, xiii, 1964, 41-3. There is a tradition that Maredudd ab Ieuan drove Hywel ab Ieuan from the castle and that his kinsman, Ieuan ap Maredudd, of Ysbyty Ifan utilised the sanctuary as a base for attack on Maredudd. *Gweithiau Gethin*, pp. 282-3, 304-5. These lands had rights of sanctuary which were flagrantly abused by perpetrators of crime. W. Rees, *The Order of St. John in Wales* (1947), pp. 63-7; *HW*, ii, p. 690. Their influence was felt throughout the Hiraethog area and as far south as the grange of Gwanas, south of Dolgellau, and Dinas Mawddwy (then in Powys). It is interesting that the author and Lewys Môn described the lordship in the same terms: 'Llai draw nyth lladron weithian'. ('There is now less danger from that nest of thieves yonder'). *GLM*, xlviii, p. 173; *Gweithiau Gethin*, 273. For more detail see E. Roberts, 'Teulu Plas Iolyn', 59-63 et seq.; *Welsh Church from Conquest to Reformation*, pp. 241, 321-2, 553-4.

52.10-11 a receptacle of thieves and murderers: These marauders were not brigands or *banditti* in the normal sense but modest gentry, pressurised by social and political conditions, such as the families in the vicinity of Cefn Digoll, Gwern-y-gof and Y Drum Ddu in Powys. E. Roberts, *Dafydd Llwyd o Fathafarn* (1981), p. 11; K. Williams-Jones, 'A Mawddwy Court Roll, 1415-16', *BBCS*, xxiii (pt. iv), 1970, 329-7.

52.23 about the four and twentieth year of his age: i.e. c.1485-90.

52.30 he should find elbow room: The author's explanation is partial and over-simplified. Maredudd was far more than a mere fugitive escaping from the terrorism of his home. He was aware of the benefits that would accrue from leasing Crown bond lands in a period of intense competition for property. J. B. Smith, 'Crown and Community', 165-7; *MWS*, pp. 46-8. By the end of the fifteenth century bondage had declined to very serious propositions in Caernarfonshire and elsewhere in north Wales, many families having vacated their tenements which escheated to the Crown. Ambitious lay proprietors cast a greedy eye upon them and it is conceivable that Rhys ap Maredudd of Plas Iolyn and Maredudd ab Ieuan were rivals because Rhys had obtained lands from Henry VII in Hiraethog for services rendered. 'Teulu Plas Iolyn', 42-3. In view of the adverse reaction to the settlement of Welsh families within the borough of Caernarfon it may have been that Maredudd chose to exploit the land-market more profitably. Smith, op. cit. 159-71. The new opportunities seized by prospering Welshman in the vicinity of Edwardian boroughs were resented and John Spicer (half-brother of Maredudd's first wife), among other prominent burgesses, was indicted in March 1532 for granting lands to Welshmen in the vicinity of Caernarfon. *CCQSR*, lxxv (n. i); *BMW*, p. 90 [see 50. 9-10n.].

52.36 John Owen ap John ap Maredudd: Of Ystumcegid. A grandson of John ap Maredudd. He was known as John Owen ap John and was as turbulent and contentious as his father and grandfather and was also a bitter rival of the Collwyn clan of Bron-y-foel. See 46, 19-20n.

52.37 Hywel ap Madog Fychan: A descendant of Madog ab Ieuan ab Einion (Collwyn) who lived c.1400. This Madog founded the estate of Abercain near Llanystumdwy which was known as 'Bercyn'. Hywel ap Madog (fl. 1441) and his son Rhys ap Hywel held the Crown lands of Ffriwlwyd (1469) and Rhys's son, Madog Fychan (fl. 1485) inherited them. The holding of Ffriwlwyd by Crown lease on the opposite side of the river Dwyfor gave the family some prominence among Eifionydd landowners. To these properties could be added other adjacent lands in the family's possession held principally by *gwely* tenure. Madog Fychan was a man of influence in his neighbourhood and his material interests were seriously threatened by the Owen family of Ystumcegid. His lands in Abercain were close to those of the Owens and encroachment caused resentment. As in the case of intermarriage between the Gesail Gyfarch and Bron-y-foel families bitterness and feud also occurred between these families in spite of the fact that Hywel ap Madog Fychan had married John Owen's first cousin, Margaret, daughter of Ieuan ap John ap Maredudd of Bryncir. *PACF*, p. 170; *Eifionydd*, pp. 187-8. Land meant wealth and wealth meant power and authority in those days; therefore, John Owen, true to the reputation of his house, attacked 'Bercyn'. Loc. cit. See 30.16n.

53.1 the heir of Bron-y-foel: i.e. Maredudd and Rhys ap Hywel ap Rhys who helped in the building of Gwydir in its early stages. See 47.10n.

53.7-8 Ieuan ap Robert ap Maredudd's sister: i.e. Maud, daughter of Robert ap Maredudd and sister of Ieuan ap Robert. Hywel's grandmother, therefore, was Maredudd's aunt. Maredudd and Hywel were first cousins once removed. *PACF*, p. 170.

53.12-13 Owen ap John ap Maredudd: John Owen's father, Owen ap John ap Maredudd, was a younger brother of Morus ap John ap Maredudd. The author's grandmother was Elin Llwyd, daughter of Morus, and John Owen was, therefore, her first cousin. *PACF*, pp. 232, 281. She was renowned for her hospitality at Dolwyddelan and Gwydir which her husband, John Wyn ap Maredudd, inherited in 1525, and Morus Dwyfech, Simwnt Fychan, Wiliam Cynwal and Wiliam Llŷn composed elegies in her memory. The episode recorded at this point in the *History* is yet again a classic example of how internecine jealousies and rival interests could cause lasting embitterment within the kindred structure.

53.19 his mother: Margaret, daughter of Hywel ab Einion ap Hywel Coetmor. *PACF*, pp. 170, 318.

53.23 Dafydd Llwyd [ap] Gruffudd Fychan: Wynn has become confused and misleading at this point. The person cited as Gruffudd Fychan was not Ieuan ap Robert's eldest son by his second wife Gwenhwyfar (or Mallt), daughter of Madog Fychan of Llwyndyrus. *WG* (1400-1500), v, p. 850; *PACF*, pp. 231, 281. That Gruffudd Fychan was Maredudd ab Ieuan ap Robert's half-brother, and Dafydd Llwyd, his son, was Maredudd's nephew and the author's great-uncle (not uncle). Wynn has obviously confused two persons named Gruffudd Fychan (alias Wynn) at this point, both linked with Cwm Ystradllyn. The Gruffudd Fychan (alias Wynn) referred to in this context was Hywel ap Madog Fychan's second cousin who resided at Talhenbont, Llanystumdwy. Dafydd Llwyd (Ieuan ap Robert's grandson), however, lived in Cwm Ystradllyn. *Eifionydd*, pp. 15, 148-9. See 40.30n.

53.26 Hywel ap Madog Fychan: He was married in 1512 to Margaret, daughter of Ieuan ap John ap Maredudd of Ystumcegid, and had a son, Hywel, born in 1517. This Hywel ap Madog was killed in that year. *PACF*, p. 170; *Eifionydd*, p. 188.

53.28 Coming to Abercain: The estate was situated in the township of Abercain and was to become extensive. The house appears as 'Aberkeyn' in *RC*, p. 40, 200; *ELISG*, p. 50.

53.30 *cocherie:* Fr. 'coucherie' ('lying abed'): described as a 'long boarded bed placed with a proper inclination from the side of the room which was the common dormitory of the servants'. *HGF (1878)*, p. 77; i.e. lying huddled together on a dais beside the long table in the hall.

54.2 was compounded for: i.e. settled by mutual consent. Hywel ap Madog Fychan died of his wounds some time after the affray and symbolised yet again a heroic chieftain determined to foster his property interests in an age of transition and even to die in that cause.

54.5 his aged father: i.e. Owen ap John ap Maredudd of Ystumcegid.

54.8-9 'This is a sorry sight: did you accomplish that which is worthy of you?'

54.11-15 i.e. since his sons had not succeeded in besieging the house of Bercyn without loss of their own blood. Owen ap John of Maredudd, based at Ystumcegid, had regarded himself as the dominant landowner in Pennant. *Eifionydd*, pp. 23-4.

54.17-18 the one lineally descended of Owain Gwynedd: i.e. the kindred related to Ieuan ap Robert and the ancestors of the Wynn family of Gwydir. C. A. Gresham states that 'Glasfryn or Cwmstrallyn' was a later addition to the text but this is not so. Ca. MS.83 (MS.4.101). 104v. In his view the author's meaning here is that Glasfryn fawr (a cadet house of Y Gesail Gyfarch) can also be added to the four mentioned as a house which owned ancestral lands in Cwm Ystradllyn. *Eifionydd*, p. 16. It was in the author's interests to stress the two main ancestral groupings among the major families in Eifionydd descended from Collwyn ap Tangno and Owain Gwynedd respectively and also to show forcefully how the forbears of the Wynns resolutely defied and defeated their enemies. The repetition encountered in the text demonstrates the author's intention in this respect, and served as well to highlight the benefits which accrued from the divergent course taken by Maredudd ab Ieuan ap Robert in Nanconwy.

54.21-2 the other sect descended of Collwyn: i.e. the kindred of Hywel ap Rhys, rival of Ieuan ap Robert. Collwyn ap Tangno was reputed to be the lord of Eifionydd, Ardudwy and part of Llŷn. *Royal Tribes of Wales*, pp. 184-8. Emphasis is placed on the honourable descent of both kindred groupings; they were free clans which had originally settled upon *gwely* lands in the twelfth century. Economic pressures in the fifteenth century, however, had forced smaller houses to struggle for their survival and the larger houses to seize the main chance and fortify their privileged position. The author at this point draws attention only to those families which had become well-established and whose owners were on the upgrade in the pre-Tudor period. Doubtless it was property that lay at the root of most kindred animosities, the persistent practice and serious consequences of *cyfrannu* often creating bitter feuds because property shares had become less economically viable in each succeeding generation. The township of Chwilog is in the parish of Llanystumdwy, Abercain and Gwynfryn in the township of Rhwng-Dwyfor-a-Dwyfach and Talhenbont in the township of Brynbras. *Eifionydd*, passim.

54.24-5 Hugh Gwyn ap John Wyn ab William: He lived at Pennarth fawr, in the township of that name (east of the parish of Abererch), and obtained the inheritance of Ieuan ab Einion ap Gruffudd of Chwilog. Wynn is misleading at this point. It was Einion, not Ieuan, who was the brother of Sir Hywel y Fwyall. Both Ieuan and Einion were sheriffs of Caernarfonshire in 1385-9 and 1351-5, 1358-9 respectively. Hugh Gwyn was sheriff of Caernarfonshire (1599-1600) and a prominent Justice of the Peace, and he extended the *plasty* of Pennarth fawr. *LS*, p. 248; *RCAM, Caerns. Central*, pp. 112-3; *WG* (1400-1500), ii, pp. 431-433.

54.30 taken by the Black Prince: The author here contends that it was the Black Prince and not Sir Hywel who captured the French King on the battlefield. See 17.16n.

54.30 Yeomen of the Crown: servants or attendants in the royal household.

55.1 Sergeant Roberts: John Wynn Roberts of Croes-y-foel, Yeoman of the Crown and subsequently Sergeant-at-Arms. *HPF*, iii, p. 42. He married Elizabeth, co-heiress of Humphrey Dimoke of Withington. She was the half-sister of Sir William Gerard of Ince, Lancashire, Lord Chancellor of Ireland, and the author's father-in-law. *DNB*, xxi, pp. 225-6.

55.4 Robert Turbridge: Of Caerfallen in the parish of Llan-rhudd, near Ruthin, Queen's Surveyor of North Wales. *CWP*, nos. 77-9; Dwnn, ii, p. 351. He married Jane, co-heiress of Humphrey Dimoke of Withington. She was a sister to John Wynn Roberts's wife.

55.12-13 he took the French King prisoner: A reference again to the tradition which persisted that Sir Hywel y Fwyall had captured the French King. The Welsh were skilled as foot soldiers with lances and in particuar the long bow. A. D. Carr, op. cit., 23-4. See 17.18-19n.

55.18 he built his house in Penamnen: Very little remains of the apparently extensive original house called Tai Penamnen and 'Parlwr Penamnen' by the older residents of Dolwyddelan to this day, the parlour only having survived (but now in complete ruin). *RCAM, Caerns. East.*, p.83; *Gweithiau Gethin*, pp. 307-8. It is reputed that Ieuan ap Rhys Gethin had a house at Penamnen. *Royal Tribes*, p. 22 [See 19.11n.]. The existing meadowland in Penamnen is still regarded by local farmers as having been at one time of the best quality in the parish owing to its high ground. The author states that the new tenant at Bwlch Cynnud [See 57.6n] felled eighteen oaks in one day to build the house which was sited in a good defensive position, commanding a good view of Carreg Alltrem opposite. To the north and south-west of Cwm

Penamnen respectively stand Bwlch-y-groes and the heights of Y Rowen over which the threat from Ysbyty Ifan was likely to come. Cwm Penamnen consisted approximately of 1,800 acres, mainly of rough pasture suitable for grazing purposes, of which fifty-five acres were considered suitable as meadow or even arable land sufficient to supply Maredudd's household with corn. He was a patron of bards at Penamnen, and Tudur Aled, Lewys Môn and Lewys Daron applauded his hospitality and military prowess. *GLM*, xlviii, p. 172; Ca. MS.83 (MS. 4.101), 28v-29v. Such powerful eulogies boosted his reputation in Nanconwy at a crucial time in his career.

55.20-1 he removed the church of Dolwyddelan: The original church of St. Gwyddelan was situated probably at Bryn-y-bedd in the vicinity of Bod-y-groes and the burial ground adjacent to St. Elizabeth parish church (now demolished), but there is no trace of it. On the north wall of the chancel of the old church (in its new location) appears a brass memorial to Maredudd in three sections consisting of a kneeling figure, coat-of-arms (Collwyn quartering Owain Gwynedd), and an inscription in Gothic lettering. *RCAM, Caerns. East*, p. 79. The effigy is described as follows in *HGF* (1878), p. xiv. 'The effigy . . . is bare-headed, with the hair clubbed in the fashion which prevailed in the early part of the reign of Henry VIII. Round the neck is worn a collar of mail. The body-armour consists of a globular breastplate with angular-shaped tuilles attached to the shirt, and beneath these is an apron of mail of that peculiar kind represented on Welsh sepulchral effigies. On the shoulders are pass-guards, the arms above and below the elbows are protected by epaulieries and vambrances, the elbows by coudes, the hands are uncovered; the thighs are protected by cuisses, the knees by genouilleres, the legs by jambs, the feet by sollerets, broad-toed and apparently laminated . . . On the left side is a sword, and the right a dagger; the hands are conjoined, as in prayer'. The religious house at Beddgelert was an Augustinian priory established on an old sixth-century Celtic site. C. A. Gresham, 'The Parish of Beddgelert', *TCHS*, xxx, 1969, 21-8; C. N. Johns, 'The Celtic Monasteries of North Wales,' ibid, xxi, 1960, 26-7.

55.24-5 Robert Wynn: Of Plas Mawr, Conwy; he was a younger brother of the author's father, Morus Wynn. He obtained lands from his father, John Wyn ap Maredudd, in Dolwyddelan and also owned properties in Nanhwynan. He prospered at Dolwyddelan by farming the *ffriddoedd* and township, and settling at Bryn Moel which he probably built c. 1572. There exists a reference to him as being of that place in an elegy composed by Morus Dwyfech on his mother's death in that year. NLW. MS.9054E. 513, Llansteffan MS. 122,498.

> A Rhobert, oleubert lys
> O'r Bryn Moel, irbren melys.

For his tenure of land in Dolwyddelan and his disputes with his nephew, Sir John Wynn, see 'Wynn of Gwydir Estate' 148, 152-3; idem, 'John Wynn and his Tenants: the Dolwyddelan and Llysfaen Disputes', 1-7. As a younger son Robert Wynn would be expected to maintain a modest estate and pursue a profession. Where he obtained his military instruction is not known but his exploits on the continent, as recorded in the *Memoirs* [see pp. 66-8], had certainly caught his nephew's imagination. He lived most of his life in the borough of Conwy and married twice (See 66.29n.). He was buried in St. Mary's parish church in the town, part of which betrays remains of the old Cistercian abbey of Aberconwy which was moved to Maenan in the Conwy valley by Edward I soon after 1282. *RCAM, Caerns. East*, pp. 43-4. In spite of what appeared to be a successful military career abroad and his hold over many lands in the commote of Nanconwy it was evident that he, more than his blood-brothers, favoured an urban way of life and his fortunes were eventually established in the borough of Conwy where he built his mansion, Plas Mawr, the first part of which was erected in 1570. *RCAM, Caerns. East*, pp. 58-64; A. and H. Baker, *Plas Mawr* (1888), pp. 17-70, 123-7, 130-1. He served Sir Philip Hoby at the siege of Boulogne July— September 1544. See *Memoirs*, p. 66. The south chapel, entered into from the chancel, was added by Robert Wynn.

55.25 the glass window: The church was built c.1500 and nearly sixty fragments of stained glass are found in the east window of the chancel. It is said that the glass was put in the window twelve years after the church was built. *RCAM*, op. cit., pp. 76-80; C. E. Breese, 'Old Stained Glass in St. Beuno's Church, Penmorva', *AC*, 1905, 147-52; H. H. Hughes and H. L. North, *The Old Churches of Snowdonia* (1924), pp. 132-3. A fragment of the eastern window of Penmorfa church (subsequently moved to the west window) contained a memorial to Maredudd ab Ieuan ap Robert and Margaret, his third wife. *HGF* (1878), p. 85 (n.5); Breese, loc. cit.

55.30 like a trivet: i.e. in this case three equally spaced and located defensive pivots. Dolwyddelan castle, the re-sited church and Tai Penamnen stood, in the form of a triangle, one mile distance from each other.

55.17-56.10 A remarkable piece of defensive strategy which historians have dismissed as pure imagination or hearsay on the author's part. Judging by the difficult terrain and the nature of the opposition to Maredudd's settlement near the eastern frontiers of the Principality there may well be much truth in what Wynn has to say at this point. A simple but effective strategy of this kind would probably have given Maredudd the extra defensive cover that he needed to ward off marauding bands of brigands. Y Garreg Big (also called Maen-y-gwylwyr) is situated opposite Carreg Alltrem and immediately above Tai Penamnen. It is in a commanding position from which can be viewed both the church and Maredudd's residence together with the areas immediately north of Dolwyddelan towards the Conwy valley. This rock can also be seen clearly through the south-east window of the old church. This paragraph may have been based on the author's reading of bardic testimony. Lewys Môn, for example, was aware of the dangers which beset Maredudd as he related in the opening passages of his eulogy. His followers, he said, would warn him in good time, because his defensive tactics were effective. *GLM*, xlviii, p. 173.

> Ar hyd dau gwm y rhout gyrch,
> A Nanconwy'n un cynnyrch . . .
> Llai treisir gywir a gwan,
> Llai draw nyth lladron weithian;

(Along two valleys and in Nanconwy thou didst conduct thy campaign. There is less oppression of the honest and weak and fewer dens of thieves.)

56.6 twenty tall archers: Tenants who were well-trained in self-defence, especially in forested areas, were usually expert bowmen and most were experienced soldiers. Owing to disorder in the March it was legislated in 1534-5 (St. 26 Henry VIII c.6) that weapons (including long and cross bows) were not to be brought to any court held in Wales or the March, nor to any town, fair, church or other assembly. *SW*, p. 57. How much effect this legislation would have had on rural areas is difficult to estimate, but in an age when so much depended on the expertise of the common man with his weapons and on the need for musters in every shire to maintain the defensive power of the realm, to forbid the use of such weapons, even in populated area, might not have been practicable. The aim of this legislation was to curb disorder in vulnerable parts of the country but, in Nanconwy, it would have had no real effect. Maredudd used his men to good purpose: to defend the commote from brigands but also to create a defensible frontier region based on the exploitation of economic opportunity. J. G. Jones, 'The Wynn Estate of Gwydir', 141-3. In spite of the suspicious background of some of his followers it is clear that Maredudd had intended to aid the cause of law and order in Nanconwy; he had sufficient mastery over these tenants to be able to subdue them, to quell disorder and repel what evil intentions they may have had and convert them into worthy and reliable subjects on his lands. In times of stress he was able to call upon them to defend their tenancies against those who attacked them, and in so doing they also learnt how to protect the best interests of a community and neighbourhood. They became respected forefathers of new families which were established in Dolwyddelan and the surrounding district as Sir John Wynn was so eager to point out.

56.9-10 in the beginning of his time: c.1485-90.

56.13-14 of them he placed colonies in the country: This colonising occurred before Maredudd purchased Gwydir, it is believed, from Dafydd ap Hywel Coetmor, a descendant of Iarddur of Arllechwedd. Whether this Dafydd survived to c.1500 (the year of purchase) is rather doubtful; it may have been that Maredudd purchased the land from Dafydd ap Hywel ab Einion ap Hywel Coetmor. It is known that Hywel ab Einion ap Hywel Coetmor lived in 2 Edward IV (i.e. 1462-3). Cheney, op. cit., p. 23. He was a Crown tenant. *WG* (300-1400), v, pp. 832-3. The bond township of Trewydir or Coed Gwedir extended from the upper Llugwy valley, north of the river, to the Conwy valley. See Gresham, *Medieval Stone Carving*, p. 207. 'Gwedir' means lowland as opposed to 'gorthir' (upland) and the form is used continually by the poets. *ELl*, p. 28. Pengraig Inco is a tenement in the uplands north of the Llugwy near Capel Curig.

56.14 filling every empty tenement: i.e. bond land. In Nanconwy only Cwmllannerch and Betws were free townships: Dolwyddelan, Penmachno, Trefriw and Trewydir were bond townships with forty-seven tenants. In 1352, according to the *Record of Caernarvon*, the township of Dolwyddelan consisted of two bond *gafaelion* called Gafael Elidir and Gafael-y-mynach, and the *ffriddoedd* were large upland vaccaries for grazing purposes which originally formed the demesne lands of the castle. *RC*, p. 10; J. Thirsk (ed.), *Agrarian History*, pp. 378-9. Encroachment on bond vills had occurred increasingly from the mid-fourteenth century onwards, and lands in Dolwyddelan and Penmachno had been encroached upon before the Glyndŵr revolt. *MWS*, p. 47.

56.5 *cessavit per biennium:* Lit. 'he has ceased for two years'. A process or writ in law (St. of Gloucester 1278 c.4) whereby a lord may recover the lands of a tenant who has, for a period of two years, neglected to perform his services or pay rents, by condition of tenure, and has insufficient goods or chattels on his lands to be distrained. G. Jacob, *A New Law Dictionary* (1782). The writ applied to a fee-farm when the lord reserved for himself and his heirs either the rent or a fourth part of the farm rent (St.6 Edward I, c.4). *Report of the Royal Commission on Land in Wales and Monmouthshire* (1896), p. 235.

56.25-6 exactions were . . . so manifold: The recurrence of plague and upheaval had devastating effects on the region, and increased fiscal demands led to the ruin of the bond population. Freeholders also felt the strain of increasing exactions and the fine of the Great Turn fell heavily on those who remained. Smith, op. cit., 152-4.

56.32 the said William: i.e. William ap Robert, the 'follower' from Is Gwyrfai. John Wyn ap Maredudd, the author's grandfather, had secured for himself a tight hold over lands in the upper Conwy valley and elsewhere. J. G. Jones, 'The Wynn Estate of Gwydir: Aspects of its Growth and Development c.1500-1580', *NLWJ*, xxii (pt. ii), 1981, 145-51.

56.37-8 King's *ffridd*, at Bryntyrch: Crown *ffridd* in the township of Trewydir. It lies east of Capel Curig below Clogwyn Mawr (behind the present Youth Hostel) and was obtained by Maredudd when he purchased Gwydir. *RC*, p. 11, 'Brentyrgh'.

57.2 the tenement of Garth: Situated in Capel Curig and in Trewydir township. Pellin (Pellyn) ap Heilin. Some members of his family served as jurors in the mid-sixteenth century. *CCQSR*, p. 311 passim.

57.3 in Rhiwgoch: A tenement again situated in Capel Curig and in Trewydir township.

57.6 in Bwlch Cynnud: Situated in Dolwyddelan township but part of it lay in Trewydir, comprising 150 acres of pasture.

57.7 in Bertheos: A *hafod* or summer pasture in the *ffriddoedd*. *RC*, p. 10 'Hauotri Partheosk'.

57.10 Fynhadog: Also called locally Nhadog, a *hafod* or summer pasture in the *ffriddoedd*. Ibid, loc. cit. 'Hautori de Danadogith'. *ELISG*, pp. 28-9.

57.14 Humphrey Jones of Craflwyn: The last clause of this sentence is provided by the author as an unnecessary addition, and indicates his keenness to establish the pedigrees of his contemporaries. Craflwyn is near Beddgelert. He was a descendant of Iolyn ap Dafydd Filwr ap Dafydd Daron, known as the Black Dean of Bangor, a supporter of Glyndŵr and founder of the Bangor family. His descendant was this Rhys ap Robert, a freeholder in Maenol Bangor, whose great grandson was Morus Jones, Baron of the Exchequer and Steward to the Bishop of Bangor (1585). Craflwyn came to his possession through his wife, daughter of Ieuan ap Richard ap Ieuan. He also acquired Meillionen and adjacent lands. He died in 1619 and was succeeded by his son Humphrey Jones who purchased lands in Cwm Ystradllyn and other lands in Merioneth. *Eifionydd*, p. 70. This Humphrey was Keeper of the Prince's Records at the Exchequer at Caernarfon and Receiver General of North Wales. *PACF*, p. 386.

57.16 my father's fosters: i.e. Morus Wynn (d. 1580). He was the eldest son of John Wynn ap Maredudd and inheritor of the Gwydir estate. He was the first to adopt the surname 'Wynn' and became a prominent public figure who served as M.P. for Caernarfonshire (1553, 1554, 1559 and 1563-7), and sheriff of the shire (1555, 1570, 1578). *DWB*, p. 1097; *LS*, p. 248; *PH*, p. 58; J. G. Jones, 'Morus Wynn o Wedir c.1530-1580', *TCHS*, xxxviii, 1977, 33-59.

57.20-1 their defender and captain of the country: This process was not uncommon in a period of economic and political dislocation. Followers, retainers or 'affinities' were often recruited by local gentry and were trained crudely in the art of warfare for their own temporary security. F. R. H. du Boulay, *An Age of Ambition*, (1970), pp. 134-5. Note Lewis Daron's tribute to him:

Pen gwlad, ein pinagl ydoedd,
Parth ein tir a'n porthiant oedd.   Ca.83.29.

(He was our chieftain and our sustainer).

He was considered to be the most notable protector of his tenants and followers in inhospitable terrain.

Nid oes i'r wlad, asur lain,
Dyn nid ydyw dan d'adain.   *GTA*, 1, liv, p. 220.

(There is no man in the region who is not in thy protection).

A 'jack' was the sleeveless padded tunic used by foot-soldiers: the 'armolet coat' was a coat of mail, and the 'chasing staves' (not 'slaves' as transcribed by Ballinger, *HGF*, p. 60) were shafts of lances or spears used to pursue the enemy.

57.29-30 he began to put back and to curb: The poets testify to his strength and his mastery over the besiegers. Lewys Môn refers to the reduction in the number of thieves ('Llai tyrfáu gwylliaid tra fych'). *GLM*, xlviii, p. 173. Lewys Daron, however, whilst complimenting Maredudd on his successes, cautioned that they might yet rise to terrorise the countryside after his patron's death. Ca. MS.83 (MS.4.101).29v. His son and heir, John Wyn ap Maredudd of Gwydir, in his capacity as sheriff of Caernarfonshire (1544-5, 1553-41, 1556-7) and justice of the peace for the county, was called upon to quell disorders on the eastern borders with Denbighshire and Merioneth. *LS*, p. 248; J. R. S. Phillips, op. cit., pp. 17-18; *CCQSR*, pp. 31(3), 64(71), 83(115), 122 (261), 176(178), 247; J. G. Jones, 'The Wynn Family and Estate of Gwydir', pp. 339-42. According to the poet Morus Dwyfech John Wynn ap Maredudd was considered to be a steadfast leader locking within his grasp three regions (presumably Caernarfonshire, Denbighshire and Merioneth). As an impartial justice of the peace, the poet maintained, he industriously bore heavily on thieves and other law-breakers. Ca.MS.20.320. See also J. Gwilym Jones, *Teulu Gwedir fel Noddwyr y Beirdd* (unpublished M.A. dissertation University of Wales, 1975), pp. 7-14.

A dôr i gloi ar dair gwlad,
Ac ustus heddwch gwastad;
Llafuriaist, gyrraist yn gaeth
Lladron ac anllywodraeth.

57.32 well appointed: i.e. well accoutred. Such a band of followers were chiefly newly-settled tenants in the upper reaches of Nanconwy who would form a 'maintained' army wearing the leader's livery.

57.34 in the country: i.e. the region or neighbourhood. In NLW MS.21253D, an early eighteenth-century text of the *HGF*, annotated by Bishop Humphrey Humphreys of Bangor, there is added an *excursus* on 'the Issue of Meredith ap Jevan ...' which supplies details of his many children, legitimate and illegitimate. It is printed in the first and second editions of the *HGF* by Daines Barrington (1770 and 1781) and in Angharad Llwyd's edition (1827), and probably derives from Humphreys's notes added to the NLW Wynnstay MS.120 copy. *HGF* (1827), pp. 97-9; J. E. Caerwyn Williams, op. cit., 281; J. G. Jones, 'Sir John Wynn and John Speed', 256-7, 264.

The *excursus* records 'The Issue of Meredith ap Jevan ap Robert of Keselgyfarch, Gwedir, com. Carn.' and lists the children born to Maredudd by his three wives respectively, namely Alice (Ales) ferch William Gruffudd ap Robin of Coch-willan (4 sons and 6 daughters), the second son, John Wyn ap Maredudd, inheriting the estate of Gwydir on his father's death; Gwenhwyfar ferch Gruffudd ap Hywel y Farf, widow of Robert Gruffudd of Porth-aml (2 daughters); Margaret ferch Morus ap John ap Maredudd of Clenennau (2 sons, 7 daughters). Then is listed his issue by two concubines, Janet ferch Siencyn Gruffudd Fychan (2 sons, 1 daughter), one of these sons, John Coetmor, being the grandfather of John Williams, goldsmith (referred to in Wynn's *Memoirs* [see p. 74]; Catherine ferch Ieuan ap John ap Heilyn of Penmachno (2 sons). In a footnote in *HGF* (1827), p. 94, Angharad Llwyd adds two other concubines who produced four more children; the last, Gwenllïan ferch Gwilym ab Ieuan Llwyd, gave birth to Catherine, the mother of Sir Thomas Wiliems, the physician and lexicographer from Trefriw ('. . . in whose MS. of Achau I found this hanes of Meredydd's children by his three wives . . .'). See also *HGF* (1878), p. 81, 84-7.

Maredudd ab Ieuan ap Robert built 'Neuadd Fredudd' at Gwydir c. 1500. It is said that he served Henry VIII at the siege of Tournai (1513) during the English expeditions in France. He is also reputed to have visited Rome on two occasions. Ca.MS.83 [MS.4.101].29v. He died on 18 March 1525 and was buried in St. Gwyddelan's church, Dolwyddelan, which he built and where his commemorative effigy is preserved. Breese, op.cit., 147-9; *RCAM, Caerns. East*, p. 79. On his death his lands in Eifionydd were divided equally by *cyfran* between his three sons John (who lived at Gwydir), Humphrey (who inherited Y Gesail Gyfarch) and Cadwaladr (who obtained Y Wenallt, the abbey of Aberconwy's land in Nanhwynan). All three adopted the surname 'Wynn'. John Wyn was Maredudd's eldest surviving son by his first wife, Alice, the other two were his sons by his third wife, Margaret, daughter of Morus ap John ap Maredudd of Y Clenennau. She bore him nine children (most of them females) although his second wife, Gwenhwyfar, daughter of Gruffudd ap Hywel, was still alive and in fact survived him! *Eifionydd*, pp. 88-9, 101, 391-2; *PACF*, p. 281; NLW.MS. 9051E.210 (dated 1528); J. G. Jones, 'Wynn Estate of Gwydir', 143-5. The Eifionydd connection was maintained by Maredudd and his son John Wyn at Gwydir through their marriages to two daughters of Morus ap John ap Maredudd of Y Clenennau.

MEMOIRS

59.4 Henry Rowlands: He was Bishop of Bangor between 1598 and 1616 and succeeded Richard Vaughan. *DWB*, p. 893; *PACF*, p. 269; J. Morgan, *Coffadwriaeth am y Gwir Barchedig Henry Rowland, D.D., Arglwydd Esgob Bangor* (1914); J. Jones, *Enwogion Sir Gaernarfon* (1922), pp. 335-6; R. Williams, *Eminent Welshmen* (1852), pp. 461-2; F. O. White, *Lives of the Elizabethan Bishops* (1898), pp. 252-3; J. G. Jones, 'Henry Rowlands, Bishop of Bangor, 1598-1616', *Jnl.Hist.Soc. of the Church in Wales*, xxxi, 1979, 34-53.

59.6-7 He was sufficiently learned: He graduated B.A. at New College, Oxford (1574) and M.A. (1577), and was appointed chaplain of the college. He obtained his B.D. (1591) at St. Mary's Hall, Oxford and D.D. (1605). A. Clarke (ed.), *Register of the University of Oxford* (1888), ii (Pt. iii), 1571-1622, p. 38; A. Wood, *Athenae Oxonienses*, ed., P. Bliss (1813-20), ii, pp. 854-6.

59.8-9 a good and provident governor: In his will he donated £20 to Bangor Cathedral for the repair of the steeple with lead and declared that the fabric still needed attention. He repaired the roof of the nave and transept in 1611 and purchased three bells for the steeple. 'What care I took for this temple while I was Bishop', he said, 'and in what estate I found it, others do know, and though I leave it in far better state than it was, yet God he knows it had need to be daily looked into having no maintenance but the Bishop's benevolence and his clergy from time to time'. Wood, ii, pp. 854-5.

59.12 *in commendam*: i.e. the portion of land assigned to a clergyman as part of his benefice. Rowlands, like other bishops of his generation, held benefices *in commendam* i.e. held with enjoyment of revenues until an incumbent was provided. Bishops were allowed to hold such livings as well as their own preferment. Rowlands held *in commendam* the livings of Trefdraeth, Anglesey, and Llanrhaeadr-yng-Nghin-meirch, Denbighshire.

59.14 and yet died rich: It is believed that he owned property to the value of £2,000. J. G. Jones, op. cit., 43 (fn.68). 'He was a most excellent good man, very charitable and conscienti-ous, and much more careful of his see and successors than any that ever sat there'. (Humphrey Humphreys, Bishop of Bangor, 1689-1701). See notes added to *Athenae Oxon.*, ii, p. 856; A. H. Dodd, *A History of Caernarvonshire, 1284-1900* (1968), pp. 85-6.

59.14-15 the commission of the peace: *CSPD*, 1603-1610, xvi, p. 261; 1611-1618, lxv, p. 53; *AC*, ix, 1878, 305; NLW Add. MS.464E, 215; Ca.MS.4.58,21; J.R.S. Phillips, op. cit., p. 21.

59.18 an almshouse. It was known as the 'Bishop Henry Rowland Charity' founded in his will. He left lands in the parish of Llansadwrn, Anglesey, to maintain 'six poor almsmen, old and impotent, of honest name and fame'. These men were to be unmarried and natives of the parishes of Pen-mynydd, Aberdaron, Mellteyrn, Bangor, Llangristiolus and Amlwch. Their weekly maintenance was to be two shillings; they were to receive 'six yards of good white frieze apiece to make them gowns towards winter, every year' and were required to attend services at the cathedral three times a week. The almshouse was the house in Bangor where the Registrar, George Steele, had lived; and it remained there until 1805 when the present almshouses were built on a different site south of the cathedral. M. L. Clarke, *Bangor Cathedral* (1969), pp. 97-8.

59.20 two Fellowships: In his will he left lands in Eirianell in the commote of Llifon, Anglesey, to the Principal and Fellows of Jesus College, Oxford, so that they might elect two scholars, one from Botwnnog School or Friars School, Bangor, and the other from Beaumaris, to become Fellows. J. G. Jones, op. cit., 41; Morgan, op. cit., pp. 65-6; L. S. Knight, *Welsh Independent Grammar Schools to 1600* (1926), p. 41.

59.21 a free school: The grammar school at Botwnnog—once described as 'a petty school in Llŷn'—was founded in 1616. Members of prominent Llŷn families, such as Edmund Gruffudd, Dean of Bangor, of Cefnamwlch [see 73.36n] and Sir William Jones of Castellmarch [see 63.27n], together with Rowlands's successsor as Bishop of Bangor, were to be appointed feoffees responsible for the maintenance of a free Grammar School to be established either at Mellteyrn or Botwnnog. The schoolmaster was to be given 'out of the profits of the same premises for his stipend £20 yearly' and was to 'be unmarried, a good scholar, a Master of Arts of the University of Oxford and an Englishman (if it may be) for the language sake'. G. Parry, 'Hanes Botwnnog', *TCS*, 1957, 1-3; *CWP*, no. 1094. Rowlands himself was educated at a school (of which nothing is known) in the parish of Penllech.

59.30 Doctor Richard Vaughan: His dates are 1550-1607. He was a native of Nyffryn, Llŷn, and was Bishop of Bangor between 1595 and 1597. He was related to Rowlands, being his mother's first cousin. The two fathers were sons of Robert Fychan of Talhenbont (Plas Hen), a member of a prominent Eifionydd family in the sixteenth century. Before he was appointed to Bangor Archbishop Whitgift regarded him and William Morgan [see 63.11n] as 'two very worthy men, and the worthiest . . . for these two small bishoprics' (i.e. Bangor and Llandaff). *HMC*, Hatfield, v, p. 18; *Eifionydd*, pp. 230-2, 292-3.

59.30-1 the following inscription: The effigies of both bishops and the inscription are placed in the north end of the choir. The Latin dedication in memory of Richard Vaughan and Henry Rowlands (May 1616), as recorded by the author, reads as follows:

Piae Memoriae duorum Episcoporum in hac Ecclesia proxime succedentium qui fuerunt contigue Nati, Coetanei, sibi invicem cari Condiscipuli, Consanguinei; ex illustri Familia Vaughanorum de Talhenbont in Evionith Prior; Filius Thomae ap Robert

Vachan, Generosi de Niffryn in Llŷn. Qui sedem hanc
per Biennium tenuit, deinde Cestrensem per septem
Annos; postea Londinensem per Triennium tenuit, ubi
vitam Mensis Martii ultimo Anno Domini 1607
immatura Morte commutavit. Cujus Virtus post funera
vivit: Posterior, Henricus Filius Rolandi ap Robert,
Armigeri, de Mellteyrn in Llŷn, ex Elizabetha filia
Griffini ap Robert Vachan, Armigeri, de Talhenbont, qui
annum Consecrationis suae jam agit decimum
octavum, multosque agat feliciter ad honorem Dei et
Evangelii propagationem. Mutuo amore alter utrique
hoc struxit Monumentum mense Maii, Anno Domini
1616.

Orimur, Vicissim Morimur,
Qui non precesserunt, sequuntur.

60.15 born also in Llŷn: *DNB*, lviii, p. 170; *DWB*, p. 105; pp.
243, 269; *Eifionydd*, pp. 230-3; White, op. cit., pp. 352-3.
Vaughan was the son of Thomas ap Robert Fychan of Nyffryn,
Llŷn. He was educated at St. John's College, Cambridge and
graduated B.A. (1574), M.A. (1577) and D.D. (1589). T. Baker,
History of St. John's College, Cambridge (1896), i, p. 235. He
became a canon of St. Paul's (1583) and Archdeacon of
Middlesex (1588).

60.21 he lived at Chester: He was Bishop of Chester between
May 1597 and December 1604. While at Chester he was
regarded as 'a man of public spirit ... who very much
promoted the reparation of the Cathedral, as he had before
that at Bangor. He caused the bells to be new cast and hung in
the Great Tower, all the west roof to be new leaded, and the
timber work repaired.' J. Hemingway, *History of the City of
Chester* (1831), i, p. 304.

60.24-5 translated ... to London: Richard Vaughan was
Bishop of London between 1604 and 1607, the year of his
death. He is described by Browne Willis as 'a great Benefactor
to the Cathedral (as was also his excellent successor, Bishop
Rowland)'. B. Willis, *A Survey of the Cathedral Church of
Bangor* (1721), pp. 24-5, 109.

60.29 Nicholas Robinson: His dates are c.1530-85 and he was
Bishop of Bangor between 1566 and 1585. The Robinsons,
burgesses of Conwy, came originally from Cheshire and

Dolwyddelan castle *(Peter De Wint)*

(Crown Copyright Royal Commission on Ancient and Historical Monuments in Wales)

Gwydir mansion   (National Library of Wales)
(Sir Richard Colt Hoare)

members of the family held offices in the borough. *CCQSR*, pp. 19, 115, 171, 184. The bishop, on his mother's side, was a descendant from the Penmynydd family of Anglesey, the founder of the Robinson family, Sir William Norris, having married a sister of Owen Tudor. *DWB*, pp. 887-8; *PACF*, pp. 23-4; White, op. cit., pp. 179-80. He was a scholar of some repute. Note his translation into Latin of the Life of Gruffudd ap Cynan. See 1.9-13n.

60.34 an excellent scholar: He was educated at Queen's College, Cambridge (1545) and graduated M.A. (1551). Willis, op. cit., p. 107. He became chaplain to Archbishop Matthew Parker and was later appointed Dean of Bangor (1556).

60.38 at St. Paul's in London: Edmund Grindal, Bishop of London, considered Robinson, among others, as a suitable nomination for the post of Provost of Eton in December 1561, and noted that he had 'made a very good Sermon yesterday at the Cross'. J. Strype, *The Life and Acts of Matthew Parker* (1711), Bk. ii, p. 105. For Robinson's career see A. O. Evans, 'Nicholas Robinson (1530?-1585)', *Y Cymmrodor*, xxxix, 1928, 149-8.

61.2-3 left many hopeful children: He married Jane, daughter of Randle Brereton. William, his eldest son, inherited Gwersyllt Uchaf, Denbighshire, and Mynachdy in Anglesey. Humphrey became rector of Aber and Hugh was elected Fellow of New College, Oxford and appointed headmaster of Winchester School. *DWB*, pp. 887-8.

61.4 Thomas Davies: The second Elizabethan Bishop of St. Asaph (1561-73). He was descended from reputable native stock, the son of Dafydd ap Robert ap Dafydd of Caerhun in the Conwy valley and Margaret, daughter of Rhys ab Wiliam of Gorddinog, Aber. He was educated at St. John's College, Cambridge, and became Archdeacon of St. Asaph (1558-61). Dwnn ii, p. 85; *PACF*, p. 162, 233; *DWB*, p. 153; *DNB*, xiv, p. 157-8. D. R. Thomas, *History of the Diocese of St. Asaph* (1908), i, p. 225; White, op. cit., p. 171; J. G. Jones, 'Thomas Davies and William Hughes: two Reformation Bishops of St. Asaph', *BBCS*, xxix (Pt. ii), 1981, 320-2.

61.10 Gruffudd Davies: His younger brother who became sheriff of Caernarfonshire (1556, 1565, 1573). He held other offices such as M.P. for Caernarfon borough (1553); Deputy-Justice of the North Wales circuit of Great Sessions and JP (from 1542 onwards). *PH*, p. 65; *LS*, p. 248; *CCQSR*, p. 246; Phillips, op. cit., pp. 17-18; *Hist. Caern.*, p. 77; G. H. Williams, 'Estate Management in Dyffryn Conwy c.1685: the Caerhun, Baron Hill and Gwydir Estates', *TCS*, 1979, 34.

61.17 Richard Davies: He was the son of Dafydd ap Gronw, curate of Y Gyffin near Conwy. He was educated at New Inn Hall, Oxford and graduated M.A. (1530) and B.D. (1536). He became rector of Maidsmorton, Buckinghamshire (1549) and was converted to Protestantism probably at Oxford. He fled to Frankfurt in 1555 and returned in 1558. In 1559 he visited the dioceses of Wales together with Hereford and Worcester, was elected Bishop of St. Asaph (1559) and was translated to St. David's (1561). He was one of the chief exponents of Protestant humanism in Wales and, at the bishop's palace at Abergwili, formerly a manor owned by the bishops of St. David's, he assisted William Salesbury in the translation of the New Testament and Book of Common Prayer into Welsh (1567). *DWB*, pp. 147-8; *DNB*, xiv, p. 149; *WRE*, pp. 55-90; G. Williams, *Bywyd ac Amserau'r Esgob Richard Davies* (1953); D. R. Thomas, *The Life of Bishop Richard Davies and William Salesbury (1902).*

61.21 'Myn y Wyry(f) Faglog': This means presumably 'by the crutched virgin', i.e. the image of the Virgin Mary bearing a cross. She is represented in art, among other forms, as the 'Glorified Madonna' bearing a crown and sceptre or an orb and cross in rich colours and surrounded by angels. *Geiriadur Prifysgol Cymru*, i, p. 240 where 'baglog' is cited as 'yn dwyn gwaywffon, yn dwyn ffon swyddogol abad neu esgob'. It can also mean bearing a cross. In St. Benedict's parish church at Y Gyffin, Conwy, where Richard Davies's father was incumbent, there exists a thirteenth-century painted wooden barrel vault over the sanctuary which includes, among other paintings, a panel depicting the Blessed Virgin with hands crossed on the breast. This may well have been the 'crutched virgin' (posing with the hands representing a cross), which had impressed Davies since the days of childhood and had inspired the oath. H. H. Hughes and H. L. North, op. cit., pp. 66-7.

61.27-8 he gave them good maintenance and education: *WRE*, p. 181; *Bywyd ac Amserau*, p. 66. Davies was a nepotist like many of his contemporaries in the church. His three sons, Richard (Thomas according to Wynn), Peregrine and Gerson were well cared for by their father. Richard and Peregrine and one other obtained the lease of the manor of Brawdey, Painscastle, Carnllwchwr and Llwchfaen together with the prebend of Brawdy and Hampcastle chapel (1580). Peregrine was appointed Archdeacon of Cardigan (1563) and, on his resignation in 1568, obtained the lease of Llanymddyfri. The youngest son, Gerson, from a very early age was given the lease of Llanbedr Pont Steffan (1563) and later acquired the prebends of Clydai and Llanbister together with the vicarage of Penbryn. *WRE*, pp. 174, 180. In his will Davies left 'all my bookes of Homilies and Histories savinge Eccliasticall histories' to Peregrine, and his other son, Gerson, was to receive the 'Eccliasticall histories and all the rest of my bookes printed'.

61.28 He did stoutly confront: Davies was eager to defend the church's interests against greedy laymen and became involved in a bitter dispute concerning the living of Llanddewibrefi which became vacant in 1566. He wished to present it to the Chancellor, Lewis Gwyn, but the earls of Pembroke and Leicester had another in mind. Although Davies's nominee was eventually presented with the living a commission was issued to investigate concealed lands within the diocese. Sir John Perrot of Haroldston, Pembrokeshire (a reputed illegitimate son of Henry VIII) was probably an instigator of the commission. He was a powerful figure in his county and a close friend of the earl of Leicester. Carey, the chief commissioner, succeeded, in spite of Davies's opposition, in restoring the living to the Crown alleging that Lewis Gwyn had trespassed on the living. Davies opposed him violently, and although he lost the living and its dependants, the dispute had not been settled on the bishop's death. Furthermore, in 1578, the Privy Council appointed Davies to enquire into the alleged piratical activities of Sir John Perrot and Richard Vaughan of Whitland. Davies's position and the fact that the earl of Essex (Perrot's enemy) was his patron, intensified the bad feeling between Davies and Perrot, but it is probably the Llanddewibrefi case which Wynn recalls at this point. *Bywyd ac Amserau*, pp. 59-60, 76-7, 81.

61.30-1 Lord Deputy of Ireland: Perrot served as Lord Deputy of Ireland (1584-88) and was a member of the Privy Council (1589-91). *DWB*, pp. 747-8. He died in the Tower under sentence of death for treason in June 1592.

61.34 William Salesbury: A Protestant humanist scholar and the chief representative of the Renaissance in Wales. He translated most of the New Testament into Welsh in 1567. He was a native of Llansannan, Denbighshire, the second son of Ffwg Salesbury of Plas Isaf, Llanrwst, and was educated at Oxford. *DWB*, p. 898; *WRE*, pp. 192-3; *Life of Davies and Salesbury*, p. 57 et. seq. Salesbury was invited to the Bishop's Palace at Abergwili in 1565 to translate the scriptures, *Bywyd ac Amserau*, pp. 92-3; Davies, according to the poets, maintained a sumptuous court at Abergwili, *GST*, i, xxix, p. 120; no. cxx, p. 469; *GWC*, ii, no. iii, p. 534; J. Jones (ed.), *Cynfeirdd Lleyn* (1905), pp. 1-4. The poets, such as Wiliam Llŷn, Siôn Tudur, Huw Dwnn, Robert Middleton and Hywel ap Syr Mathew, were welcomed at Abergwili, and scholars like Thomas Huet, Precentor of St. David's, who assisted Davies and Salesbury by translating the Book of Revelation; *Bywyd ac Amserau*, pp. 82-4.

61.37-8 translated the New Testament: The Act for the translation of the scriptures into Welsh (St. 5 Eliz. I, c.28) was passed in 1563 but only the New Testament appeared in 1567, most of it the work of Salesbury who also translated the Psalter which was published with the Book of Common Prayer shortly before the New Testament. G. H. Jones, 'The Welsh Psalter', *Jnl. Hist. Soc. of the Church in Wales*, xvii, 1967, 56-61; *SW*, pp. 149-51.

62.3-4 the general sense and etymology of one word: Since Salesbury was well-known for his stylistic and syntactical peculiarities in Welsh ('British and mother tongue') a rift might easily have been caused for that reason between him and Davies. This tradition, first recorded by Wynn, may well have contained an element of truth. There may also have been financial considerations which accounted for the quarrel. *Bywyd ac Amserau*, pp. 107-8. For a case against accepting Wynn's explanation of this dispute see I. Thomas, *Y Testament Newydd Cymraeg* (1976), pp. 302-3.

62.12 a rare scholar: Sir Thomas Wiliems, the lexicographer and Salesbury's contemporary, says of him: 'WS I declare is the most learned Briton, not only in the British tongue, but in Hebrew, Greek, Latin, English, French, German and other languages, so much so, that it would be strange that anyone could attain such perfection in the tongues unless he studied nothing else at his life'. I. Thomas, *William Salesbury and his Testament* (1967), p. 11.

62.16 Plas-y-Person: It was situated near the rectory at Y Gyffin but has now disappeared. H. H. Hughes and R. L. North, *Old Churches of Snowdonia*, p. 72.

62.17-18 he was fain to flee ... to Geneva: There is no evidence that he lived at Geneva but rather at Frankfurt. It has been suggested that since Geneva was better known (because of its Calvinist connections) than Frankfurt it may have come first to Wynn's mind. *Bywyd ac Amserau*, pp. 17-19. Davies may have visited Geneva since there is no mention of him at Frankfurt after June 1557. He may have travelled with fellow Protestants to Geneva via Strasburg.

62.27 William Glyn: His dates are 1504-58. He was a native of the parish of Heneglwys, in the commote of Malltraeth, Anglesey. His brother was Geoffrey Glyn who obtained the lands and buildings of the suppressed Bangor Friary and who founded Bangor Grammar School. His half-brother was John Glyn, Dean of Bangor (1505-34). Willis, p. 125, *DWB*, 281; *PACF*, p. 239. William Glyn was educated at Queen's College, Cambridge where he became a Fellow (1530) and later Professor of Divinity (1544) at Trinity College. He was appointed Bishop of Bangor in 1555 and was described as 'a Person of very great Learning, as may be seen by his Disput-ations printed in Fox's Book of Martyrs'. *DNB*, viii, p. 11; *DWB*, p. 281; Willis, pp. 104-5; D. Wilson-Reid, 'William Glyn, Bishop of Bangor, 1555-1558', *TAAS*, 1950, 87-90.

62.34 Another William Glynn: He was the son of Robert ap Maredudd of Glynllifon by his first wife, Ellen Bulkeley of Beaumaris. He was appointed Archdeacon of Anglesey (1524-57) and acquired many ecclesiastical preferments, *DWB*, p. 280; *PACF*, pp. 172-3.

62.36 Bishop Skevington: Thomas Skevington (or Skeffing-ton), the absentee Bishop of Bangor (1509-33) and native of Skevington, Lancashire. He became Abbot of Waverley in Surrey. In his will he stipulated that 'the steeple and lofte of Bangor churche where the Bells doo hange be fynished, and the three Bells hanged up, and a further Belle agreeable to them be provided and hangid there, and that the roofe of that Steple to be well made, coverid with leade, and the Window in the said Steple, over the Doore, to be well Barride with yron and glased'. Clarke, p. 18; *DNB*, lii, p. 340; Willis pp. 96-8.

63.1 were sold by the Bishop: Arthur Bulkeley, Bishop of Bangor (1542-53), brother of Sir Richard Bulkeley I of Beaumaris (d. 1546-7). According to his will he sold and disposed of mitres, copes, challices and probably bells. Willis, p. 102. *DWB*, p. 57. He became a Doctor of Canon Law at Oxford (1525). He was educated at New Inn Hall, Oxford and was confirmed Bishop of Bangor in December 1541. Bulkeley was later to be granted the rectory of Llanddeusant, Anglesey (1525)and also became canon of St. Asaph about the same time. *DNB*, vii, p. 231; *Alumni Oxon*, I, p. 207; *Athenae Oxon.*, II, p. 764.

63.4 the Duke of Somerset: Edward Seymour, earl of Hertford and duke of Somerset, Lord Protector of England (1547-9). His policy of religious toleration and advanced Protestantism led to pillaging and iconoclasm on the part of ambitious landowners and royal servants. He was deprived of his office in 1549 by John Dudley, earl of Warwick (later duke of Northumberland) and was executed in 1552.

63.11 William Morgan: His dates are c.1545-1604, was elevated Bishop of Llandaff (1595-1601) and of St. Asaph (1601-04). It was he who translated the Old Testament and Apocrypha into Welsh (1588). He was born at Tyddyn Mawr, a farm in Blaen Wybrnant, in the parish of Penmachno and commote of Nanconwy, a younger son of John ap Morgan and his wife Lowri, both of whom descended from gentle stock. He entered St. John's College, Cambridge (1565) and held several livings: Llanbadarn Fawr (1572-5), Welshpool (1575-9) and Llanrhaeadr-ym-Mochnant (1578-95) where the work of translating was completed

63.13 descended of the race of the bondmen: His father, a descendant of Hedd Molwynog and Nefydd Hardd, was a tenant on the Wynn estate but it was the land held by him rather than the lineage (as Wynn seems to imply) that was servile. Even twenty years or so after the bishop's death Sir John Wynn could not conceal his bitter feelings towards him because of the fierce dispute that had occurred between them concerning church lands in Llanrwst in 1603-04. The sparsely populated Nanconwy was well known for its large bond tenements and it may be assumed that John ap Morgan was a fairly substantial tenant farmer. It is doubtless Wynn's vindictiveness at the time of writing that accounts for the sneering comment on the bishop's ancestry. Yorke, *Royal*

Tribes, pp. 188-9; *DWB*, p. 656; *DNB*, xxxix, p. 38.
G. Williams: 'Bishop William Morgan (1545-1604) and the
First Welsh Bible', *JMHRS*, vii (Pt. iv), 1976, 348-51. W.
Hughes, *The Life and Times of Bishop William Morgan*
(1891); C. Ashton, *Bywyd ac Amserau yr Esgob Morgan*
(1891); R. G. Gruffydd, 'William Morgan' in G. Bowen (ed.),
Y Traddodiad Rhyddiaith (1970), 149-74. He was probably
educated at Gwydir at the time when John Wyn ap Maredudd
was head of the family. I. Thomas, *Y Testament Newydd
Cymraeg*, pp. 303-4.

63.16 His first preferment: i.e. to the diocese of Llandaff in
1595: During his quarrel with Morgan over church lands in
Llanrwst in 1603-04 Sir John Wynn did remind Morgan of his
ungratitude and declared that it was by means of his good
services that he had been preferred. 'Hominibus ingratis
loquimini lapides. The sower went out to sowe and some of
his seede fell in stonie ground where hitt wythered because
hitt coulde take noe roote. The seede was goode but the land
nought. I may justly say soe by you. I have in all shewed my
selfe your ffreinde in soe much as yf I had not pointed you the
waye with my finger (whereof I have yett good testimonye)
you had beene styll Vycar of Llanrhayder'. Wynn had also
mediated on Morgan's behalf in his disputes with Ieuan ap
Maredudd of Lloran Uchaf, Llanrhaeadr-ym-Mochnant and
David Holland of Teirdan, Llanelian-yn-Rhos. J. G. Jones,
'Bishop William Morgan's Dispute with John Wynn of
Gwydir, 1603-04', *Jnl. Hist. Soc. of the Church in Wales*,
xxvii, 1972, 49-52, 71. See also I. ab O. Edwards, 'William
Morgan's Quarrel with his Parishioners at Llanrhaeadr-ym-
Mochnant', *BBCS*, iii (Pt. iv), 1927, 298 et. seq.; Yorke, *Royal
Tribes*, pp. 134-43 for the correspondence concerning the
dispute between Sir John Wynn and Morgan over the lease of
Llanrwst rectory.

63.17 Bishop of Llandaff: He was Bishop of Llandaff between
1595 and 1601. He was elected on 30 June 1595, confirmed on
18 July and consecrated on 20 July in Croydon Church by
Archbishop John Whitgift. W. de Gray Birch, *Memorials of
the See and Cathedral of Llandaff* (1912), pp. 364-6. He was
not the first choice for Llandaff because the see was intended
for Richard Vaughan who became Bishop of Bangor and later
of Chester and London. HMC, Hatfield, v, 18. *GCH*, iv, pp.
225, 230. See also R. G. Gruffydd, *The Translating of the Bible
into the Welsh Tongue* (1988) and I. Thomas, *William*

Morgan and his Bible (1988) for two useful general surveys of Morgan's career and scholarship.

63.17-18 afterwards translated to St. Asaph: He was Bishop of St. Asaph between 17 September 1601 and 1604 and held the archdeaconry of St. Asaph *in commendam*. He was elected on 21 July 1601, consecrated on 21 September, and died on 10 September 1604. B. Willis, *A Survey of St. Asaph* (1801), i, pp. 107-8; D. R. Thomas, *H.St.A.*, i, pp. 226-7. It was during his short period at St. Asaph that Morgan's quarrels with Wynn reached their peak, disputes which compelled the bishop to describe him unequivocably as 'a perfidiouse spoyler of my diocesse and an unnatural hindrer of preachers and good scholars'. Yorke, *Royal Tribes*, p. 134.

63.23 yet he carried the name of it all: Davies and Salesbury had started to translate the Old Testament in 1567 before they quarrelled (probably in 1575). Gruffydd, op. cit., p. 172. William Morgan, however, in his dedication of the Bible to Queen Elizabeth I in 1588, did acknowledge the contribution which both Davies and Salesbury had made to the spiritual life of the nation in 1567 and also vindicated the value of the New Testament to his fellow-countrymen. It had enabled them, he maintained, by comparing the English and Welsh versions, to attain a knowledge of the English language and to understand and accept Protestant truths more easily. W. Hughes, *The Life and Times of Bishop William Morgan*, pp. 122-3; C. Davies (ed.), *Rhagymadroddion a Chyflwyniadau Lladin, 1551-1632* (1980), pp. 65-6.

63.23-4 He repaired and slated the chancel: This is the only source which records the bishop's work in repairing the fabric of the cathedral church. He also completed a revised version of the Book of Common Prayer in 1599, and a revised translation of the New Testament shortly before his death, a work which was never published. He also took firm steps to improve preaching facilities within the parishes of the dioceses.

63.25 He died a poor man: On his death Morgan incurred many debts, particularly episcopal rates. G. J. Roberts, *Yr Esgob William Morgan* (1955), pp. 46-7. Wynn, in a letter to the lawyer Thomas Martin in 1603 during his dispute with Morgan, recalled that, before he was elevated to St. Asaph, he was 'but poore (hys translation [i.e. movement to St. Asaph] havynge stood him in muche) yett wylfull and heddy to run into suets'. J. G. Jones, op. cit., 72.

63.26 a Grecian and Hebrician: At St. John's College, Cambridge, he was probably taught Hebrew either by the French scholar Anthony Chevallier, Reader in Hebrew, or his successor Philip Bignon. Gruffydd, op. cit., pp. 162-3. On 11 December 1600 Gabriel Goodman, Dean of Westminster, informed Lord Burghley that Morgan 'is well known to be the most sufficient man in that both for his learning, government and honesty of life, and hath also best deserved of our country for his great pains and charges in translating the Bible into our vulgar tongue with such sufficiency as deserveth great commendation and reward'. John Whitgift, Archbishop of Canterbury, also commended him as 'a man of integrity, gravity and great learning, for whom he has received that testimony, both from the best of that country where he now remains, and of that also where he wishes him to be placed, that he never received for any man'. *HMC*, Hatfield, xiv,p. 144; xi, p. 282. For a full assessment of Morgan's contribution to Welsh religion and culture see G. Williams, 'Bishop William Morgan and the First Welsh Bible', 347-70.

63.27 Sir William Jones: He was born at Castellmarch, Llangïan, Llŷn in 1566 and died in 1640. He was the eldest son of William ap Gruffudd ap John and was the first of the family to adopt the surname. His mother was Margaret, daughter of Humphrey Wynn ap Maredudd of Y Gesail Gyfarch. She was Sir John Wynn's kinswoman because both their grandfathers were half-brothers. This Sir William Jones assisted in founding Beaumaris Grammar School in 1602 and he obtained his education at St. Edmund's Hall, Oxford (1580) and subsequently at Lincoln's Inn. He was called to the Bar in 1595, was elected member of parliament for Beaumaris in 1597-8, 1604 and 1614, and for Caernarfonshire in 1601, and was knighted in 1617. His promotion within the legal profession was rapid because, in that year, he was appointed Lord Chief Justice of Ireland, an office which he retained until 1620. He was highly esteemed among his colleagues, and in the following year (1621) became a Judge of Common Pleas at Westminster. Wynn, at that time, called him the 'prime man of the country'. *CWP*, no. 942; *DWB*, pp. 1138-39; *DNB*, xxx, p. 171; *PACF*, pp. 191, 236, 280-1; *PH*. pp. 10, 59, 66; *Welsh Judges*, p. 94; *Athenae Oxon*, II, p. 673; *Alumni Oxon*, II, p. 831. He aided Wynn with his many legal affairs and was well-acquainted with him. *CWP*, 262, 281, 301, 323, 325 et. seq.

63.34 Jeffrey Coetmor: In a letter to Sir William Jones on 27 January 1621 Wynn referred to this person, Jeffrey Coetmor (but not by name), whom he described as having lived at Henley-upon-Thames. It is he and not his grandfather Hywel Coetmor, incidentally, who lived there, Wynn being rather confusing at this point. A *cywydd* composed in his honour had been sent by Wynn to Jones but there is no way of identifying either the patron or the bard since the poem is no longer extant. In his letter Wynn explains: 'My unkle, Robert Wynne of Conwey, in his youthe servinge Sr. Walter Stoner, then leiuetenant of ye Towre (who dwelled neere Hentley upon Thames, as I hear his heires yet doe) tould mee that this Coytmor had a house not farr of & that it was there reputed that he was desended of ye Welshe race & yt his inheritannce went to Coparceners a litle before his cominge thither'. NLW MS.9058, 1005. Mr. E. D. Jones identified this Coytmor as Hywel Gwynedd ab Einion ab Hywel Coetmor. This is incorrect since Wynn was specifically referring to the person who is mentioned in his letter (cited above), another grandson of Hywel Coetmor (and possibly Hywel Gwynedd's brother). Hywel Coetmor assisted Owain Glyndŵr and his sepulchral effigy lies in the Gwydir chapel at Llanrwst. This Hywel also was the owner of Castell Cefel Ynghoedmor, Betws-y-coed, his brother Rhys Gethin (another ally of Glyndŵr) living nearby at Hendre Rhys Gethin. E. D. Jones, 'Howel Coytmor (Coetmor)', *NLWJ*, viii, 1953-4, 148; *RCAM* (Denbs.), p. 148; *PACF*, pp. 328, 394. As Wynn notes he was renowned for his military activities in the French wars. *IGE*, pp. 107-8; *HPF*, i, iii, p. 33; *PACF*, pp. 328, 394. It is he, and not Jeffrey Coetmor who, according to Wynn, captained a 100 Denbighshire men at Poitiers in 1356 [see *HGF* (1927), p. 66].

> Gŵr glân a gâi'n Lloegr y glod,
> I Ffrainc y curai Ffrancod.

(A resplendent soldier renowned for assisting England to defeat the French), *IGE*, p. 107. See 17.17-25n, 54.27-37n.

64.3 William Thomas: The son of Rice Thomas of Caernarfon who built up the family fortunes (later identified with Coed Alun). William Thomas was sheriff of Anglesey (1578), Caernarfonshire (1580-1) and M.P. for Caernarfonshire (1573-85). He was also Deputy-Constable of Caernarfon Castle from 1583. He was an avid accumulator of property in Llŷn, Anglesey and Caernarfonshire. It is said that he commanded 200 Welshmen under Robert Dudley, earl of Leicester, his close friend and patron, in December 1585 and was slain while serving with Sir Philip Sidney's company of volunteers in the Netherlands at the battle of Zutphen (1586). S. L. Adams, 'The Gentry of North Wales and the earl of Leicester's Expedition to the Netherlands, 1585-1586', *WHR*, vii (no. 11) 1974, 132-5, 137; *PACF*, p. 202; *DWB*, p. 935, P. Williams, *Council in the Marches*, p. 114, *LS*, p. 248, *PH*, p. 59. His company was at Rheinburg in July 1586. *CSPF*, 1586-7, pp. 110, 116, 127, 316.

64.7 Sir Thomas Morgan: He was the son of William Morgan of St. George's and Pencarn, Glamorgan, a descendant of the Morgan family of Tredegyr in Gwent. He was known as 'the warrior', who spent most of his active military life in the Netherlands (1572-93) where he became Colonel of the regiment of English volunteers. He was knighted in 1587 and his name appears frequently in State Papers relating to the Netherlands campaign. He was at Rheinburg in 1586 and was appointed Governor of Bergen-op-zoom in 1588. *CSPF*, 1586-7, p. 109; 1588, p. 71; *DWB*, p. 652; *DNB*, xxxix, p. 29.

64.7 Sir Roger Williams: The son of Thomas Williams of Penrhos, Monmouthshire. He served in the household of Sir William Herbert, 1st earl of Pembroke, but spent most of his active service as a mercenary on the continent. He was knighted by the earl of Leicester in 1586 and, in 1572 joined a company of 300 men under Captain Thomas who went to Flushing to fight against Spain. *DWB*, p. 1069; *DNB*, lxi, p. 441.

64.7-8 Sir Martin Schenk: also Shinck, Skenke etc. Colonel Maarten van Nydechem (1550-89), nobleman and commander under the duke of Parma (see 64.11n.) in the Netherlands. He played a prominent role in the revolt and in 1585 abandoned the Spaniards because he was not given the Governorship of Gueldres. *CSPF*, 1584-5, pp. 452, 470, 476. He became Governor of Venlo in the province of Limberg. Ibid, 1585-6, p. 28. He was also made a Knight of the Garter for his services to the rebels and the English cause in the Low Countries, ibid, p. 612.

64.11 Berk-upon-Rhine: Rheinburg (Berck). A small town in the Ruhr, near the left bank of the river Rhine, 6 miles north of Moers in West Germany. It is about 15 miles east of the Dutch frontier.

64.11 Prince of Parma: Alexander (Allesandro) Farnese, Prince of Parma (1545-92), son of an illegitimate daughter of Charles V. He was a Spanish Commander, diplomat and Governor-General of the Netherlands (1572-92) during the revolt. He captured Antwerp (1585) and was created duke of Parma (1586). Preparations for the siege of Rheinburg began on 25 April 1586, *CSPF*, 1585-6, p. 621. The siege continued for several months, ibid, 1586-7, pp. 87, 114, 116, 125, 276. Schenk defended the town in the summer of 1586 with Morgan and the English companies, ibid, p. 112. The town capitulated on 27 January 1590 and Mansfelt entered it on 23 January. Ibid, August 1589—June 1590, pp. 106-7.

64.17 Zutphen: A town in the province of Gelderland, east-central Netherlands, at the junction of the rivers Ijssel and Berkel. The battle was fought on 22 September 1586 between English forces aided by the Dutch who, under the command of the earls of Leicester and Essex and Lord Willoughby, unsuccessfully besieged the town.

64.17-18 Sir Philip Sidney: His dates are 1554-86. He was the son of Sir Henry Sidney, Lord Deputy of Ireland and President of the Council in the Marches (1559-86). He was a diplomat, military leader and literary figure who typified the Renaissance spirit in Elizabethan England, his chief works being *Arcadia* (1580) and the *Defence of Poesie* (1595). He was shot in the thigh at Zutphen and died at Arnhem 26 days later. *DNB*, liii, pp. 219-10.

64.30 Gruffudd Wynn: Of Berthddu, Llanrwst, second son of John Wyn ap Maredudd and uncle of Sir John Wynn. He acquired most of his estate through his marriage to Gwen, daughter and co-heiress of Robert Salusbury of Cae'r Milwr and Berthddu. *PACF*, pp. 184, 281. Her uncle was William Salesbury, humanist and translator of the New Testament into Welsh. See 61.34n. Gruffudd Wynn was born at Gwydir and acquired Berthddu after his marriage. He also accumulated lands in the commote of Uwchdulas, principally in the townships of Llanrwst, Garthgyfannedd, Mathebrwd, Tybrith and Garthgarmon, and acquired his younger brother, John Gwynn's lands. For further details see J. G. Jones, 'Wynn Estate of Gwydir', 147-8.

64.32 Sir Edmund Knevett: Of New Buckenham Castle, Norfolk. The family was well known in Norfolk, its ancestor having married the heiress of Sir John Clifton, benefactor of Wymondham Abbey. Sir Edmund's mother was Elizabeth Howard, daughter of the second duke of Norfolk. He was, therefore, a cousin to both Anne Boleyn (executed in 1536) and Katherine Howard (executed in 1542), the second and fourth wives of Henry VIII respectively. W. Land, *Kett's Rebellion: the Norfolk Rising of 1549* (1977), pp. 102-3.

64.40 Cadwaladr ap Maredudd: Cadwaladr Wynn ap Maredudd ab Ieuan ap Robert by his third wife Margaret, daughter of Morus ap John ap Maredudd of Clennenau. He obtained Y Wenallt, Nanhwynan as part of his father's inheritance together with other properties in the township of Pennant. *Eifionydd*, pp. 13, 15-16, 89; *PACF*, pp. 281, 345.

64.40-65.1 John . . . and Dafydd Llwyd: Both were the sons of Rhys Wyn who was the son of Maredudd ab Ieuan ap Robert by his first wife, Ales, daughter of William Gruffudd ap Robin of Cochwillan. *PACF*, pp. 280-1. Rhys Wyn settled at Llwynbedw, Llanberis, after his marriage to Margaret, heiress of Robert of Llwynbedw. Ibid, p. 193. His son John married Annes, daughter of John ap Robert of Castellmarch, ibid, p. 191. Both sons are mentioned as beneficiaries in their father's will.

65.2 Thomas Williams: Founder of the Williams family of Y Faenol, Bangor (d. 1592). *PACF*, pp. 186, 190. He was a younger son of William Williams the elder of Cochwillan, the first of the family to assume the surname.

65.4 Edward Williams: Of Maes-y-castell, parish of Caerhun, Conwy valley, younger brother of the above. He fought at the siege of Boulogne in 1546 against the French. *PACF*, p. 190. He was sheriff of Caernarfonshire (1570-1), *LS*, p. 248. He was a 'captain of cannon' in 1588. *CWP*, no. 114. Sir William Paget was, at the time, Henry VIII's ambassador in France. He was first Baron Paget of Beaudesert (1505-63) who, together with Edward Seymor, first earl of Hertford, served as Henry VIII's chief adviser. *DNB*, xliii, p. 60.

65.7-8 Robert ap Hugh: Robert Pugh I of Penrhyn Creuddyn, sheriff of Caernarfonshire (1560-1) and a member of a well-known recusant family. He married Jane, daughter of Sir Richard Bulkeley II of Beaumaris. *PACF*, p. 372; *LS*, p. 248; E. G. Jones, *Cymru a'r Hen Ffydd* (1951), pp. 18-21, 30, 41.

65.12 the rebels of Norfolk: In July 1549 the Norfolk rebels set up a camp at Hingham, a village mid-way between Norwich and Watton. This camp was attacked successfully by Sir Edmund Knevett who returned with his troops to Buckenham Castle. Land, op. cit, p. 102.

65.25 the marquess of Northampton: William Parr, marquess of Northampton (1513-71), brother of Catherine Parr, Henry VIII's sixth and last wife who outlived him. He was created earl of Essex (1545) and marquess of Northampton (1547). He supported Edward Seymour, who became Lord Protector, and also the duke of Northumberland. As Lord Lieutenant of the five eastern counties it was his duty to restore order in 1549, but his military experience on the battlefield was very limited. Land, op. cit., pp. 84-5; *DNB*, xliii, p. 367.

65.27 the Lord Sheffield: Edmund Sheffield, first Baron Sheffield (1521-49). A courtier who had served Thomas Cromwell, and a poet and musician. He was created Baron Sheffield of Butterwick at the coronation of Edward VI and was the only nobleman to be killed in Ket's rebellion during the assault on Norwich on August 1, 1549. It was he, and not Knevett, as Wynn states, who suffered an untimely death, being only 28 years of age at the time. Land, op. cit., pp. 95-6.

65.23-36 the battle that was fought: Northampton was sent with 1,400 men to rescue Norwich from the rebels. The siege occurred in August 1549 and Sheffield was second-in-command. Robert Ket, a landowner in Wymondham, became the popular leader of the rebellion and was put to death. *DNB*, xxxi, p. 76. The rising was finally suppressed by John Dudley, earl of Warwick (later to become duke of Northumberland) in August.

65.30 Capapee: (Old Fr. cap a pie): armed from head to foot.

65.33 withers: The ridge between a horse's shoulder-blades.

66.1 Framlingham Castle: In Suffolk. It was Howard property at this time, the family being related to Sir Edmund Knevett's mother. N. Pevsner, *The Buildings of England; Suffolk* (rev. E. Radcliffe) (1974), pp. 218-20.

66.2 the Lady Mary: i.e. Mary Tudor, daughter of Catherine of Aragon.

66.8-9 as appeareth by the chronicle: Nicholas Sotherton *The Commoyson in Norfolk* 1549 or possibly Alexander Neville's *De furoribus Norfolciensium Ketto Duce* (1575) (translated into English in 1615 by Richard Woods, entitled *Norfolke Furies*). The Latin account was added to Christopher Ocland's *Anglorum Praelia* (1582). Also of importance are Raphael Holinshed's *Chronicles* (1578) and Sir John Haywood, *Life and Reign of King Edward the Sixth* (1610).

66.11-12 Ket was slain: Ket, in fact, was convicted of treason and hanged in chains in Norwich castle on 7 December 1549. Land, op. cit., pp. 142-3.

66.14 'Glas Ket': i.e. 'Ket's small grey horse or pony' ('caseg las').

66.16-17 William, earl of Pembroke: William Herbert (1501-70), 1st earl of Pembroke of the second creation, who led the forces which suppressed Sir Thomas Wyatt's rebellion (1554) *DWB*, p. 350; *DNB*, lxiii, p. 187.

66.18 old William Mostyn: William Mostyn (d. 1576) was the son of Thomas Mostyn of Flintshire. He also served under Pembroke in Wyatt's Rebellion. He was M.P. for Flintshire (1553-1554, 1572), sheriff of the county (1560-1, 1565-6, 1570-1), and of Caernarfonshire (1567-8), *LS*, p. 254; *PH*, p. 85. He was one of the royal commissioners appointed to hold an *eisteddfod* at Caerwys in 1567-8. *RWM*, i, p. 291-2. A. D. Carr, 'The Mostyns of Mostyn, 1540-1642' *Flints. Hist. Soc. Jnl.*, xxviii, 1977-8, 24-5.

66.20 Doctor [John] Gwynn: A lawyer (d. 1574), a younger brother of Gruffudd Wynn and the son of John Wyn ap Maredudd. He was educated at Queens' College, Cambridge (1545) and became a Fellow of St. John's College (1551) and graduated Ll.D. (1560). He became an Advocate of the Doctors Commons and moved into the Middle Temple. He left his estate to his brother Gruffudd. *CWP*, no. 54; Baker, *Hist. of St. John's*, i, pp. 421-2; *PACF*, pp. 184, 281; *DWB*, pp. 329-30.

66.28 and was wealthy withal: The references are all to Gruffudd Wynn who was sheriff of Merioneth (1591-2) and of Denbighshire (1593-4). *LS*, pp. 251, 260. His lands were increased in Uwchdulas on his marriage, particularly in the townships adjacent to Llanrwst. A rental of his lands in the counties of Caernarfon, Merioneth and Denbigh (1603) revealed that they were valued at £397 12s. 2d. UCNW (Bangor) Mostyn MS. 301.

66.29 Robert Wynn: Another of Gruffudd Wynn's younger brothers, who inherited and purchased lands in Dolwyddelan and who settled at Bryntyrch and Brynmoel in the township. His subsequent fortunes, however, were to be established in the borough of Conwy. *PACF*, p. 281 [see 68.9-10n]; *RCAM, Caerns. (East)*, p. 82.

66.30 Sir Philip Hoby: His dates are 1505-58. He was a diplomat who was knighted after the siege of Boulogne (1544). He was appointed ambassador to Charles, the Holy Roman Emperor (1548), and Privy Councillor. *DNB*, xxvii, pp. 54-5.
- -

66.33-4 the siege of Boulogne: This occurred between 19 July and 30 September 1544 when Henry VIII captured the city during the third Anglo-French War of his reign. Charles Wriothesley, *A Chronicle of England during the Reigns of the Tudors, 1485-1559*; W. D. Hamilton (ed.), *Camden Soc.*, i, 1875, pp. 148-9.

67.3 Sir William Gruffudd of Penrhyn: Chamberlain of North Wales (1508-31) and son of his namesake, Chamberlain of North Wales (1483-90). *PACF*, pp. 184, 186; 280-1; *DWB*, p. 1125.

67.4 William Williams: He was a brother to Thomas Williams. See 65.2n. His wife was Dorothy, daughter of Sir William Gruffudd of Penrhyn (c.1480-1531). See 67.3n. *PACF*, pp. 185, 190.

67.8 Thomas Dymock: Of Wellington, a township in the commote of Hanmer, Maelor Saesneg. The family was descended from Tudur ap Rhys Sais. She was Dorothy, daughter of Edward (not Thomas, as Wynn has it) by his second wife, Maud, daughter of Roger Puleston. Dwnn, ii, pp. 313-4.

67.16 orifice: i.e. the aperture of a wound.

67.28-9 the winning and burning of Edinburgh and Leith: Under the command of the earl of Hertford between 1-16 May

1544 both Leith (the port of Edinburgh) and the city were burnt and occupied. Camden Soc., *op. cit.*, p. 147; *CSPD*, xix (Pt. ii), 1944, passim.

67.30 the chronicles: Probably Charles Wriothesely's *A Chronicle of England during the Reigns of the Tudors, 1485-1559*, or William Patten's *The Expedition into Scotland* (1548).

67.32 Musselburgh: It is a town near Edinburgh in north-east Midlothian on the Firth of Forth at the mouth of the river Esk. It is probably a reference to the battle of Pinkie (a locality in N.E. Midlothian near Edinburgh, south of Musselburgh) in September 1547 when the earl of Hertford defeated the Scots. Henry VIII died on 28 January 1547. W. K. Jordan (ed.), *The Chronicle and Political Papers of King Edward VI* (1969), pp. 6-8.

67.34 his master was sent ambassador: He was appointed ambassador to the court of Charles V in April 1548. *DNB*, xxvii, p. 54; *CSPF*, 1547-53, p. 20.

67.36 Soleiman the Turk: Suleiman II, the Magnificent (who reigned between 1520 and 1566), was the son of Selim, and a menacing threat to the security of the Holy Roman Empire. In 1526 he defeated Hungary at the battle of Mohacs and later, in 1542, pacified that country and annexed it to the Ottoman Empire. In 1551, however, war broke out between the Turks and Ferdinand (who was to succeed his brother Charles as Holy Roman Emperor in 1555) when he attacked Transylvania in eastern Hungary. R. E. Dupuy & T. N. Dupuy (ed.), *The Encyclopaedia of Military History* (1970), 497, pp. 500-01.

67.39 being revoked by Queen Mary: Wynn is incorrect in his statement that Hoby ceased to serve Mary Tudor. He was, in fact, appointed ambassador in Flanders in 1553 and kept in close touch with the Queen and Philip II.

68.9-10 Robert Wynn . . . built a goodly house: He built the famous Plas Mawr in the borough of Conwy in 1576. *RCAM, Caerns. (East)*, pp. 58-64; A. & H. Baker, *Plas Mawr*, pp. 17-20, 23-7; 30-1; R. Williams, *The History and Antiquities of the Town of Aberconwy and its Neighbourhood* (1835), pp. 83-4; *PACF*, p. 281. He was sheriff of Caernarfonshire in

1590-91 and a county magistrate. *LS*, 248; Phillips, op. cit., pp. 20-22. See 55.24-5n.

68.14 another for his first wife: A stone plate (1586) in memory of Dorothy, wife of Robert Wynn, is found in the west wall of the nave in St. Mary's Church, Conwy, as well as a stone tomb in memory of Robert Wynn (d. 30 November 1598), both bearing their coats of arms. *RCAM*, op. cit., p. 44.

68.15 Hugh Gruffudd: Gruffudd John Gruffudd of Cefn-amwlch, Penllech, Llŷn was the first of his family to achieve prominence in county affairs. He became sheriff of Caernarfonshire (1589-90). *LS*, p. 248; *PACF*, p. 169; *DWB*, p. 288.

68.24 the Dunkirks: A. H. Dodd, *Hist. Caern.*, p. 31. 'Dunkirks' were privateers from Dunkirk on the coast of French Flanders. He was apprenticed to a London merchant and developed a profitable business with Spain, not all of which was legal. It appears that his father and brother-in-law, William Jones of Castellmarch, the future judge, had also participated in this illicit practice.

68.25 Hugh Owen: His dates are 1538-1618. He was a Roman Catholic conspirator and a member of an old family from Plas Du, Llanarmon, Llŷn, descended from Collwyn ap Tangno. He was implicated in the Ridolphi Plot (1571) to assassinate Elizabeth I. He advised the Netherlands government on English affairs and assisted Spain. He died in the English College at Rome in 1618. *DWB*, p. 697; E. G. Jones, op. cit., pp. 13-15, *PACF*, p. 205.

68.29 the earl of Arundel. Henry Fitzalan, 12th earl of Arundel and lord of Oswestry. Hugh Owen, early in his career, attended the Diet of Augsburg (1566) and was influenced by his employer to plot on behalf of Mary Queen of Scots.

68.30 in the duke of Norfolk's action: i.e. the Ridolphi Plot (1571). Thomas Howard, fourth duke of Norfolk (1536-72), was one of the instigators of the plot and was executed for treason although he denied having been a papist. *DNB*, xxviii, p. 69.

68.37 letter of mark: i.e. letters of marque and reprisal. Originally a licence granted to a subject to make reprisals on his country's enemies, but later it acquired the meaning, as in this context, of a licence granted, usually to privateers, to fit out an armed vessel for the purpose of capturing merchant enemy ships.

71.9 Argier: i.e. Algiers.

71.12 double pistoletts: i.e. small fire arms.

71.13-14 bull's pessel: i.e. bull's pizzle, the penis of the bull, used as an instrument for whipping.

71.19 Sir Maurice Gruffudd: He was the son of William Gruffudd of Plas Mawr, Caernarfon, and grandson of Sir William Gruffudd of Penrhyn. *PACF*, p. 125. He served in Ireland and was knighted in July 1603. His mother was Margaret, daughter of John Wyn ap Maredudd.

71.21-2 He served in the realm of Ireland: In 1606 he succeeded Sir Richard Trefor in command of Newry, *CSPI*, 1603-06, pp. 541-2. In 1610 he was appointed Constable of Drumruske Castle, (Connaught Castle), ibid, 1608-10, p. 508 and was known as Captain. In 1612 he was referred to as a burgess of Carricdrumruske (Carrick-on-Shannon) co. Leitrim, ibid., 1611-14, p. 294; and in 1620 the castle and lands were granted to Sir Maurice Gruffudd for 21 years at 40/- Irish money annually, ibid., 1615-25, pp. 285, 343; ibid, 1623, 406. At the time he was considered suitable for the office 'since the place requires the continual presence of an able man' and was described as 'a very honest and discreet gent', one that 'hath been long experienced in that part'. Connaught (Connacht), one of the historic provinces of Ireland, included Galway, Leitrim, Mayo, Roscommon and Sligo. Elizabeth I established a Presidential Council under Sir Edward Filton in 1570 to aid the administration of justice within the province and to divide it into shires. E. Hogan, *The Description of Ireland in Anno 1598* (1878)), p. 122. Gruffudd was a member of this Council.

71.27 Captain Prichard: Of Madryn Isaf, Llandudwen, Llŷn. *PACF*, p. 243.

71.32 Sir Richard Wynn: Richard Gwynn(e) of Hirdrefáig, Penmynydd, Anglesey, who married the widow of Captain William Thomas of Coed Alun who died at Zutphen (1586).

See 64.3n. She was Elen, daughter of William Gruffudd of Plas Mawr, Caernarfon (71.19n). He was the son of John Wynn, sheriff of Anglesey (1573-4). *LS*, 236. His connection with Bryncir, in the parish of Dolbenmaen, was established through his grandfather, Ieuan ap John ap Maredudd of that place. *PACF*, p. 25. He was appointed to conduct a conscript company from Wales to Flushing and in 1584 became muster-master in Gwynedd. Flenley, *Calendar*, pp. 218-20; Adams, *op. cit.*, 133.

71.36-7 Sir Henry Sidney: He was Lord Deputy of Ireland on three occasions (1566, 1568, 1575) and Lord President of the Council in the Marches (1559-86). *DNB*, lii, p. 210.

72.8 Gruffudd Williams: His dates are 1587-1673. He was a native of Treflan near Caernarfon and was educated at Jesus College Cambridge (1606-8) where he graduated D.D. (1621). He was appointed rector of Llanllechid (1616-26) and Tref-draeth (1626) and served as absentee Dean of Bangor (1634). In 1641 he was appointed Bishop of Ossory in Ireland. *DWB*, p. 1038; *DNB*, lxi, p. 401; W. J. Jones, *Old Carnarvon* (1882), p. 131. He was a close ally of Sir John Wynn during his quarrel with Bishop Lewis Bayly. J. G. Jones, 'Bishop Lewis Bayly and the Wynns of Gwydir, 1616-27', *WHR*, vi (no. iv), 1973, 408, 421.

72.10 the Reverend Father Lewis: i.e. Lewis Bayly, Bishop of Bangor (1616-31) and author of the famous devotional work *The Practice of Piety* (1611). *DWB*, p. 289; *DNB*, iii, p. 448. See A. H. Dodd, 'Bishop Lewes Bayly, c.1575-1631', *TCHS*, xxviii, 1967, 13-36; idem, *Hist. Caerns.*, pp. 101, 113, 163.

72.12 William Glynn: The son of Thomas Glynn of Glyn-llifon who was knighted in Dublin in 1606 for his military services in Ireland. He died in 1620. *DWB*, pp. 280-1.

72.13-14 John Wynn ap Hugh: Of Bodfel, Llŷn. He was the Standard-Bearer to John Dudley, earl of Warwick, at the battle of Dussindale near Norwich (1549). He served as sheriff of Caernarfonshire (1550-51, 1559-60). *LS*, p. 248; *PACF*, p. 171.

72.18-19 John, earl of Warwick: John Dudley (1502-53), created earl of Warwick (1547) and duke of Northumberland (1551). He governed England during the latter part of the reign of Edward VI (1549-53) and was executed (1553) for resisting the succession of Mary Tudor to the throne. *DNB*, xvi, p. 109.

72.27 the Isle of Bardsey: John Wynn ap Hugh was notorious for his piratical activities and was described in a Star Chamber suit against him as 'a man of evill disposicon, principall captayne, cheefe and onlie supporter, defender and maynteyner of all pirates'. PRO St. Cha. 18/1 Eliz. J. G. Jones 'Documents relating to certain aspects of Local Government in Stuart Caernarvonshire', *BBCS*, xxiv (Pt. iv), 1972, 504-5. Bardsey island was granted to him on 15 April, 1553. *CPR*, 1547-53, v, p. 109.

72.32-3 Doctor of the Arches: See 66.20n. The Court of the Arches was the court of the official Principal of the Archbishop of Canterbury. It was the chief court of the Archbishop dealing with ecclesiastical causes such as diocesan jurisdiction and ecclesiastical appeals. Northumberland was arrested, on behalf of Queen Mary, by the earl of Arundel at Cambridge on 24 July 1553 on a charge of conspiring to place Lady Jane Grey on the throne. A. F. Pollard, *The History of England, 1547-1603* (1911), p. 93.

72.38 gathered a great estate: His agent, John Williams of Penmachno, kept a carefully recorded account of his financial affairs in 1572-3, a document which illustrates his comfortable circumstances, UCNW (Bangor) Mostyn MS.6624. See 66.20n. He attended Trinity College, Cambridge, and became a Fellow of St. John's College. In his will (1574) he assigned £40 annually from his Maenan lands for the maintenance of 3 Fellows and 6 Scholars (and not 2 Fellows and 3 Scholars, as recorded by the author, at St. John's, preference for fellowships to be given to Llanfair Dyffryn Clwyd, Maenan, the commote of Nanconwy and the three counties of Caernarfon, Merioneth and Denbigh. Scholars were to be selected from Friars School, Bangor. NLW MS 9051E 54; Baker, op. cit., i, pp. 421-2; H. Baker & H. Lewis, op. cit., 170-1. Gwynn's executors soon realized, however, that the original endowment was insufficient and it was decided that the bequest should support only two Fellows and three Scholars. UCNW Mostyn MSS. 308, 1291, 1298. J. G. Jones, 'Educational Activity among the Wynns', 20-1.

73.5 the Right Honourable John Williams: 1582-1650: Dean of Westminster (1620), Lord Keeper of the Great Seal and Bishop of Lincoln (1621), Archbishop of York (1641-50). He was a native of Conwy and a descendant, on his father's side, of the house of Cochwillan and Penrhyn and, on his mother's side, of Gwydir, she being Mary, daughter of Owen Wynn of Eglwysbach. *PACF*, p. 186. He was educated at St. John's College, Cambridge (1601) where he became a Fellow (1603), and obtained the degree of Doctor of Divinity in 1617. *DWB*, p. 1045.

73.7 Owen Wynn: The third son of Gruffudd Wynn of Berth-ddu and nephew (not brother as Wynn states) of Dr. John Gwynn who founded scholarships and was elected fellow of St. John's. He was appointed 18th Master of St. John's in 1612 and graduated D.D. in 1612. *DWB*, p. 1093; *PACF*, pp. 184, 281; Baker, op. cit. i, pp. 198-210, 245-6, ii, pp. 615-9; Venn, ii, p. 278, iv, p. 482.

73.10 James Ellis: The son of Elisa ap Maurice of Clenennau, a kinsman to Sir John Wynn. By his second wife, Janet, daughter of Sir James Owen, Penhilfa, Pembrokeshire, he had James Maurice (or Ellis), who was alive in 1595. He served as rector of Llandwrog, Caernarfonshire, and Llanfwrog, Denbighshire, and Chancellor of Peterborough Cathedral. *PACF*, p. 218; *DWB*, p. 621.

73.14 William Gruffudd: A brother of Sir Maurice Gruffudd and youngest son of William Gruffudd of Maes Mawr, Caernarfon.

73.17-18 Maurice Glynn: Son of Robert ap Maredudd of Glynllifon by his first wife, Ellen Bulkeley of Beaumaris. He became Archdeacon of Merioneth, his brother, William Glyn, becoming Archdeacon of Anglesey. *DWB*, p. 280; *PACF*, p. 172.

73.23-4 Gruffudd Williams: See 72.8n. He became a Lecturer at St. Peter's and St. Paul's, London and rector of St. Bennet Sherhog (1612-16). *DWB*, p. 1038. He was a renowned preacher, and often denounced Puritanism.

73.32-3 Owen Meredith: The son of Maredudd ap Thomas Gruffudd of Mynachdy Gwyn, Clynnog who became vicar of Clynnog. His brother, Humphrey Meredith, was sheriff of Caernarfonshire (1613-14) and a prominent local administrator. *LS*, p. 248; Phillips, pp. 23-8.

73.36 Edmund Gruffudd: His dates are 1570-1637. He was a younger son of Gruffudd ap John Gruffudd of Cefnamwlch, Llŷn. He was appointed rector of Llanbedrog (1604), Dean of Bangor (1613) and Bishop of Bangor (1633), and was educated at Brasenose College, Oxford (1589-99). *PACF*, pp. 169, 271; *DWB*, p. 291; *DNB*, xxiii, p. 230.

73.40 William Bryncir: He was a younger son of Robert Wynn of Bryncir. His mother, Ann, daughter of Morus ab Elisa of Clenennau, was the sister of Sir William Maurice of Clenennau. He became rector of Llaniestyn and Llanaelhaearn (d. 1627-8). His eldest brother, Ellis Bryncir, was sheriff of Caernarfonshire (1623-4) and a prominent justice of the peace. *PACF*, pp. 28, 251, E. Breese, *Kalendars of Gwynedd* (1873), p. 54; Phillips, pp. 26-8.

TABLE A

LINEAL DESCENT OF THE WYNN FAMILY OF GWYDIR FROM GRUFFUDD AP CYNAN

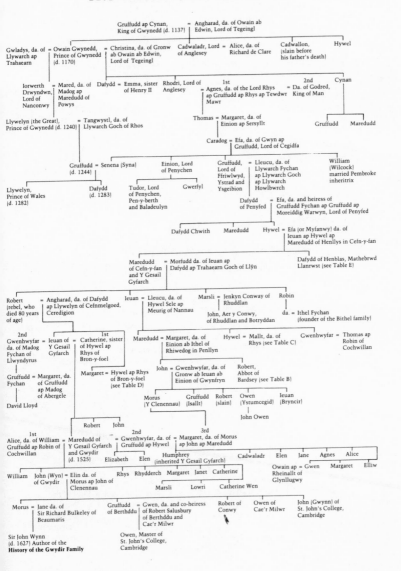

TABLE B

THE DESCENDANTS OF ROBERT AP MAREDUDD, ABBOT OF BARDSEY

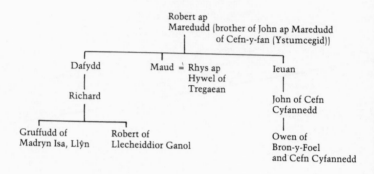

TABLE C

THE ANGLESEY CONNECTIONS OF HYWEL AB IEUAN AP MAREDUDD

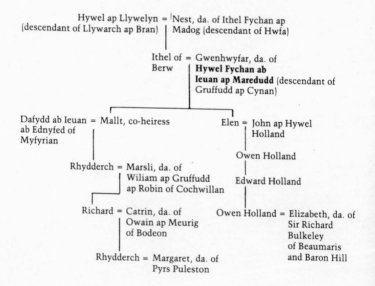

TABLE D

THE BRON-Y-FOEL FAMILY

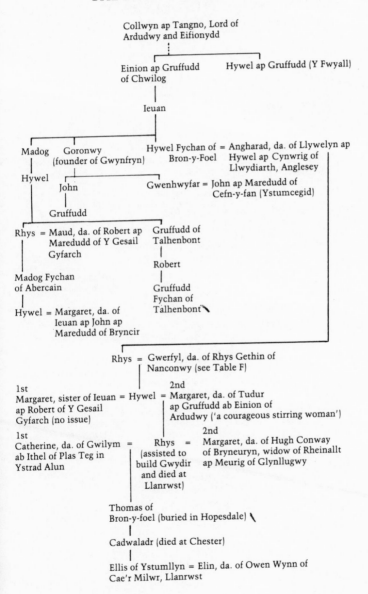

Collwyn ap Tangno, Lord of
Ardudwy and Eifionydd

Einion ap Gruffudd   Hywel ap Gruffudd (Y Fwyall)
of Chwilog

Ieuan

Madog   Goronwy   Hywel Fychan of = Angharad, da. of Llywelyn ap
       (founder of Gwynfryn)   Bron-y-Foel   Hywel ap Cynwrig of
Hywel   Llwydiarth, Anglesey
      John   Gwenhwyfar = John ap Maredudd of
                           Cefn-y-fan (Ystumcegid)
    Gruffudd

Rhys = Maud, da. of Robert ap   Gruffudd of
      Maredudd of Y Gesail   Talhenbont
      Gyfarch
                           Robert
Madog Fychan
of Abercain   Gruffudd
                           Fychan of
Hywel = Margaret, da. of   Talhenbont
      Ieuan ap John ap
      Maredudd of Bryncir

Rhys = Gwerfyl, da. of Rhys Gethin of
     Nanconwy (see Table F)

1st   2nd
Margaret, sister of Ieuan = Hywel = Margaret, da. of Tudur
ap Robert of Y Gesail   ap Gruffudd ab Einion of
Gyfarch (no issue)   Ardudwy ('a courageous stirring woman')

1st   2nd
Catherine, da. of Gwilym = Rhys = Margaret, da. of Hugh Conway
ab Ithel of Plas Teg in   (assisted to   of Bryneuryn, widow of Rheinallt
Ystrad Alun   build Gwydir   ap Meurig of Glynllugwy
                and died at
                Llanrwst)

Thomas of
Bron-y-foel (buried in Hopesdale)

Cadwaladr (died at Chester)

Ellis of Ystumllyn = Elin, da. of Owen Wynn of
Cae'r Milwr, Llanrwst

TABLE E

THE LINE OF IEUAN AP HYWEL AP MAREDUDD OF HENLLYS IN CEFN-Y-FAN AND DAFYDD AP HYWEL OF HENBLAS, MATHEBRWD

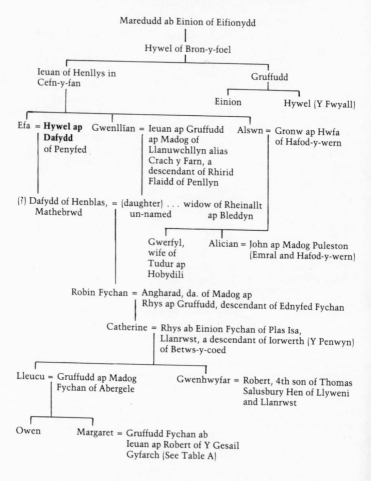

Maredudd ab Einion of Eifionydd

Hywel of Bron-y-foel

Ieuan of Henllys in Cefn-y-fan

Gruffudd

Einion   Hywel (Y Fwyall)

Efa = **Hywel ap Dafydd** of Penyfed   Gwenllïan = Ieuan ap Gruffudd ap Madog of Llanuwchllyn alias Crach y Farn, a descendant of Rhirid Flaidd of Penllyn   Alswn = Gronw ap Hwfa of Hafod-y-wern

(?) Dafydd of Henblas, Mathebrwd = (daughter) un-named . . . widow of Rheinallt ap Bleddyn

Gwerfyl, wife of Tudur ap Hobydili   Alician = John ap Madog Puleston (Emral and Hafod-y-wern)

Robin Fychan = Angharad, da. of Madog ap Rhys ap Gruffudd, descendant of Ednyfed Fychan

Catherine = Rhys ab Einion Fychan of Plas Isa, Llanrwst, a descendant of Iorwerth (Y Penwyn) of Betws-y-coed

Lleucu = Gruffudd ap Madog Fychan of Abergele   Gwenhwyfar = Robert, 4th son of Thomas Salusbury Hen of Llyweni and Llanrwst

Owen   Margaret = Gruffudd Fychan ab Ieuan ap Robert of Y Gesail Gyfarch (See Table A)

TABLE F

THE LINE OF HYWEL COETMOR AND RHYS GETHIN OF NANCONWY

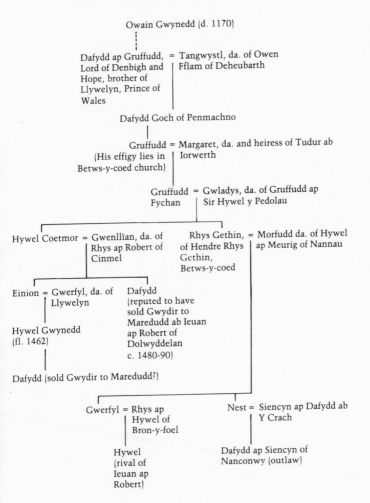

Owain Gwynedd (d. 1170)

Dafydd ap Gruffudd, = Tangwystl, da. of Owen
Lord of Denbigh and   Fflam of Deheubarth
Hope, brother of
Llywelyn, Prince of
Wales

Dafydd Goch of Penmachno

Gruffudd = Margaret, da. and heiress of Tudur ab
(His effigy lies in   Iorwerth
Betws-y-coed church)

Gruffudd = Gwladys, da. of Gruffudd ap
Fychan   Sir Hywel y Pedolau

Hywel Coetmor = Gwenllïan, da. of   Rhys Gethin, = Morfudd da. of Hywel
Rhys ap Robert of   of Hendre Rhys   ap Meurig of Nannau
Cinmel   Gethin,
                        Betws-y-coed

Einion = Gwerfyl, da. of   Dafydd
Llywelyn   (reputed to have
                     sold Gwydir to
Hywel Gwynedd   Maredudd ab Ieuan
(fl. 1462)   ap Robert of
                     Dolwyddelan
                     c. 1480-90)

Dafydd (sold Gwydir to Maredudd?)

Gwerfyl = Rhys ap   Nest = Siencyn ap Dafydd ab
Hywel of   Y Crach
Bron-y-foel

Hywel   Dafydd ap Siencyn of
(rival of   Nanconwy (outlaw)
Ieuan ap
Robert)

BIBLIOGRAPHY

A ORIGINAL SOURCES

The British Library (BL)
Add. MS. 8533

National Library of Wales (NLW)
Add.MS. 464E.215
       465E.375
       14866
MS. 5281
MSS. 9051E 463(b), 210
MS. 9054E.513
MS. 9058E.1005
MS. 9061E.1504

Cwrtmawr MS. 11
Llansteffan MSS. 179, 722
Peniarth MSS. 134, 136, 139, 176, 177
Wynnstay MS. 120

South Glamorgan County Library (Ca. MS.)
MS. 4.58
MS. 51
MS. 83 [4.101]

University College of North Wales (UCNW)
Mostyn MSS. 308, 1291, 1298, 1855, 5440, 5972, 6624

B PRINTED SOURCES

Ballinger, J. (ed.), *Calendar of Wynn (of Gwydir) Papers, 1515-1690* (1926)
Ballinger, J. (ed.), *The History of the Gwydir Family* (5th ed. 1927)
Banks, R. W. (ed.), T. Dineley, *The Account of the Official Progress of Henry the First Duke of Beaufort through Wales in 1684* (1888)
Barrington, Daines (ed.), *The History of the Gwydir Family* (1st ed. 1770)
Barrington, Daines (ed.), *The History of the Gwydir Family* (2nd ed. pub. in the editor's *Miscellanies* 1781)
Bliss, P (ed.), A. Wood, *Athenae Oxonienses* (1813-20)
Board of Celtic Studies, *Mynegai i Farddoniaeth Gaeth y Llawysgrifau* (1978)
Bowen, I. (ed.), *The Statutes of Wales* (1906)
Brewer, J. S., Dimock, J. F. and Warner, G. F. (ed), *Giraldi Cambrensis Opera*, Rolls Series (1861-91)
Calendar of Letters and Papers Foreign and Domestic, Henry VIII (1862 ff)
Calendar of Patent Rolls (1891 ff)
Calendar of State Papers Foreign (1863 ff)

Calendar of State Papers Ireland (1858 ff)

Calendar of State Papers Domestic (1856 ff)

Clarke, A. (ed.), *Register of the University of Oxford* (1888)

Croft, H. H. S. (ed.), T. Elyot, *The Governor* (1883)

Davies, C. (ed.), *Rhagymadroddion a Chyflwyniadau Lladin, 1551-1632* (1980)

Dugdale, W. (ed.), *Monasticon Anglicanum* (1665-73)

Edwards, I. ab O. (ed.), *A Catalogue of Star Chamber Proceedings relating to Wales* (1929)

Edwards, J. G. (ed.), *Littere Wallie* (1940)

Ellis, H. (ed.), *Registrum vulgariter nuncupatum* (The Record of Caernarvon) (1838)

Elyot, T., *Castel of Helthe* (1541)

Evans, D. S. (ed.), *Historia Gruffud Vab Kenan* (1977)

Evans, J. G. (ed.), *Reports on Manuscripts in the Welsh Language* (1898-1910)

Flenley, R. (ed.), *A Calendar of the Register of the Council in the Marches of Wales, 1569-1591* (1916)

Foster J. (ed.), *Alumni Oxonienses* (1891-2)

Griffith, J. E., *Pedigrees of Anglesey and Carnarvonshire Families* (1914)

Halliwell, J. O. (ed.), *An Ancient Survey of Penmaenmawr* (1859) [reprint 1906 by W. Bezant Lowe]

Hamilton, W. D. (ed.), C. Wriothesley, *A Chronicle of England during the Reigns of the Tudors, 1485-1559*, Camden Society, 1825

Hardy, T. D. (ed.), *Rotuli Chartarum* (1837)

Hardy, T. D. (ed.), *Rotuli Litterarum Clausarum* (1844)

Historical Manuscripts Commission: *Calendar of the Manuscripts of the Marquis of Salisbury (Hatfield MSS)*, (1883-1965)

HMSO, Report of the Royal Commission on Land in Wales and Monmouthshire (1896)

Hogan, E. (ed.), *The Description of Ireland in Anno* 1598 (1878)

Howlett, R. (ed.), *Chronicles of the Reigns of Stephen, Henry II and Richard I* (1884-8)

James, B. L. (ed.), Rhys Meurig, *Morganiae Archaiographia* (1983)

Jones, E. G. (ed.), *Exchequer Proceedings Concerning Wales: Henry VIII—Elizabeth* (1939)

Jones, G. P. (ed.), *The Extent of Chirkland, 1391-93* (1933)

Jones, G. P. and Owen, H. (ed.), *Caernarvon Court Rolls, 1361-1402* (1951)

Jones, J. (ed.), *Cynfeirdd Lleyn, 1500-1800* (1905)

Jones, O., Williams E and (Pugh), W. O. (ed.), *The Myvyrian Archaiology of Wales* (1870)

Jones, T. (ed.), *Brut y Tywysogion: Peniarth MS. 20* (1941)

Jones, T. (ed.), *Brut y Tywysogion or the Chronicle of the Princes: Peniarth MS. 20 Version* (1952)

Jones, T. G. (ed.), *Gwaith Tudur Aled* (1926)

Jones-Pierce, T. (ed.), *Calendar of the Clenennau Letters and Papers in the Brogyntyn Collection. NLW Jnl. Supp.*, Series iv, pt. i, 1947.

Jordan, W. K. (ed.), *The Chronicle and Political Papers of King Edward VI* (1966)

Leland, J., *De Rebus Britannicis Collectanea* (1774)

Lewis, H., Roberts, T., Williams, I. (ed.), *Cywyddau Iolo Goch ac Eraill* (1937)

Llwyd, A. (ed.), *The History of the Gwydir Family* (3rd ed. 1827)

Luard, H. R. (ed.), Matthew Paris, *Chronica Majora* (1877)

Meyricke, S. R. (ed.), Lewys Dwnn, *Heraldic Visitations of Wales and Part of the Marches* (1846)

Owen, H. (ed.), George Owen, *The Description of Penbrokshire* (1906)

PRO Lists and Indexes no. ix: *List of Sheriffs for England and Wales* (1898)

Phillips, J. R. S. (ed.), *The Justices of the Peace in Wales and Monmouthshire 1541 to 1689* (1975)

Powel, D., *Historie of Cambria* (1969 ed.)

Rees, U. (ed.), *The Cartulary of Haughmond Abbey* (1985)

Rees, W. (ed.), *Calendar of Ancient Petitions relating to Wales* (1975)

Royal Commission on Ancient Monuments in Wales and Monmouthshire: *Denbighshire* (1914); *Merioneth* (1921); *Caernarfon East* (1956); *Caernarfon Central* (1960); *Caernarfon West* (1964)

Record Commission, *Rotuli Parliamentorum* (1783 ff)

Roberts, A. (ed.), *The History of the Gwydir Family* (4th ed. 1878)

Roberts, E. (ed.), *Gwaith Siôn Tudur* (1978)

Roberts, T. (ed.), *Gwaith Tudur Penllyn ac Ieuan ap Tudur Penllyn* (1958)

Roberts, T. and Williams, I. (ed.), *The Poetical Works of Dafydd Nanmor* (1923)

Robertson, J. C. and Sheppard, J. B., (ed.), *Materials for the History of Thomas Becket* (1875-85)

Rowlands, E. I. (ed.), *Gwaith Lewys Môn* (1975)

Rymer, T. (ed.), *Foedera, Conventiones, Litterae . . .* (1819-69)

Smith, L. Toulmin (ed.), John Leland, *Itinerary in Wales, 1536-1539* (1906)

Smith, T., *De Republica Anglorum* (1970 ed.)

Strype, J., *The Life and Acts of Matthew Parker* (1711)

Thorpe, L. (ed.), *Gerald of Wales: The Journey through Wales / The Description of Wales* (1978)

Vinogradoff, P. and Morgan, F. (ed.), *Survey of the Honour of Denbigh, 1334* (1914)

Williams, I. and Williams, J. Ll. (ed.), *Gwaith Guto'r Glyn* (1939)

Williams, J. (ed.), *Annales Cambriae*, Rolls Series (1860)

Williams-Jones, K., 'Llywelyn's Charter to Cymer Abbey in 1209', *JMHRS*, iii, 1957.

C   SECONDARY MATERIAL

Adams, S. L., 'The Gentry of North Wales and the earl of Leicester's Expedition to the Netherlands, 1585-1586', *WHR*, vii (no. ii), 1974

Ashton, C., *Bywyd ac Amserau yr Esgob Morgan* (1891)

Baker, A. and H., *Plas Mawr* (1888)

Baker, T., *History of St. John's College, Cambridge* (1896)

Bartrum, P., *Welsh Genealogies, 300-1400* (1974)

Bartrum, P., *Welsh Genealogies, 1400-1500* (1983)

Boase, F. (ed.), *Modern English Biography, 1851-1900* (1965)

Boulay, F. R. H. du, *An Age of Ambition* (1970)

Bowen, D. J., *Gruffudd Hiraethog a'i Oes* (1958)

Bowen, D. J., 'Ail Eisteddfod Caerwys a Chais 1594', *Llên Cymru*, iii (no. iii), 1955

Bowen, E. G. (ed.), *Wales: an Historical, Regional and Physical Geography* (1957)

Bowen, G. (ed.), *Y Traddodiad Rhyddiaith* (1970)

Breese, E. (ed.), *Kalendars of Gwynedd* (1873)

Breese, C. E., 'Old Stained Glass in St. Beuno's Church, Penmorva', *AC*, 1905

Bromwich, R. (ed.), *Trioedd Ynys Prydain* (1961)

Burke, *Peerage, Baronetage and Knightage*, ed. P. Townend (1967)

Carr, A. D., *Medieval Anglesey* (1982)

Carr, A. D., 'Welshmen and the Hundred Years War', *WHR*, iv (no. i), 1968

Carr, A. D., 'The Mostyns of Mostyn, 1540-1642', *Flints. Hist. Soc. Publns.*, xxviii, 1977-8

Caspari, F., *Humanism and the Social Order in Tudor England* (1964)

Charles, B. G., *Non-Celtic Placenames in Wales* (1938)

Charles, B. G., *George Owen of Henllys* (1973)

Cheney, C. R., *Handbook of Dates* (1978)

Chrimes, S. B., Ross, C. D., and Griffiths, R. A., *Fifteenth-Century England, 1399-1509* (1972)

Chrimes, S. B., *Lancastrians, Yorkists and Henry VII* (1966)

Chrimes, S. B., *Henry VII* (1977)

Clarke, M. L., *Bangor Cathedral* (1969)

Clive, R. H., *Documents connected with the History of Ludlow and the Lords Marcher* (1841)

Cokayne, G. E. (ed.), *Complete Baronetage* (1983 ed.)

Davies, G., *Noddwyr Beirdd ym Meirion* (1974)

Davies, J. H. (ed.), *Catalogue of Manuscripts* (NLW, 1921)

Davies, R. R., *Lordship and Society in the March of Wales, 1282-1400* (1978)

Davies, R. R., *Conquest, Coexistence and Change: Wales 1063-1415* (1987)

Davies, R. R., 'The Twilight of Welsh Law, 1284-1536', *History*, li, 1966

Davies, R. R., 'Race Relations in Post-Conquest Wales: Confrontation and Compromise', *TCS*, 1974-5

Dictionary of National Biography (1885-1900)

Dictionary of Welsh Biography (1959)

Dobson, R. B. (ed.), *The Peasants' Revolt of 1381* (1970)

Dodd, A. H., *A History of Caernarvonshire, 1284-1900* (1968)

Dodd, A. H., 'Bishop Lewes Bayly c.1575-1631', *TCHS*, xxviii, 1967

Dupuy, R. E. and Dupuy, T. N. (ed.), *The Encyclopaedia of Military History* (1970)

Earle, P., *The Life and Times of Henry V* (1972)

Edwards, F., 'Penrhyndeudraeth', *JMHRS*, i (no. iii), 1951

Edwards, I. ab O., 'William Morgan's Quarrel with his Parishioners at Llanrhaeadr-ym-Mochnant', *BBCS*, iii (Pt. iv), 1927

Edwards, J. G., *The Principality of Wales, 1267-1967* (1967)

Edwards, J. G., 'Sir Gruffydd Llwyd', *EHR*, xxx, 1915

Edwards, J. G., 'The Normans and the Welsh March', *Proceedings of the British Academy*, xlii, 1956

Ellis, M., 'Angharad Llwyd, 1780-1860', *Flintshire Hist. Soc. Publns.*, xxvi, 1973-4

Ellis, T. P., *Welsh Tribal Law and Custom in the Middle Ages* (1926)

Emerson, B., *The Black Prince* (1976)

Evans, D. L., 'Some Notes on the History of the Principality of Wales in the time of the Black Prince, 1343-1376', *TCS*, 1925-6

Evans, E., *Some Specimens of the Poetry of the Antient Welsh Bards* (1764)

Evans, H. T., *Wales and the Wars of the Roses* (1915)

Evans, H. T., *Modern Wales* (1934)

Fox, L. (ed.), *English Historical Scholarship in the Sixteenth and Seventeenth Centuries* (1956)

Fussell, E. M., 'Some Aspects of Monasticism in Anglesey', *TAAS*, 1921

Fussner, F. S., *The Historical Revolution, 1580-1640* (1962)

Gibbs, V. (ed.), *Complete Peerage* (1910 ff)

Glenn, T. A., *The Family of Griffith of Garn and Plasnewydd in the County of Denbigh* (1934)

Gluckman, M., 'The Peace in the Feud', *Past and Present*, viii, 1955

Gray Birch, W. de, *Memorials of the See and Cathedral of Llandaff* (1912)

Gresham, C. A., *Medieval Stone Carving in North Wales* (1968).

Gresham, C. A., *Eifionydd: a study in Landownership from the Medieval Period to the Present Day* (1973)

Gresham, C. A., 'The Aberconwy Charter', *AC*, 1939

Gresham, C. A., 'Platform Houses of North-West Wales', *AC*, 1954

Gresham, C. A., 'The Townships of Gest, Treflys and Ystumllyn', *TCHS*, xviii, 1957

Gresham, C. A., 'Townships in the Parish of Llanystumdwy', *TCHS*, xix, 1958

Gresham, C. A., 'The Bolde Rental (Bangor MSS. 1939)', *TCHS*, xxvi, 1965

Gresham, C. A., 'The Parish of Beddgelert', *TCHS*, xxx, 1969

Gresham, C. A., 'The Aberconwy Charter: Further Considerations', *BBCS*, xxx (Pts. iii and iv), 1983

Griffith, W. P., 'Beth oedd y Dyn Tuduraidd?' in D. G. Jones and J. E. Jones (ed.), *Bosworth a'r Tuduriaid* (1985)

Griffiths, R. A. (ed.), *Boroughs of Medieval Wales* (1978)

Griffiths, R. A., 'Gentlemen and Rebels in Later Medieval Cardiganshire', *Ceredigion* v, 1965

Gruenfelder, J. R., 'The Wynns of Gwydir and Parliamentary Elections in Wales, 1604-40', *WHR*, ix (no. ii), 1978

Gruffydd, R. G., 'The Life of Dr. John Davies of Brecon', *TCS*, 1971 (Pt. ii)

Gruffydd, R. G., 'William Morgan' in G. Bowen (ed.), *Y Traddodiad Rhydiaith* (1970).

Gruffydd, R. G., *The Translating of the Bible into the Welsh Tongue* (1988)

Hays, R. W., *The History of the Abbey of Aberconway, 1186-1537* (1963)

Hemingway, J., *History of the City of Chester* (1831)

Hobsbawn, E. and Ranger, T. (ed.), *The Invention of Tradition* (1983)

Holmes, G. A., *The Estates of the Higher Nobility in Fourteenth-Century England* (1957)

Hughes, H. H. and North, H. L., *The Old Churches of Snowdonia* (1924)

Hughes, W., *The Life and Times of Bishop William Morgan* (1891)

Jack, R. I., *The Sources of History: Studies in the Uses of Historical Evidence: Mediaeval Wales* (1972)

Jacob, G., *A New Law Dictionary* (1782)

Jarman, A. O. H. and Hughes, G. R. (ed.), *A Guide to Welsh Literature*, ii (1979)

Jenkins, D., *Cyfraith Hywel* (1978)

Jenkins, D., *Hywel Dda, The Law, 1986.*

Jenkins, D., 'Kings, Lords and Princes: the nomenclature of authority in thirteenth-century Wales', *BBCS*, xxv (Pt. iv), 1976

Jenkins, D. and Owen, M. E. (ed.), *The Welsh Law of Women* (1980)

Jenkins, D. E., *Bedd Gelert: its Facts, Fairies and Folklore* (1899)

Johns, C. N., 'The Celtic Monasteries of North Wales', *TCHS*, xxi, 1960

Jones, D. C., 'The Bulkeleys of Beaumaris, 1440-1547', *TAAS*, 1961

Jones, E. D., 'Howel Coytmor (Coetmor)', *NLWJ*, viii, 1953-4

Jones, E. D., 'The Family of Nannau (Nanney)', *JMHRS*, ii, 1953

Jones, E. G., *Cymru a'r Hen Ffydd (1951)*

Jones, E. G., 'County Politics and Electioneering, 1558-1625', *TCHS*, i, 1939

Jones, E. G., 'Sir John Wynn of Gwydir', *The Welsh Review*, v, 1946

Jones, F., 'An Approach to Welsh Genealogy', *TCS*, 1948

Jones, G. E., *The Gentry and the Elizabethan State* (1977)

Jones, G. H., 'The Welsh Psalter', *Jnl. Hist. Soc. of the Church in Wales*, xvii, 1967

Jones, I., *Modern Welsh History* (1934)

Jones, J., *Enwogion Sir Gaernarfon* (1922)

Jones, J. G., 'Diddordebau Diwylliannol Wynniaid Gwedir', *Llên Cymru*, xi (nos. i-ii), 1970

Jones, J. G., 'Caernarvonshire Administration: the Activities of the Justice of the Peace 1603-1660', *WHR*, v (no. ii), 1970

Jones, J. G., 'Documents relating to certain aspects of local government in Stuart Caernarvonshire', *BBCS*, xxiv (Pt. iv), 1972

Jones, J. G., 'Bishop William Morgan's Dispute with John Wynn of Gwydir, 1603-04', *Jnl. Hist. Soc. of the Church in Wales*, xxvii, 1972

Jones, J. G., 'Bishop Lewis Bayly and the Wynns of Gwydir, 1616-27', *WHR*, vi (no. iv) 1973

Jones, J. G., 'Syr John Wynn o Wedir: ei Gymeriad a'i Gefndir', *TCHS*, xxxvi, 1975

Jones, J. G., 'Morus Wynn o Wedir c. 1530-1580', *TCHS*, xxxviii, 1977

Jones, J. G., 'Priodoleddau Bonheddig yn Nheulu'r Wynniaid o Wedir', *TCS*, 1978

Jones, J. G., 'Sir John Wynn of Gwydir and John Speed: Aspects of Antiquarian Activities', *NLWJ*, xx (no. iii), 1978

Jones, J. G., 'Henry Rowlands, Bishop of Bangor, 1598-1616', *Jnl. Hist. Soc. of the Church in Wales*, xxxi, 1979

Jones, J. G., 'The Welsh Poets and their Patrons c, 1550-1640', *WHR*, ix (no. iii), 1979

Jones, J. G., 'The Wynn Estate of Gwydir: Aspects of its Growth and Development c.1500-1580', *NLWJ*, xxii (Pt. ii), 1981

Jones, J. G., 'Thomas Davies and Williams Hughes: two Reformation Bishops of St. Asaph', *BBCS*, xxix (Pt. ii), 1981

Jones, J. G., 'Educational Activity among the Wynns of Gwydir', *TCHS*, xlii, 1981

Jones, J. G., 'Sir John Wynn and his Tenants: the Dolwyddelan and Llysfaen Disputes', *WHR*, xi (no. i), 1982

Jones, M. H., 'Wales and Hungary', *TCS*, 1968 (Pt. i)

Jones, O. G., *Gweithiau Gethin* (1884)

Jones, T., *History of Brecknockshire* (1909-30)

Jones, T., *Gerald of Wales* (1947)

Jones, T. A., *Without my Wig* (1945)

Jones, W., *Plwyf Beddgelert: ei Hynafiaethau a'i Gofiannau* (1862)

Jones, W. J., *Old Carnarvon (1882)*

Kelso, R., *The Doctrine of the English Gentleman in the Sixteenth Century* (1964)

King, D. J. C., 'Henry and the Fight at Coleshill', *WHR*, ii (no. iv), 1965

Kingsford, C. L., *Prejudice and Promise in Fifteenth-Century England* (1962)

Knight, L. S., *Welsh Independent Grammar Schools to 1600* (1926)

Land, W., *Kett's Rebellion: the Norfolk Rising of 1549* (1977)

Lander, J. R., *The Wars of the Roses* (1965)

Lander, J. R., *Conflict and Stability in Fifteenth-Century England* (1969)

Lloyd, J. E., *A History of Wales from the Earliest Times to the Edwardian Conquest (1939)*

Lloyd, J. E., *Owen Glendower* (1931)

Lloyd, J. E. (ed.), *A History of Carmarthenshire* (1935)

Lloyd, J. E., 'The Death of Llywelyn ap Gruffudd', *BBCS*, v (Pt. iv), 1931

Lloyd, J. E., 'The Mother of Gruffudd ap Llywelyn', *BBCS*, i (Pt. iv), 1923

Lloyd, J. Y. W., *History of the Princes of Powys Fadog* (1881-87)

Lloyd-Jones, J., *Enwau Lleoedd Sir Gaernarfon* (1928)

Mckisack, M., *The Fourteenth Century, 1307-99* (1959)

Mckisack, M., *The Medieval History in the Tudor Period* (1971)

Masterman, N., 'The Massacre of the Bards', *The Welsh Review*, vii, 1948

Morgan, J., *Coffadwriaeth am y Gwir Barchedig Henry Rowland, D.D., Arglwydd Esgob Bangor* (1914)

Morgan, P., *The Eighteenth-Century Renaissance (1981)*

Morris, T. E., 'The Castle of Deudraeth', *AC*, 1927

Newcome, R., *An Account of the Castle and Town of Ruthin* (1836)

O'Neil, B. H. St. J., 'Criccieth Castle, Caernarvonshire', *AC*, xcviii (Pt. i), 1944

Ormerod, G., *History of Cheshire* (1819)

Owen, D. H., 'The Englishry of Denbigh: an English Colony in Medieval Wales', *TCS*, 1974-5

Owen, G. D., *Elizabethan Wales: the Social Scene* (1962)

Owen, L., 'The Population of Wales in the Sixteenth and Seventeenth Centuries', *TCS*, 1959

Parry, B., 'Hugh Nanney Hen (c. 1546-1623), Squire of Nannau', *JMHRS*, v, 1967

Parry, G., 'Hanes Ysgol Botwnnog', *TCS*, 1957

Parry, T., 'Siôn Dafydd Rhys', *Y Llenor*, ix, 1930

Pevsner, N (ed.), *The Buildings of England: Suffolk* (rev.) E. Radcliffe (1974)

Pollard, A. F., *The History of England, 1547-1603* (1911)

Powicke, F. M., *The Thirteenth Century* (1953)

Prys-Jones, A. G., *Gerald the Welshman* (1955)

Rees, W., *South Wales and the March, 1284-1415* (1924)

Rees, W., *The Order of St. John in Wales* (1947)

Rees, W., *The Union of England and Wales* (1948)

Rhys, J. (ed.), T. Pennant, *Tours in Wales* (1883)

Rhys, J. and Brynmor-Jones, D., *The Welsh People* (1909)

Richards, G. M., *Welsh Administrative and Territorial Units* (1969)

Richards, G. M., 'Sgeibion, Llanynys', *TDHS*, ix, 1960

Richter, M., *Giraldus Cambrensis: the Growth of the Welsh Nation* (1972)

Richter, M., 'David ap Llywelyn, the first Prince of Wales', *WHR*, v (no. iii), 1971

Roberts, E., *Dafydd Llwyd o Fathafarn* (1981)

Roberts, E., 'Siôn Tudur', *Llên Cymru*, ii, 1952

Roberts, E., 'Seven John Conways', *Flints. Hist. Soc. Publns.*, xviii, 1960

Roberts, E., 'Teulu Plasiolyn', *TDHS*, xiii, 1964

Roberts, G., *Aspects of Welsh History* (1969)

Roberts, G., 'Biographical Notes', *BBCS*, xvii (Pt. i), 1956

Roberts, G. J., *Yr Esgob William Morgan* (1955)

Roberts, R. F., 'Y Dr. John Davies o Fallwyd', *Llên Cymru*, ii, 1952

Roberts, P. R., 'The "Act of Union" in Welsh History', *TCS*, 1972-3

Rowlands, E. I., 'Tri Wiliam Gruffudd', *Llên Cymru*, ii, 1952-3

Simon, J., *Education and Society in Tudor England* (1967)

Smith, J. B. (ed.), T. Jones Pierce, *Medieval Welsh Society* (1972)

Smith, J. B., *Llywelyn ap Gruffudd: Tywysog Cymru* (1985)

Smith, J. B., 'Crown and Community in the Principality of North Wales in the Reign of Henry Tudor', *WHR*, iii (no. ii), 1966

Smith, J. B., 'The Regulation of the Frontier of Meirionnydd in the Fifteenth Century', *JMHRS*, v (no. ii), 1966

Smith, J. B., 'Owain Gwynedd', *TCHS*, xxxii, 1971

Smith, Ll. B., 'The Gage and the Land Market in Late Medieval Wales', *Economic History Review*, xxix (no. iv), 1976

Somerville, R., *History of the Duchy of Lancaster, 1265-1603* (1953)

Stephens, T., *The Literature of the Cymry* (1876)

Stephenson, D., *The Governance of Gwynedd* (1984)

Stone, L., *The Crisis of the Aristocracy, 1558-1641* (1965)

Stone, L., *Social Change and Revolution in England, 1540-1640* (1965)

Stow, J., *A Survey of London* (1842)

Thirsk, J. (ed.), *The Agrarian History of England and Wales*, vol. iv, 1500-1640 (1966)

Thirsk, J., 'Younger Sons in the Seventeenth Century', *History*, liv, 1969

Thomas, D. Ll., 'Further Notes on the Court of the Marches', *Y Cymmrodor*, xiii, 1900.

Thomas, D. R., *The Life of Bishop Richard Davies and William Salesbury* (1902)

Thomas, D. R., *History of the Diocese of St. Asaph* (1908-13)

Thomas, I., *William Salesbury and his Testament* (1967)

Thomas, I., *Y Testament Newydd Cymraeg* (1976)

Thomas, I., *William Morgan and his Bible* (1988)

Waters, W. H., *The Edwardian Settlement of North Wales in its Administrative and Legal Aspects, 1284-1343* (1935)

White, F. O., *Lives of the Elizabethan Bishops* (1898)

Wiliam, A. Rh. (ed.), *Llyfr Iorwerth* (1960)

Williams, A. H., 'The Old Endowed Grammar Schools of Denbighshire', *TDHS*, ii, 1953

Williams, D., *A History of Modern Wales* (1965)

Williams, E. N., 'Sir William Maurice of Clenennau', *TCHS*, xxiv, 1963

Williams, G., *Bywyd ac Amserau'r Esgob Richard Davies* (1953)

Williams, G., *The Welsh Church from Conquest to Reformation* (1962)

Williams, G., *Owen Glendower* (1966)

Williams, G., *Welsh Reformation Essays* (1967)

Williams, G. (ed.), *Glamorgan County History*, vol. iv, 1500-1640 (1974)

Williams, G., *Religion, Language and Nationality in Wales* (1979)

Williams, G., *Recovery, Reorientation and Reformation: Wales c. 1415-1642* (1987)

Williams, G., 'The Deprivation and Exile of Bishop Richard Davies', *Jnl. Hist. Soc. of the Church in Wales*, i, 1947

Williams, G., 'Bishop William Morgan (1546-1604) and the First Welsh Bible', *JMHRS*, vi (Pt. iv), 1976

Williams, G. A., 'The Succession to Gwynedd, 1238-47', *BBCS*, xx (Pt. iv), 1964

Williams, G. A., 'Edmwnd Prys (1543/4-1623): Dyneiddiwr Protestannaidd', *JMHRS*, vii, 1980.

Williams, G. H., 'Estate Management in Dyffryn Conwy c.1685: the Caerhun, Baron Hill and Gwydir Estates', *TCS*, 1979

Williams, I., *Enwau Lleoedd* (1945)

Williams, J., *Ancient and Modern Denbigh* (1856)

Williams, J. E. C., 'Thomas Wiliems, Y Geiriadurwr', *Studia Celtica*, xvi-xvii, 1981-2

Williams, M. L., 'The Portionary Church of Caergybi and Jesus College', *TAAS*, 1947

Williams, P., *The Council in the Marches under Elizabeth I* (1958)

Williams, P., 'The Welsh Borderland under Queen Elizabeth', *WHR*, i (no. i), 1960

Williams, R., *The History and Antiquities of the Town of Aberconwy and its Neighbourhood* (1835)

Williams, R., *Eminent Welshmen* (1952)

Williams, S. J. and Powell, J. E. (ed.), *Cyfreithiau Hywel Dda yn ôl Llyfr Blegywryd* (1942)

Williams, W. Ll., *The Making of Modern Wales* (1919)

Williams, W. O. (ed.), *Calendar of the Caernarvonshire Quarter Sessions Records*, vol. i, 1541-1558 (1956)

Williams, W. O., 'The Survival of the Welsh Language after the Union of England and Wales: the First Phase, 1536-1642', *WHR*, ii (no. i), 1964

Williams, W. O., 'The Social Order in Tudor Wales', *TCS*, 1967 (Pt. ii)

Williams, W. R., *The Parliamentary History of the Principality of Wales, 1541-1895* (1895)

Williams, W. R., *The History of the Great Sessions in Wales 1542-1830 together with the Lives of the Welsh Judges* (1899)

Willis, B., *A Survey of the Cathedral Church of Bangor* (1721)

Willis, B., *A Survey of St. Asaph* (1801)

Wilson, F. P. (ed.), *The Oxford Dictionary of English Proverbs* (1970)

Wilson-Reid, 'William Glyn, Bishop of Bangor, 1555-1558', *TAAS*, 1950

Wormald, A. and Wright, C. E., *The English Library before 1700* (1958)

Wright, L. B., *Middle-Class Culture in Elizabethan England* (1935)

Wynne, W. W. E., 'Lists of Constables of Harlech Castle', *AC*, 1846.

Wynne, W. W. E., 'Sheriffs for the County of Merioneth', *AC*, 1847

Yorke, P., *The Royal Tribes of Wales* (1887)

D   UNPUBLISHED DISSERTATIONS

Jones, J. G., 'The Wynn Family and Estate of Gwydir: their Origins, Growth and Development up to 1674' (Ph.D. Dissertation, University of Wales, 1974)

Jones, J. Gwilym, 'Teulu Gwedir fel Noddwyr y Beirdd' (M.A. Dissertation, University of Wales, 1975)

Jones, R. L., 'Astudiaeth Destunol o Awdlau, Cywyddau ac Englynion gan Wiliam Cynwal' (M.A. Dissertation, University of Wales, 1969)

Owen, D. H., 'The Lordship of Denbigh, 1282-1425' (Ph.D. Dissertation, University of Wales, 1967)

GENERAL INDEX